GET TO
MARKET
NOW!

GET TO MARKET NOW!

Turn FDA Compliance into a Competitive Edge in the Era of Personalized Medicine

John Avellanet

LOGOS PRESS

Get to Market Now!
Turn FDA Compliance into a Competitive Edge in the Era of Personalized Medicine
John Avellanet

Published in The United States of America
by
Logos Press, Washington DC
www.Logos-Press.com
info@Logos-Press.com

10 9 8 7 6 5 4 3 2 1

ISBN-13: 978-1-934899-12-0

Library of Congress Cataloging-in-Publication Data

Avellanet, John.
  Get to market now! : turn FDA compliance into a competitive edge in the era of personalized medicine / John Avellanet.
      p. cm.
  Includes bibliographical references and index.
  ISBN 978-1-934899-12-0
  1. Drugs--United States--Marketing. 2. Pharmaceutical industry--United States. 3. New products--Marketing. I. Title.
  HD9666.5.A88 2010
  615.1068'1--dc22
                        2010005206

Contents

Figures

Disclaimer

This book is designed to provide information about the subject matter covered. It is sold with the understanding that the publisher and the author are not rendering specific legal advice within this book. Information in this book draws on a variety of sources, including published reports, interviews, and research, which may or may not have been prepared or conducted by the author or the publisher. This text is not a substitute for personalized advice from a knowledgeable professional. The advice and strategies contained herein may not be suitable for your situation. Adherence to your company's (and any governing regulatory agency's) policies regarding medicinal product development, quality systems, regulatory affairs, records retention, and compliance is your responsibility.

It is not the purpose of this book to reprint all the information that is otherwise available, but to complement, amplify, and supplement other texts and resources. For more information, see the many references in the Appendix and in the Bibliography.

Every effort has been made to make this book as complete and as accurate as possible. However, there *may be mistakes*, both typographical and in content. Therefore, this text should be used only as a general guide and not as the ultimate source of developing and bringing a medicine to market and/or developing and implementing a quality system and regulatory compliance program. Furthermore, this book contains information on developing a new medicine and complying with regulatory expectations only up to its printing date.

While the publisher and the author have used their best efforts in preparing this book, they make no representations or warranties with respect to the advice in this book. Neither the publisher nor the author shall be liable for any loss or damage caused or alleged to be caused directly or indirectly by the information contained in this book.

*To Jacob and Chloe, who stand to benefit far more from the
ideas in this book than their parents*

Men in their proceeding—and so much the more in great actions—should consider the times and accommodate themselves to them.

– Discourses on Livy, Niccolo Machiavelli

Acknowledgements

The advice of numerous friends and colleagues enriched and sharpened this book, and I would like to thank Brad Rickelman, Akos Bartha, Eric Lawson, Nancy Singer, Andy Villers, Clinton Hallman, Eric Dawnkaski, and Bill Cope for their suggestions and attention. Sadly, Bill passed away three weeks shy of seeing the final manuscript and my adoption of his fine critiques and insights. I would also like to thank Kim Trautman, Barry Cherney, and Peter Byron who indulged far too many of my questions. And I would like to acknowledge in particular Michael Blum for his generosity of spirit: every depiction of the new product funnel in this book is due to his work.

I owe a considerable debt to Jim Koessler for providing me support, Cheryl Avellanet and Mark Kessler for always standing by me, Bob and Peggy Ruffner for providing a temporary home away from home and reminding me, some time ago, that the best written book is a finished book, and my parents, Ralph and Susan, for always expecting great things. I hope I have not disappointed any of them.

I cannot begin to sufficiently acknowledge my editor, Yali Friedman, who has wonderfully steered and fostered this book, and I am grateful to him for his keen insight, patience, and strong encouragement.

Finally, for reasons that cannot, and need not, be enumerated here, I thank my wife, Sheila, and my two children, Jacob and Chloe, for their incredible forbearance, encouragement, support, and pride. This has been their labor as much as it has been mine.

Introduction

Today's compliance and quality systems, with their emphasis on standardization and prescriptive rules, are rooted in a command-and-control philosophy from the 1900s. As we move forward in the 21st century into an era of medicines customized to individuals and particular patient populations, how well served are we with a one-size-fits-all mindset?

To foster innovation and medicine personalization, we need compliance infrastructures—from regulatory affairs, quality systems, and corporate policies—that work alongside our research and development programs as partners, not policemen.

For biopharmaceutical and device organizations to succeed in the coming decades, executives need a compliance program that is flexible and cost-effective, a regulatory strategy that balances rule-adherence with risk-taking, and a quality system that helps scientists and engineers build in safety, efficacy, and quality from day one. And, as I will show in this book, many executives have already started and many industries have faced similar challenges. Your advantage lies in being able to review their experiences and to pick and choose tactics that best suit you and your organization.

One thing is certain: executives who select a "wait and see" strategy will watch as their chances to successfully adapt and profit in the era of personalized medicine shrink with each passing year. The average time to bring a new drug or biologic to market is now almost 13 years; to bring a new device to market requires at least eight.[1] To adapt even some of the strategies and tactics in this book to new medicinal product development and regulatory compliance structures, executives need to start right now. The sooner a firm begins, the better its results, the faster its new product time to market, and the lower its costs.

These lessons are also relevant beyond individual companies and executive teams. Our industry needs new ways of thinking about regulatory compliance, quality systems, and medicinal product development that reflect the changing reality of the 21st century. And we need to start adopting those new strategies *now*.

WHO ARE THE EARLY ADOPTERS

As I will show in the pages that follow, companies, along with their executives, are trying to adapt to the challenges of personalized medicine by restructuring their research and development (R&D) programs and their compliance infrastructures to be more in synch.

A number of these early stage adapters already exist:

- Husseini Manji, a vice-president in Johnson & Johnson's global research and development group, is committed to integrating personalized biomarkers and diagnostics tools as early in development as possible. This in turn is making their entire research and development process more efficient and more effective.[2]
- Mark Fishman, head of Novartis AG, has led his company's large investment (in 2002 alone, over $4 billion) in genetics-focused medicinal research. The result: a June 2009 approval for Novartis' new genetic-based drug, Ilaris, ahead of market expectations.[3]
- AstraZeneca's vice-president of oncology research, Alan Barge, is scrutinizing the genetics of cancer to discover drugs that target those genetic profiles, establishing a model of future biologics and pharmaceutical drug development with the potential to dramatically reduce side effects and earn AstraZeneca strong patient loyalty.[4]
- Sanofi-Aventis CEO, Chris Viehbacher, has introduced Sanofi's new model of drug research and development that looks first at patient needs, and then regional healthcare issues, before tackling the science; as a result, medicine development is increasingly patient focused.[5]
- Precision Therapeutics, a small Pennsylvania company, has demonstrated the use of predictive diagnostic modeling to identify how a patient's genetic makeup

will respond to various available treatments. The result:
cancer patients have a 40% greater chance of survival
and a 300% greater likelihood of cancer-free survival.
These results alone have netted the company $42 million
in investor funding.[6]

And there are dozens more examples of companies adopting tactics
espoused in this book to develop personalized drugs and device products.

WHAT ARE THE FORCES AT PLAY

Underlying the need for changes in R&D and compliance infrastructures are powerful forces at play in the early 21st century, including:

KNOWLEDGE SPECIALIZATION

Over the past twenty years, our scientific and technical knowledge has
dramatically increased, from decoding the human genome to mastering
the building of nanoscale materials. As a result, professional expertise
has dealt with this revolution of knowledge and technological ability
through an increase in specialization, sub-specialization and even sub-
sub-specialization. Toxicologists have begat neurotoxicologists who
have begat proteomic-neurotoxicologists.

Specialization adds two significant problems in any organization:

1. Each specialized professional vies for his or her share of
    limited company resources, thus reducing the amount
    for everyone else
2. Ever more narrowly focused information makes it more
    difficult to see patterns and linkages

These two problems alone make coping with the complexity of personalized medicine challenging. Additionally organizational politics
and personal egos can frustrate integration of disciplines and knowledge-sharing; because knowledge is power, executives frequently have
little incentive to share information.

The result: without careful shepherding, new medicine development, regulatory compliance, and quality systems programs become mired in organizational politics and silos of specialization.

VIRTUAL COMPANIES

Beginning in the 1990s, a new type of company emerged: the virtual corporation. Virtual companies depend heavily on the Internet, computers, and telecommunications. They are made up of contractors, freelancers, part-time workers, and multiple suppliers and partners. They take advantage of their virtual structure to keep costs low and drive product development through outsourcing most or all of their research and development functions; these are not physical, "brick and mortar" companies you can visit in order to resolve a problem.

As globalization and technological capabilities have grown, the prevalence of virtual companies has also grown, including in the biopharmaceutical and device sectors.

While regulators expect biopharma and device executives to "own" their suppliers, those same executives are facing increasing challenges trying to bring complex new medicines to market using a chain of outsourced company functions, independent contractors, and virtual vendors around the world. How does one enforce rules or inspect a company whose only tangible physical presence is a website?

GENERATIONAL FACTORS

Much has been written about the generational challenges companies face trying to juggle retiring baby-boomers, rising Gen-Xers, and the new Gen-Y or Millenials now entering the workforce. The implications for product development, quality systems, and compliance are significant.

Senior scientists, engineers, and compliance professionals are watching their hard-earned knowledge and expertise become obsolete. Their expectation of doing things "the company way" is being replaced by Gen-X and Gen-Y professionals who are much more willing to try new technological tools, take risks, and ignore convention. They are, in other words, more entrepreneurial. This mindset shift is good news for increasing innovation, but how does this work when it comes to creating new medicines? How does one take highly entrepreneurial people and tell them to innovate, develop, and design in a tightly controlled environment in constant compliance with regulatory rules, boundaries and expectations?

Consider that Gen-Ys have never known a time without computers, without the Internet, without wireless access, without file-sharing and swapping sites, and without pocket-sized cell phones. Gen-Ys see no difference in working with someone halfway around the world whom they only know by an alias and in working with someone the next desk over. And they certainly struggle with why they shouldn't ignore current copyright regulations and download music and software created and owned by others. Thus, not only do executives need to worry about how these new workers will innovate new medicines under current regulatory expectations and their firm's standard operating procedures, executives also need to consider how to protect nascent intellectual property *before* the company lawyer is even aware there is something new to patent!

ECONOMICS AND HEALTHCARE

Our global population is simultaneously aging and expecting better healthcare that is customized and tailored to the individual. But personalizing such cutting-edge medicine comes at a cost.

In my workshops on speeding personalized medicine development, I frequently note that we have less of a "healthcare crisis" in the world than we have a "healthcare funding crisis." Proof lies not in all the detailed statistics but rather in a simple question that I pose to each of the executives in my workshops:

> *Today, we have the technology and the drugs to keep*
> *you alive deep into your 100's—in fact, I'd be willing*
> *to bet, we could probably keep you alive almost forever.*
> *Now, admittedly, you'll spend your time lying in your*
> *hospital bed hooked to more machines than you have*
> *organs, and you'll get pumped with chemicals and*
> *biologics continuously, but we can keep you alive. So...*
> *here's the question: who will pay for you?*

To the aging population around the globe, add the declining birth rates in the Western world, the increasing cost of developing a new medicine, and a vacillating global economy, and biopharmaceutical and device executives are left with a conundrum: the population who can afford to pay for expensive new treatments is shrinking while the demand for new, customized treatment is growing.

How will firms lower costs, improve personalization, and make a profit selling smaller amounts of new medicines to ever-smaller sub-populations? Part of the answer comes from increasingly relying on cutting-edge information and technology, and yet this also comes with its own perils.

DIVERSION OF TECHNOLOGY AND REGULATION

The US Food and Drug Administration (FDA)—along with its international counterparts—is modernizing the regulations under which firms develop and bring new medicines to market. However, government efforts are too slow compared with the speed at which business must act to stay afloat.

In 1997, the FDA published a regulation laying out its expectations and rules for companies adopting electronic or digital signatures and/or records (instead of paper and ink). This regulation, Title 21 of the Code of Federal Regulations Part 11 (21 CFR Part 11 or "Part 11"), quickly grew out of control in its scope and its application—not because of the agency or the industry, but because of a growing gap between technological realities and regulatory expectations.

New computer-based products emerge every month. Moore's Law states that every 24 months computing power and capability double. Apple's iPhone contains more computing power than all of the computers worldwide in 1990. So why are we still using medicinal development methodologies developed before 1990 as our default strategies? It is no wonder then that new drugs and devices take so long to develop, and that keeping them safe, efficacious, and compliant costs so much.

How quickly do regulations evolve to accommodate technology that doubles in capacity and capability every two years? At the time of writing, the FDA's Part 11 has still not been updated or revised after more than twelve years.

Imagine a company not buying any new computers or software until the FDA had published its final version of the revised 21 CFR Part 11. Would such a company still exist by the time the agency published its new rules? This growing gap between regulatory expectations and marketplace capabilities is only accelerating. Despite the FDA's best efforts, the agency is not expected to complete its first pass at modernizing the regulations until at least 2012. At such a pace, "modernized" regulations risk obsolescence before they've been approved for publication. Given the long timeline required to bring a new drug or device to market, one can hardly afford to wait to explore new technologies and processes until the FDA has finished its regulatory revisions.

GLOBALIZATION

At the beginning of this century, regulatory agencies around the world began pushing to align their rules and regulations with each other. Through international working groups such as the International Conference on Harmonization (ICH) and the Global Regulatory Task Force (GHTF), regulations and expectations have been harmonized to standardize much of the regulatory requirements for drugs, biologics and devices. Ironically, because these changes necessitated compromises and reinterpretations by the FDA, this harmonization has made many biopharmaceutical and device compliance and quality systems out of date.

If the 20th century's industrial-based compliance systems are struggling, the question becomes, what will work? And how much will it cost? A simple economic analogy can clarify this. Think of your organization as a microcosm of the overall economy. Your regulatory affairs and quality management systems are part of your organization's service sector (along with other support functions such as information technology, human resources, finance and accounting, legal, and so forth). What then are your manufacturing sectors?

Most people draw the conclusion that an organization's "manufacturing" sector is its production areas (*e.g.*, factories and production lines). And in the 20th century, that would have been correct. By 2003, however, 85% of the average company's value was based not on goods produced by its factories and production lines, but on intangible intellectual property produced in offices and laboratories.[7] *The Economist* completed an analysis showing that for US companies alone, 75% of their value was solely based on intangible information and services.[8] In the 21st century's economy, an organization's "manufacturing" sector is its laboratories, clinical sites, engineering departments, etc.; the areas of the company that produce the intellectual property which production lines turn into pills, gels, defibrillators, and parenterals.

These cutting-edge, knowledge-creation "factories" require an advanced, dynamic quality system and compliance infrastructure to keep up with them and help guide them.

INCREASED COMPLIANCE BURDEN

Thirty years ago, approximately 100 clinical trials were held in the US in an average year. Today, more than 41,000 clinical trials occur annually worldwide, with 4,000 – 6,000 in the US alone.[9] As we customize medicines to fit patient profiles, the number of clinical trials will continue to rise, perhaps doubling or tripling within the next 12–17 years.

With increased medicine customization will come increased liability for the executives involved; patients will claim that companies should have done a better job testing for and optimizing their new medicines based on genetic profiles. Is there any doubt that this will further increase the need for multiple clinical trials?

As the number of clinical trials increases, the overall cost to bring a new medicine to market will increase. Even if clinical trials become smaller as they multiply, the in-depth analysis work will increase as compliance, medical affairs, and quality management executives will be forced to juggle multiple trials and objectives, where before they might only have faced a single trial at a time.

Long before a company needs to figure out how to manufacture and distribute a personalized medicine, executives need to determine how to allocate resources to shepherd personalized medicine candidates through the development pipeline, into the marketplace, and into post-market monitoring.

In the era of personalized medicine, one drug or biologic trade name may need multiple variations and approvals to cover multiple drug versions, each tailored to a specific genetic population. The years ahead promise significant upheaval for quality systems predicated on single formulations, single production runs, single procedures, and single products.

OVERLY RIGID QUALITY SYSTEMS

Many standard operating procedures (SOPs) and policies make business adaptability all but impossible. We are all familiar with seemingly inane procedures that had to go through lengthy change and approval processes just to adapt to a minor business condition or technology change since the SOP was first crafted. In the era of customized medicine, the more SOPs and policies that have outlived their usefulness, the farther behind a company will fall.

Business flexibility is a vital survival mechanism, and so some companies routinely ignore their own rules, or write memos to the file to get around their SOPs, or engage in round-the-clock SOP-revision projects. Inevitably, this sloppiness results in regulatory agency enforcement actions. And, at least in the US, FDA Form 483 observations and warning letters are the least of a company's problems: more and more quality system and compliance failures are causing financial declines, investor lawsuits, and bankruptcies.[10] Lawsuits (investor-led, or based on product-liability claims) against companies and executives citing their failure to adapt the firm's product development, quality systems, and compliance plans are expected to continue to increase in the decade ahead.

COMPLIANCE AS A COMPETITIVE EDGE

To succeed in the global era of personalized medicine, executives need to make it easy for regulators to approve a new product; to make it easy for consumers and patients to understand why they should buy that new medicine over competing products; to make it easy for prospective partners, collaborators, and investors to understand why working with the company improves their odds of success and return on investment; and to make it easy for employees and suppliers to comply with the regulations and company quality system expectations.

Executives can achieve compelling results by developing a flexible, cost-effective compliance infrastructure that builds safety, efficacy, and quality into new medicines from day one. Such a proactive program is vital for having effective discussions with investors and healthcare reimbursement agencies, fast-tracking a new medicine's development, negotiating with regulators, launching the new medicine ahead of industry expectations, and competing successfully in a globalized marketplace.

Given the landscape challenges we face over the next decade, compliance as a competitive edge will be both complex and demanding. Bringing together quality management, scientific development, regulatory compliance, and a host of different company sub-cultures, and then expecting them to work cooperatively and cross-functionally from pre-clinical research through post-market monitoring and improvements will be an immense challenge.

You can succeed by using a wide portfolio of tactics, tools, and strategies—many of which I've outlined in the pages that follow. Taken individually, these techniques—virtualization, voice of the customer, rapid prototyping, intellectual property espionage protection, defensible documents, quality by design, and others—are not new. It is their unique combination under a holistic framework that provides the results.

The more strategies and suggestions in this book that you adopt, the more innovative, more agile, and ultimately, more successful you, your colleagues, and your organization will become. Compliance as a competitive edge will help you develop your potential, taking you to the next level where few of your competitors will be able to follow.

GETTING STARTED

This book is organized into two parts:

> Part one—chapters one through four—summarizes the landscape today, including the traditional models of medicinal product development and the roles of regulatory compliance and quality systems, and then looks at the larger landscape in which compliance and product development must exist, from the rise of the informed patient to the increase in executive liability. Throughout, I blend current analyses with forecasts for how these trends and factors will evolve over the next decade.

> Part two—chapters five through ten—lays out the strategies, tactics, and techniques to cope with, adapt to, and succeed in the decades ahead to bring safe, efficacious personalized medicines to market, stay compliant, and turn a profit.

At the end of each chapter, I have also added a "to do" checklist to either reinforce the takeaways or provide a step-by-step review to simplify implementation.

To strengthen the book's practical, "how to" mindset, I have created a dedicated website (http://www.Get2MarketNow.com) with bonus material, downloads, and supplemental information, including:

- Free articles
- Checklists and templates
- Sample policies and standard operating procedures
- Subscription forms to my blog and newsletter
- Information about new events and publications
- Free mini-seminars

TWO QUESTIONS

When I speak to organizations and executives about these topics, two questions almost always arise:

- *Why are you discussing drugs, biologics, and devices altogether as if they are similar?*
- *Why do you use terms like "compliance," "quality systems" and "quality management" interchangeably?*

For the latter question, consistently stating *"regulatory affairs, quality assurance, quality control, quality management, quality systems, quality management systems, records and document controls, computer security, electronic information integrity controls, corporate policies, and so on"* seems more than unwieldy. As a result, I try to use the phrase "compliance infrastructure" or "compliance programs" to encapsulate all these different aspects of medicinal product compliance. You will need to tailor these terms to your environment. When I do specifically describe a particular strategy component to be carried out by your "regulatory affairs department" or your "quality department," I do mean those specific groups.

In terms of conflating drugs (including biologics) and devices (including diagnostics), there are six reasons to consider these together as I lay out a proactive, holistic compliance framework:

- FDA officials have repeatedly stated that "we got it right with device regulations" and their desire to make drug regulations more aligned with the device regulations
- Genetic segmentation of potential patient populations increasingly relies on incorporating diagnostics into treatments—in other words, blending devices and drugs
- Biologics account for more and more of the new drugs

on the market, and because of the problems associated
with taking biologics orally, these new drugs often rely
upon devices for administration

- Many of the trends in the 21st century regulatory
landscape affect drug, biologic, and device firms
similarly

- A majority of the tactics and strategies in this book apply
equally to firms that develop new medicines, be they
drugs, biologics, devices, or combinations thereof

- Increasingly, both innovation and compliance rely on
the convergence of technologies such as data sharing and
telemedicine

I will show the details of each of these as the book unfolds.

Additionally, while this book uses FDA requirements and expectations as its baseline, the compliance strategies, tactics, and tools I
outline are designed to meet, with some degree of modification, regulatory agency expectations in Europe, Japan (and other parts of Asia),
Australia, Canada, and elsewhere. A book like this cannot hope to fully
address every regulatory requirement worldwide, so you will need to
judge the specifics to be tailored to your organization, its products, and
the environments you face.

NEXT STEPS

From reading this book, I hope you take away two key realizations:

- Without a flexible, cost-effective, proactive regulatory
compliance infrastructure covering the preclinical
through the postmarket product lifecycle, companies
cannot hope to bring a personalized drug, biologic, or
device to market at a sustainable cost

- The combination of this type of flexible, cost-effective,
proactive compliance infrastructure with an adaptive,
customer-oriented medicinal development program is
required if a company is to compete effectively—and
survive—in the coming decades

These realizations reflect the growing gap between our 21st century knowledge and our 20th century, industrial-era mindset. And this gap presents enormous vulnerability, but also historic opportunities. Readers of this book will have access to many of the strategies and tools to capitalize on these opportunities. This book will give you the techniques and tactics to enable 21st century competitiveness while still adhering to regulations, rules, and interpretations largely laid down in the previous century.

If this book merely provokes discussions amongst your colleagues and company, the book is a disappointment. My humblest hope is that you will adopt at least some of the tactics and tools in this book to help speed your time to market with new medicines over the next decade.

My challenge to you is to map out your own timeline for adapting as many of the strategies and suggestions in this book as possible so you can bring your new medicines to market now.

1 — Today's Regulatory Landscape

T his book is about the future of drug, biologic and device compliance—whether in terms of quality systems, records control, or regulatory affairs—and its role in enabling innovation and new medicinal marketplace success.

In this chapter, I describe the major changes in the regulatory landscape. Each of these changes has traditionally been seen in isolation by outside observers specializing in one particular compliance aspect. With a broader view, we can see the evolution of the larger landscape to which we must adapt our development plans, regulatory approval strategies, and quality systems programs. Not only can we then stay compliant, but we can give ourselves a chance to be proactive with the ultimate result of gaining a competitive edge.

Executives have already started reacting to the dramatic transitions in drug, biologic, and device development that has unfolded over the past few decades. However, without a holistic strategy, firms have been left to struggle forward in a confused manner.

To provide a clear framework for success—one that you can adopt and adapt to your specific needs—I will look first at the four major regulatory compliance trends placing companies and their new medicine development plans in significant jeopardy:

1. Evolution of onerous safety, efficacy, and quality expectations from regulators
2. Rising role of reimbursement concerns in new drug or device marketability
3. Increasing emphasis on records, document, and data integrity controls
4. Declining levels of experienced compliance personnel

SAFETY, EFFICACY, AND QUALITY EXPECTATION EVOLUTION

To shed light on the new landscape, the first step is to summarily review how regulatory oversight from the US Food and Drug Administration (FDA) has evolved since the 1980s.

ROLE OF THE FDA

While regulation of drugs started back in the days of the Lincoln administration, the FDA as we think of it today began with the 1938 Food, Drug and Cosmetic Act (FDCA) during the Franklin Roosevelt administration. The legal statutes of the FDCA and subsequent acts of the US Congress provide the basis for the FDA and its authority over drugs, devices, and biologics. In terms of actual requirements for how these medical product sectors should comply with the law, these statutes only cover the high level requirements (*e.g.*, do not produce unsafe products). Instead, Congress has left it to the FDA to create practical rules. And for executives and investors in the industry, it is these rules that matter most.

To achieve the mandates of the legislation, the FDA has crafted a series of regulations or rules under Title 21 of the Code of Federal Regulations (21 CFR). These regulations, covering various activities involved in the discovery, design, development, testing, production, sales, and distribution of drugs, biologics, and devices, lay out the minimum requirements for life sciences organizations. Depending on the types of activities undertaken, a company may be subject to just a few parts of 21 CFR (*e.g.*, the manufacture of drugs is specifically governed by 21 CFR Parts 210 and 211), or the full panoply of FDA regulations and expectations.

In the 1980s, critics of the FDA claimed that this ever-escalating set of regulations was inadvertently impeding innovation—the more a company tried to move innovative ideas through its research and development (R&D) pipeline to market, the more regulations it had to comply with, thus driving up costs and diminishing incentives. Despite the ongoing need for some level of protection for consumers from unsafe products and/or unscrupulous executives (*i.e.*, the 1950s Thalidomide tragedy and the more recent push by some pharmaceutical executives to hide or downplay poor clinical studies results), criticism that medical innovation was at risk did not fall on deaf ears at the FDA.

Beginning in the 1990s, the agency held a series of meetings with executives from other industries that had faced the dilemma of balancing public safety and product reliability with innovation and business profitability. Executives from industries as diverse as aerospace, automotive, semi-conductor, telecom, and information technology met with the agency and reviewed their struggles and achievements. In 2002, the FDA released a concept paper on 21st century Good Manufacturing Practices.[11] With the assistance of several biopharmaceutical firms, pilot programs were started to explore the viability of revising 20th century regulations to meet 21st century demands.

In conjunction with this 2002 concept paper, the FDA tackled another concern of critics and agency personnel: the growing difficulty of adhering to FDA regulations in the US while also developing and making products for other markets around the globe. Each nation's regulatory agency governing medicinal products was different enough to cause major headaches both for companies and for agencies trying to coordinate inspections and compliance from medicine manufacturers based overseas. As part of its deliberations for the 2002 concept paper and in subsequent progress reports, the agency referenced its work with other regulatory agencies in Japan and the European Union to harmonize scientific standards and regulatory operations on medicine quality.[12]

Meanwhile, the FDA had struggles of its own. Budget limitations and the exploding rate of scientific knowledge (the human genome was decoded in June 2000), meant the agency was forced to make tradeoffs—not every product could be analyzed, not every manufacturer or researcher could be inspected. Originally, the FDA had focused on keeping unsafe medicines off the market; as the agency's own inspection manuals simply stated, the FDA's mission was "to prevent the distribution of unsafe or ineffective products."[13] By the early 2000s, however, the agency had increasingly shifted into prioritization mode. In the 20th century, inspections of companies were done in a prescriptive manner, with checklists drawn from a line-by-line comparison of the regulations. By 2004, according to Helen Winkle, Director of the Office of Pharmaceutical Science, and Thom Savage, Director of the Office of Regulatory Compliance, FDA inspectors started to be trained to assess a company less on a black-and-white adherence to specific regulatory wording and phrasing, and more on the firm's ability to maintain—and demonstrate—a consistent "state-of-control."[14]

This mindset shift coincided with the publication that same year of two FDA reports, "Introduction or Stagnation: Challenge and Opportunity on the Critical Path to New Medical Products,"[15] and "Pharmaceutical cGMPs for the 21st Century—A Risk-Based Approach."[16] The reports identified many of the challenges facing the biopharmaceutical sectors in the era of globalized medical product development and manufacture. The FDA followed its reports with discussions of steps the agency would take over the next decade to ensure medicinal product safety, efficacy, and quality while still fostering innovation in the industry. While much of the resulting reports revolve around internal agency dynamics and activities, for biopharma and device executives, four major components stand out:

1. The revision of current regulations to incorporate new scientific knowledge and techniques
2. The increased level of international harmonization with other non-US health agencies
3. The adoption of a risk-based philosophy of oversight and inspection
4. The push for companies to design quality, safety, and efficacy into their new medical products as early as possible (*e.g.*, quality by design)

Medical device and diagnostics executives familiar with 21 CFR Part 820 Quality Systems Regulations (QSRs) who review these two FDA papers will be pleasantly surprised at the similarities with Part 820. Indeed, at a 2007 pharmaceutical industry conference, FDA official Kim Trautman expressly conducted a cross-comparison between the regulations governing devices and those governing drugs and biologics, concluding, "We got it right with the device QSRs."[17]

More recently, in publications and speeches (some of which are discussed in this chapter), regulatory officials have argued that not only do life sciences companies need to make fundamental changes by 2020 to get to market with new medicines, but also that life sciences executives "do not have the option to go slow."[18]

As I will show throughout the rest of this book, there should be little doubt that FDA regulations governing pharmaceuticals and biologics will look increasingly like the regulations governing medical devices and diagnostics, with an emphasis on risk-based controls, quality by design, and international cooperation. Several of these initiatives bear similarity to long-held philosophies of other national health agencies such as the European Medicines Agency, and were clearly influenced by the FDA's involvement in two international regulatory alignment groups starting in 1990: the International Conference on Harmonization and the Global Harmonization Task Force.

ROLE OF THE INTERNATIONAL CONFERENCE ON HARMONIZATION (ICH)

The FDA, along with the European Union's European Medicines Agency and Japan's Ministry of Health, Labor and Welfare (MHLW), became a founding member of the International Conference on Harmonization (ICH) in January 1990. Other members include the major pharmaceutical trade groups in each of these three regions, plus Health Canada and the World Health Organization.

The ICH essentially drafts harmonized regulatory guidelines covering biopharmaceutical quality, safety, and efficacy. A miscellaneous category of guidelines also exists, tackling items such as common medical terminology and a common technical document format (the CTD) for regulatory submissions, thereby streamlining the submissions process in all member states.

Each ICH guideline goes through multiple revisions before it is published in final form by the ICH and released by its respective national health agency (i.e., the FDA in the US) as a formal regulatory guideline for industry. Of critical importance to biopharmaceutical executives was the announcement in 2007 that the FDA was going to start enforcing ICH guidelines by the end of 2008. And in April 2008, the first warning letter was issued citing failure to comply with an approved ICH guideline.[19]

ROLE OF THE GLOBAL HARMONIZATION TASK FORCE (GHTF)

In 1992, the FDA also became a founding member of a similar harmonization effort, this time for medical devices and diagnostics, the Global Harmonization Task Force (GHTF). Other members include health agencies from the European Union, Canada, Japan, and Australia.

Like the ICH, the GHTF has broken down guidelines into categories designed to be harmonized across all regions. The GHTF has organized its categories around the position of the medical device in its overall lifecycle—development ("clinical safety/performance"); submission for approval ("premarket evaluation"); production and distribution ("post-market surveillance and vigilance")—plus operational considerations ("quality systems" and "auditing").

At the time of writing, FDA officials are debating whether to enforce GHTF guidelines. FDA inspectors are being trained in GHTF expectations and rules.[20] It seems certain, given increasing pressure on the agency to strengthen medical device requirements, that compliance with GHTF guidelines is inevitable. While compliance may only initially be limited to firms in the device, diagnostics, or combination product marketplaces, as we will see, in the era of personalized medicine, few executives will be able to win an argument claiming complete exemption from GHTF compliance.

Long-Term Implications

Harmonization will continue as regulatory oversight agencies confront the realities of overseeing a global marketplace. No regulatory agency has the necessary staffing, expertise, and budget to inspect every purveyor of medical products. International cooperation is a necessity. As the regulations are increasingly harmonized, I expect a commiserate increase in joint inspection and oversight responsibilities; inspections by Health Canada or the European Medicines Agency will be accepted by the FDA and vice versa.

For the drug, biologic, or device executive, experience with FDA regulations is no longer enough. Even for a firm planning to develop and market its new medicine in the US only, FDA regulations only make up half the required device or drug rules. Compliance with ICH or GHTF (or both if a company is developing a combination drug and device) is now a necessity.

Three key implications can be drawn from this reshaping of the regulatory safety, efficacy, and quality landscape. First, hiring of personnel and outside compliance experts with only FDA expertise puts firms at a disadvantage in an internationally harmonized regulatory environment. Second, medical product development plans and compliance strategies need to incorporate—and design controls around—building quality, safety, efficacy, and harmonization as early as possible. And third, the traditional approaches to compliance-related issues, from FDA enforcement responses to the submission of applications to market a new drug or device, are increasingly out of date. Executives who fail to adapt their 20th century philosophies to the new realities of the 21st century regulatory landscape will find the odds increasingly stacked against them.

MEDICINAL REIMBURSEMENT AND MARKETABILITY

Most of the industrialized world has some form of government-sponsored healthcare. These government agencies play a significant role in controlling drug prices. In the US, the Centers for Medicaid and Medicare Services (CMS) accomplishes price regulation indirectly; in the U.K., the National Health Service is more active through its National Institute for Health and Clinical Excellence (NICE), and in the rest of Europe, the Committee for Medicinal Products for Human Use (CHMP) controls prices with its emphasis on risk-benefit ratios.

ROLES OF NICE IN THE UK AND CHMP ELSEWHERE IN EUROPE

Under the UK's national health insurance program, biopharmaceutical firms must submit their product's cost-effectiveness information to NICE for analysis and review. Part of this effectiveness information includes the quality-of-life-adjusted-year (QALY) tool that analyzes how a prospective treatment affects patient quantity of life (*e.g.*, how much does it extend life?) and quality of life (*e.g.*, how much better is a person following treatment?). Typically, NICE takes approximately 18 months to assess a new drug or biologic. If NICE determines that claims of effectiveness are not supported—for instance, the cost of the new drug is 30% more than a drug already on the market in the UK but the new drug's effectiveness is only 5% greater than the existing drug—NICE will not approve coverage of the drug.[21] In other words, proof of efficacy *and* proof of cost-efficiency are required for reimbursement and sales in the UK.

The European Medicines Agency has a similar framework, although because each member state has different reimbursement mechanisms, Europe's CHMP focuses on the risk-benefit ratio in regards to effectiveness and safety data.

How does this play out in terms of personalized medicine? Consider the example of Amgen's cancer drug Vectibix. In May 2007, the CHMP refused to grant approval based on clinical trial data that did not demonstrate a clear level of effectiveness. Amgen promptly appealed. In its appeal, Amgen provided a biomarker analysis of its previous Phase 3 study plus a Phase 3 extension study. Amgen showed that patients with a *KRAS* gene mutation were resistant to the drug (approximately 35% of prospective patients).[22] By excluding those patients with the genetic mutation from any effectiveness conclusions, Amgen was able to demonstrate that its biologic had a significantly improved risk-benefit ratio. In other words, for patients with the non-mutated *KRAS* gene, Vectibix was highly effective and cost-efficient. The European Medicines Agency then granted Amgen marketing approval for patients with the non-mutated *KRAS* gene.

Whether it's an analysis of the risk-benefit ratio or a review of comparative cost-effectiveness, NICE and CHMP serve as gatekeepers in their respective markets to control healthcare costs.

ROLE OF CMS IN THE US

In the same way that decisions by CHMP and NICE are reviewed by other health reimbursers throughout Europe, so too do private health insurers in the US take their cues from the reimbursement levels assigned to new medications by CMS.

CMS's underpinnings for reimbursement categorization can be confusing—indeed, an entire cottage industry of reimbursement consultants has arisen to help executives sort through the confusion of CMS (*e.g.*, how to appeal financial rulings and private insurer decision-making). An understanding of reimbursement expectations is critical for new medical product development and innovation. While US regulatory approval and marketplace launch may not be impacted directly by CMS reimbursement classification, a company's sales and marketplace success are impacted. Private insurers look to CMS reimbursement rates and set their own reimbursement rates accordingly.

Therefore, the earlier that reimbursement classification estimations can be defined, the sooner biopharmaceutical and device executives can start to gather data supporting reimbursement goals.

ROLE OF VENTURE CAPITALISTS

In addition to regulatory healthcare agencies, venture capitalists also play an increasingly influential role in new medical product innovation. Gone are the days—if they ever truly existed—where venture capitalists would provide money to a scientist or biomedical engineer with simply a "good idea." Increasingly, venture capitalists are experienced in the realities of new medical product development, from the poor chances of success to the enormous costs involved and to the long timelines.

A 2009 University of Maryland study found that venture capitalists pay little to no attention to the academic credentials and scientific research successes of medical product scientists and engineers who want to become entrepreneurs.[23] Instead, since 2000, venture capitalists have focused more on commercial execution rather than research credentials, providing more and more funding to those startups planning to develop the new molecule, biologic or device *up until* it can be licensed or sold away.[24]

Today's venture capitalists have an average time horizon of approximately 3 years in which to obtain a return on their investment.[25] Indeed, the number one question that life science entrepreneurs are asked is "What is your end game?" In other words, the venture capitalists understand that the odds of a nascent company independently launching a new medicine is extremely unlikely. So is the strategy to focus on research and license the intellectual property? Or to bring the new drug/device through early clinical trials and then license, sell, or partner?

Unless a company can provide compelling evidence that a new product is marketable—including laboratory testing results, clinical results, comparative product analyses, and reimbursement likelihoods—company executives are going to run out of time and money. The pressure for both financial returns and R&D productivity has only increased with the rising number of biotechnology and device entrepreneurs all around the world, from China and India to Europe and Latin America. Excluding long-time biotechnology industry observers, few scientists and entrepreneurs realize that less than a third of all biotechnology firms are in the US.

LONG-TERM IMPLICATIONS

For the drug, biologic, or device company executive, being able to appropriately factor in reimbursement realities and financial trends with compliance and development strategies is now an essential skill. Failure to adopt cost-efficiencies within regulatory compliance, quality systems, and medical product development strategies will put firms, shareholders, investors, and prospective patients in jeopardy.

Over time, I expect some form of the UK's NICE and Europe's CHMP to expand into other English-speaking nations such as Canada, Australia, and India, not to mention other countries such as China and Brazil. NICE has already consulted on a non-profit basis with more than 60 countries on how to ensure affordable medicines.[26] The US will not be exempt from this. As I noted in the introduction, we have the technology and science available to extend life considerably; what we do not have are the resources to match; trade-offs are inevitable.

The FDA also plays a role in helping determine cost-efficiencies of new medicines. In August 2008, the agency issued a procedural guidance document entitled *Integrated Summary of Effectiveness*.[27] This document laid out the specific expectations of the FDA for comparisons and analyses of efficacy results in clinical trials, including any comparative effectiveness data between competing products. While the FDA currently cannot use cost-effectiveness information in its approval decisions on new medicines, by encouraging companies to develop this type of specific information in their clinical packages, the FDA fosters the creation, and ultimately the awareness, of this information. Whether such information then directly or indirectly influences CMS or private insurer reimbursement is unclear; however, executives would be wise not to discount the possibility.

Analysis of further financial issues impacting medical product development falls beyond the scope of this book. Such financial examinations require a depth of analysis that goes well beyond the boundaries of regulatory compliance, quality systems, and regulatory affairs, and so I will briefly touch upon further financial impacts and trends only insomuch as they help illustrate observations or recommendations in the book. Readers looking for more in-depth analyses of the behind-the-scenes financial details can find these in some of the resources listed in the bibliography.

RECORDS MANAGEMENT AND DATA INTEGRITY

Executives must keep in mind that the pressure to produce compelling evidence of new product marketability increases the temptation to skirt the rules. Fraudulent clinical and laboratory results have been on the rise over the past few years, and the FDA trains its inspectors and reviewers to spot records fraud.

Since 2006, more than 95% of FDA enforcement actions and denials of marketing approval have been motivated by inadequate records integrity.[28] Whether it is the integrity of data in a regulatory submission, or the ability to control the documentation and information in your own company, it seems that regulatory approval is predicated upon the ability to control the reliability and quality of records.

The increasing importance of new medical product innovation and compliance emphasizes three crucial needs:

1. Intellectual property protection
2. Data integrity
3. Records controls

INTELLECTUAL PROPERTY PROTECTION

Intellectual property protection is typically left to lawyers; unfortunately, this assumption unintentionally endangers discoveries, proprietary processes, and other forms of intellectual property.

As I have written before, "Intellectual property is the greatest asset of any company; it must be thoroughly protected and secured."[29] Whether a discovery in the lab, a revelation from patient research, an engineering blueprint, or a unique production method, intellectual property forms the core of the 21st century drug, biologic, and device company. The medicine itself is really just a tangible form of the underlying intellectual property.

In the context of traditional FDA compliance professions—regulatory affairs and quality management—the goal of the former has been to bring this medicinal intellectual property to market successfully in a compliant manner, while the goal of quality management personnel has been to ensure this medicinal intellectual property was produced and maintained in a controlled manner.

Understanding that confidential information encompasses far more than patented intellectual property—that it includes drug interaction data, internal quality audit results, biologics production processes, critical manufacturing control parameters, and so on—gives us opportunities to incorporate controls throughout the product lifecycle. Quality management, regulatory affairs, and other compliance executives are perfectly poised to easily incorporate intellectual property (IP) controls into any compliance program.

Executives who ignore the interplay between intellectual property, regulatory compliance, and quality systems do so at their firm's peril. In December 2008, Pfizer was penalized US\$38.7 million for stealing clinical drug interaction and comparative-use data on the drug Bextra. Pfizer had obtained this confidential information through a former employee of another organization.[30]

The intricacies of intellectual property and its protection are beyond the scope of this book. However, as I will show in chapter five, there are several steps that quality management, regulatory affairs, and other compliance executives should be taking on a regular basis to help protect their organization's intellectual property.

When I speak to organizations on preventing theft of their intellectual property and trade secrets, I start by asking attendees to list basic questions they might consider incorporating into their internal quality audits or due diligence reviews of new suppliers and partners. A few, tentative suggestions—typically involving some variation of "ask the lawyer"—are voiced. I follow by offering two simple questions every compliance-based due diligence or internal audit should include:

1. Are visitors required to sign in with specific information, such as which company they are from and whom they are visiting?
2. Does the lab director or the clinical investigator enforce a clear desk policy regarding confidential information?

These two examples alone tend to spark thoughtful discussions by attendees on what each member of a due diligence or internal audit team could do better to improve the security of their firm's intellectual property and confidential information. Given that quality, regulatory affairs, and other compliance executives are at the forefront of due diligence and internal audits, those who do not include at least some assessment of intellectual property controls unwittingly place their company and their investors at undue risk.

Data Integrity

Not long ago, quality of data integrity was judged by how well a firm managed its laboratory notebooks and batch production records. The sooner a researcher's notes and test results were reviewed, witnessed, and signed off by his/her supervisor, the better the integrity.

As paper notebooks have given way to electronic lab notebooks and laboratory information management systems, data integrity is no longer about who witnessed what when. Electronic information is time and date stamped the moment it is created, and again when it is saved. Today's uncertainties center on the amount of integrity inherent in any given information set. Have the data been tampered with? Are all the data present, or have negative results been omitted or obscured? Whether it is production batch records, analytical lab test results, or adverse event reports, regulatory officials increasingly scrutinize a company's records and documents for integrity... or a lack thereof.

To FDA regulators, medical product and compliance records are reliable and trustworthy if they are accurate, legible, attributable to a particular individual, original, complete, and contemporaneous (*i.e.*, the information was recorded at the time of the actual activity, such as a lab test or production run).

In 2007, FDA directors revealed that agency inspectors had been receiving specialized training on "uncovering data integrity, data manipulation and fraud."[31] A year later, Edwin Rivera-Martinez, of the agency's Office of Compliance, noted that one-third of all pre-approval inspections—the FDA onsite inspections conducted prior to granting approval for a new medicine—are initiated because of record integrity issues.[32] And whistleblowers who allege data manipulation and fraud increasingly find a receptive outlet in the FDA.

Data integrity issues become increasingly difficult considering how long much of the information needs to be retained. Different types of product safety, efficacy, and quality information may be required, by regulation, to be retained for more than two decades. Paper records, when properly maintained, last at least several hundred years. No one knows how long digitally-stored information will last. So far, most forecasts have fallen dramatically short. Compact discs (CDs), for instance, were supposed to last indefinitely. Then it was determined that a typical lifespan might be 20-25 years. Today, we know that the chemical reactions that occur when you record information onto a CD degrade far more rapidly than originally thought, causing the CD to fail regardless of how it is cared for and stored. A recorded CD will last, on average, only 8-10 years. Given the long horizon involved in new medical product development, the retention of product safety, efficacy, and quality records is yet another new aspect of the regulatory landscape of the 21st century, and one to which we will return in chapter nine.

RECORDS CONTROLS

The integrity of information can be maintained, intellectual property can be protected, and proof of a new medicine's safety, efficacy, and quality can be demonstrated as long as your company's records are controlled. Records are your proof. They either support your assertions, or they reveal the invalidity of your claims.

Analysis of 294 warning letters made publicly available since 2007 reveals that 271 of the 294 letters cite firms for records control-related issues such as "firm was unable to provide documentation"[33] and "firm does not keep adequate records to determine each batch, lot, or unit is manufactured in accordance with the Quality Systems regulations."[34]

Establishing standard operating procedures, and training personnel to employ them, is only the beginning. Unfortunately, for many executives accustomed to 20th century expectations, the bar has been raised; simply having a written procedure and holding a training session to explain it is not enough. Records must exist that prove that the procedure was followed, and those records must be maintained over time. To establish and maintain that proof, requires records controls.

Each FDA regulation has a subsection within it spelling out the types of records the agency expects companies to retain and control. From laboratory notebooks and clinical investigator reports, to production lot files and adverse event reports, each record type has different retention periods and requirements. As such, companies need to set up records retention schedules and define governing policies and controls procedure.

Compliance executives are natural leaders for these efforts. After all, it is their responsibility to ensure that the company has defensible documents. Such defense goes far beyond simply having a standard operating procedure. Defensible records require controls. Executives who ignore the expectations encapsulated in the recent warning letters cited above, and who try to define their role in the context of last century's regulatory expectations, do so at their peril.

LONG-TERM IMPLICATIONS

For the drug, biologic, or device executive, familiarity with basic good records management and control practices is a must. Just as medieval knights lived and died by the sword, today's executives succeed or fail by the record.

While the stock prices of firms rise and fall by as much as 40% based on public FDA enforcement actions[35], many of us have also seen the conviction of executives and firms in the court of public opinion in the news of court cases involving GlaxoSmithKline, AstraZeneca, Merck, Wyeth, Boston Scientific, Bristol Myers Squibb, and countless others. In each of these cases, documents and records that reflected poorly on these companies and their executives were disclosed in the courtroom. In the case of embarrassing public exposure such as this, an FDA warning letter may be the least of a company's concerns. Financial penalties, bad publicity, and ruined careers linger far longer than FDA Form 483 observations and wounded pride.

I expect records integrity to continue to dominate the regulatory landscape in the 21st century. Development of personalized medicine is complicated, with subtle differences having significant impacts on safety, efficacy, and quality. Records are your proof that you understood these risks, put in place appropriate controls, and have maintained both effective controls and suitable documentation. When inspectors arrive at your facility, few will be interested in hearing about how wonderful your processes are. Instead, expect to be asked to "prove it."

CHANGING COMPLIANCE EXPERTISE

At the same time that all of these shifts are occurring in the regulatory landscape, the ability of companies to cope with these shifts is at risk. Demographics are working against the industry.

US REGULATORY AFFAIRS AND QUALITY MANAGEMENT DEMOGRAPHICS

A 2006-2007 survey by the University of Southern California (USC) found that two-thirds of experienced compliance professionals in the US—those with more than 10 years of experience—are preparing to retire between 2015 and 2020.[36] Some of these individuals will stay engaged in the field through speaking and advisory roles, yet how interested will these semi-retirees be in accumulating the substantial set of new skills required to navigate records controls, reimbursement strategies, and the globally harmonized, stricter regulatory expectations of personalized medicine?

As a part of preparing this book, I conducted a topic review of the various industry certification programs and graduate degree programs available to rising professionals within quality systems and regulatory affairs. To date, within these programs each of the major trends I identified above—the need to incorporate reimbursement elements within regulatory strategies, the changing expectation of FDA to incorporate quality by design and regulatory harmonization, and the criticality of records integrity—is given minimal attention, if they are discussed at all.

The implication that compliance personnel are not being developed with the requisite skills necessary for success in the 21st century is borne out by the USC study. More than 48% of companies express difficulty in filling compliance positions with personnel who have experience beyond the traditional textbook view of regulatory affairs and quality systems.[37]

FDA PERSONNEL SHIFTS

Concurrent with this loss of private industry expertise, the FDA is set to experience its largest knowledge transfer, with the retirement of nearly 50% of its workforce by 2020.[38] The significant loss of tacit knowledge, just as the agency is revising its regulations might be disconcerting, were it not for the shift noted above of increasing global harmonization and cooperation. As a result, while industry struggles to adapt to all the shifts in the regulatory landscape, FDA officials can rely on assistance from their colleagues in other regulatory agencies around the world. The result will be more international harmonization, more multinational inspections, and more knowledge sharing between regulatory health agencies, just as companies are confronting a dearth of knowledge and expertise.

Witness the industry's frustration with the UK's NICE. Because of growing reliance upon non-FDA agencies to offer advice and expertise on regulatory requirements, I expect officials from non-traditional medical product oversight agencies such as NICE and CMS may obtain greater say over which products will be approved and which products will not. The rising influence of healthcare reimbursers on approval decisions is one reason why medical product effectiveness so easily correlates to cost-effectiveness. If healthcare reimbursement agency personnel question a new medicine's effectiveness, expect doubts to creep into the FDA reviewers' minds as well.

LONG-TERM IMPLICATIONS

For the drug, biologic, or device executive, there are several lessons to be gleaned from this trend of declining expertise. In the short term, company development programs will need to make up for the inability of industry and educational certifications to keep up with the knowledge required in the 21st century. This can be accomplished with formal employee development programs, or executives can look at and adopt the recommendations in the second half of this book to provide compliance personnel with practical frameworks in which they will naturally develop crucial knowledge. Ideally, a company will adopt both, providing a robust system to ensure development of effective compliance personnel.

As global harmonization proceeds, companies will increasingly have the opportunity to outsource basic regulatory affairs and quality systems activities. Outsourcing basic tasks is something that other industries have adopted, and there is little doubt that device makers and biopharmaceutical firms will also proceed down this path. Today, regulatory agencies are actively harmonizing their submissions formats for requests to market a new medicine. If a regulatory submission is largely similar regardless of whether it is for the US, Canada, the EU, and so on, then companies can quickly and easily gain efficiencies by outsourcing the bulk of such work to regulatory affairs professionals in India, Australia, or China and then complete minor amendments for the US, Canada, or the EU. This is one way I expect companies to adapt to declining compliance expertise in the US. That such outsourcing also dovetails with the outsourcing of clinical trials and manufacturing overseas only supports its inevitability.

In the 21st century compliance roles will be split between those more easily outsourced because the work is relatively operational with a high degree of consistency due to regulatory harmonization (for instance, CTD formatting, supplier due diligence auditing, and regulatory training) and those compliance roles less easily outsourced because the work is unique to a company and its products (for instance, developing a clinical regulatory integrated strategic plan for a newly created medicine, ensuring that the reimbursement, efficacy, and safety characteristics of a new medicine are verified under a compliant quality system, and so on).

SUMMARY

As I noted at the beginning of this chapter, there are four trends shaping the regulatory landscape today:

1. Declining expertise in compliance
2. Increasing emphasis on records controls and integrity
3. Globalized expectations to incorporate safety, efficacy, and quality in new medicine development
4. Increasing relevance of reimbursement issues

These four trends cover large, structural, systemic evolutions. And not a single one was evident throughout most of the 20th century. Executives who do not change how their compliance infrastructures and strategies support new medicine development and launch are not likely to succeed in the 21st century landscape.

A company's quality systems and regulatory compliance infrastructure for the 21st century must include reference to, and be compliant with, ICH guidelines and/or GHTF guidelines. The FDA, along with other regulatory agencies around the world, has moved away from proscriptive oversight to a more principled approach that focuses on looking at the justifications that prove your controls meet or exceed expectations. As I will show you later in the book, the wise executive can use this to his or her company's advantage.

Developing a new medicine is highly regulated with rewards increasingly controlled by public healthcare agencies with considerable interests in equating medicinal price with efficacy. Because clinical development and medical product production are intimately involved with efficacy, regulatory affairs and quality systems executives will be increasingly asked to incorporate elements of reimbursement strategies in any compliance strategy; this is yet another aspect of using compliance as a competitive edge.

And determining how to gather, organize, and control all of this proof is a core consideration in your product development and regulatory compliance strategies. Quality systems and regulatory affairs have not traditionally tackled records management issues. In this century, executives unwilling to expand outside of traditional compliance roles will lead their companies and product development efforts to failure.

Understanding these trends allows us to grasp why companies are

increasingly having difficulty hiring regulatory, quality, and other compliance personnel who are able to think beyond the traditional landscape, and why such companies are increasingly at risk. To stay current,
more outsourcing of compliance-related tasks is inevitable. And to succeed in launching a new medical product, executives will need to blend
their newfound flexibility of compliance with an understanding of the
trends shaping new drug, device, or biologic development; topics which
are covered in the next chapter.

EXECUTIVE'S CHECKLIST FOR CHAPTER ONE

Understanding the major trends impacting the regulatory compliance
landscape in which new medicines are developed is the first step toward
success in the 21st century. Here's a step-by-step to-do list:

- ☐ Download and review the FDA's reports on its Critical
  Path initiative and Quality by Design (copies of these
  can be obtained from the FDA or from the book's
  website at http://www.Get2MarketNow.com)
- ☐ Visit the ICH and GHTF websites to determine which
  rules apply to your organization (links to these websites,
  plus to those of the FDA, the European Medicines
  Agency, Health Canada, and other agencies, are on the
  book's website and in appendix two)
- ☐ Update any consultant and personnel selection and
  hiring processes to clarify that familiarity with ICH and/
  or GHTF are mandatory
- ☐ Decide what comparative effectiveness data you will plan
  to assess during development
- ☐ Read Chapter 5, "Improving Innovation," on ways in
  which you can incorporate basic intellectual property
  protection mechanisms into your compliance and
  medicinal product development activities
- ☐ Verify you have an effective and up-to-date records
  retention program that defines, at minimum, how long
  all FDA and ICH/GHTF required record types are
  retained
- ☐ Read Chapter 9, "Driving a Holistic Compliance
  Framework," to learn how to put in place a compliant

records management program

☐ Review due diligence and internal audit questionnaires with your legal department to identify which corporate espionage controls you should be regularly assessing

☐ Ask your colleagues to assess their level of comfort with ICH and/or GHTF requirements

☐ Map an ICH and/or GHTF professional development program with your human resources/personnel department

2 — Today's New Drug, Biologic and Device Development Landscape

On a warm July day, Drs. Cox and Demian announced in their company's monthly product development review that their device—the inhaler their firm was designing in tandem with several biopharmaceutical partners—was capable of producing nanoparticles. And, noted Dr. Cox, not only could it produce those nanoparticles to carry medicine, but, given some further tinkering and testing, it could deliver those nanoparticles to any particular spot in the lung.

This exciting news was shared with collaborators in Europe, the United Kingdom, and the US. Scientists, quality assurance, regulatory affairs, and all the different product developers thrilled at the news. Business development and marketing executives were absolutely giddy. Imagine how easily lung cancer could be excised; picture how simply asthma and emphysema could be eased if not reversed. These were just a sampling of the electrifying possibilities the various groups raved about.

And yet, in less than six months, after new combination product development efforts had been established, further development ground to halt. In the United Kingdom one of the collaboration teams had held their semi-annual cross-functional product development review, and in it a medical affairs specialist threw cold water on the idea of targeting nanoparticle-sized medicines to specific locations in the lung.

"So what?" he asked. "So what if you can target medicine anywhere in the lung. There is no technology today—and nothing on the horizon—that will tell us *where* in the lung to put that medicine. Without the diagnostics, you have a delivery mechanism that needs an actual target. How are you going to get that?"

And from there, the finance department and reimbursement folks chimed in, "How much will it cost to develop these diagnostics? And how long will that take? Will health agencies be willing to reimburse us or patients? For any reimbursement negotiations, we need an idea of effectiveness. This sounds like brand new, untested technology with new medicines—how are we to gauge effectiveness?"

Needless to say, the much heralded nanotechnology capabilities of the inhaler were shelved.

In developing 21st century medicines, it is no longer a question of: If we build it, will the patients come? Now the question is: If we build it, will we know what to do with it and can patients afford it? This is a far cry from the past 100 years of "follow the science." To appreciate this widening gap—and figure out how best to bridge it—we need to take a look at the most common drug, biologic, and device development model.

For the purposes of this book, I will use the traditional new product development funnel (see Figure 1) to illustrate the different stages of new medicine development. In its simplest form, the development funnel provides a visual representation of how various ideas and discoveries move from the initial conception stage (the wide end of the funnel, on left), through multiple layers or gates of sorting and discarding (the middle parts of the funnel), to the selection of the one or two that will eventually make it to the marketplace. One can then further narrow the funnel by identifying those products that will break even financially and those products that will make the company a significant profit.

In the general product development landscape, for every 1,000 ideas or product concepts that are created, less than 10 to15 will make it onto the market, and only 1 or 2 will make the company more than a 3% profit. When it comes to the new medicine development landscape, the success rate is even lower. Only 1 out of every 250 new biologic and drug candidates will make it to market[39], and of those, only one-third will break even financially.[40] While FDA critics like to point to the FDA as the main culprit of this low innovation success rate, the numbers given above point to a different cause: poor innovation prospects start early in the development process, years before the FDA becomes involved.

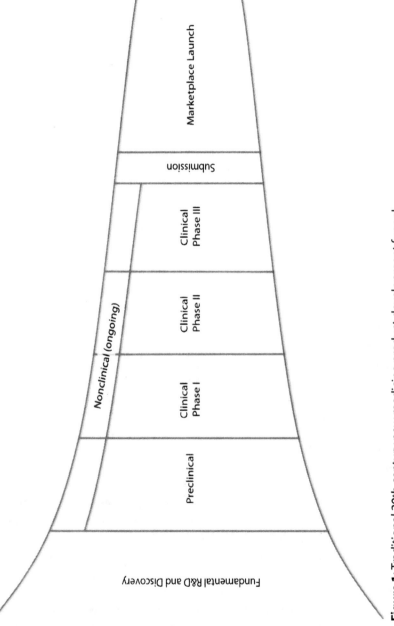

Figure 1: Traditional 20th century new medicine product development funnel

BASIC RESEARCH AND DEVELOPMENT

The multi-year process of drug discovery and device design starts in the basic research and development (R&D) phase. Also known as "fundamental" or "early-stage" R&D, in this phase activities are directed at a disease, molecular, or physical target. Because this phase of development does not use humans as test subjects, the FDA does not regulate basic R&D.

DRUG DISCOVERY

Throughout most of the 20th century, drug researchers relied on random testing of chemical compounds against known disease targets. This painstaking, trial and error approach has produced more than 90% of the drugs on the market today.[41]

Over the past thirty years, knowledge, techniques, and technological advances in biology, genetics, biochemistry, and engineering have transformed drug discovery. Molecular targets are increasingly preferred over general disease characteristics. This allows better screening of possible drug candidates. Synthetic chemical creation capability has also increased, expanding the pool of potential new drugs. And new biomedical engineering techniques using recombinant DNA (rDNA), combinatorial chemistry, and other methods have helped further transform the field.

By exponentially increasing the number of potential drug compounds, researchers have improved their likelihood of finding a viable drug candidate. In his book *Science Business*, Gary Pisano points out that under traditional drug discovery, a medicinal chemist took one month to create and test four possible new drug compounds. Today, medicinal chemists can use new knowledge, technologies, and automation to produce and test 3,300 compounds a month.[42]

If the availability of new technologies and automation were all that has improved over the past thirty years, then drug development would have dramatically sped up. We would be screening out 3,296 additional compounds per month. Unfortunately, our knowledge and awareness of potential compounds and our ability to create new compounds have far outstripped our screening automation. We understand more about the interplay of chemical compounds and the human body than we have the medical laboratory equipment or capability to screen out. In other words, while the equipment today might be able to screen against 3,300 known compounds, how do we screen for the compounds discovered or invented *after* the equipment was purchased and installed?

Genomics—the understanding of DNA sequences and the genetic functions of different parts of our bodies—has dramatically expanded the number of potential drug targets. Despite early hopes that genomics would lead us to discover the "bad" gene for various diseases, organ failures, and so on, we now know that things are not so simple. Most diseases and conditions result from a complex interplay of genetics, proteins (they translate information from genes into biological functions), and environmental factors.

As a result, what was once hoped to be a means to refine the potential disease target (*e.g.*, screen for that one bad gene) has turned into a complicated, multi-dimensional problem that only grows the more we learn. According to Dr. Barry Cherney of the FDA Center for Drug Evaluation and Research, "There are times when I wonder if all those techniques like rDNA and combinatorial chemistry have allowed us to do is just keep pace with all the new drug targets we keep uncovering."[43]

Today, biopharmaceutical companies screen millions of chemical compounds to produce less than 300 potential drug candidates. From these, a further winnowing produces 1-2 optimized lead candidates. It is these optimized compounds that will enter preclinical, then clinical trials, and then, hopefully, be launched as a new drug or biologic.

To get through the discovery end of the product development funnel typically takes 3-7 years and costs well in excess of US$12 million.[44] Only 1 in 6,000 compounds in the discovery R&D stage ever make it to market launch[45], making the discovery phase a costly numbers game for biopharmaceutical firms, their investors, and their prospective patients.

DEVICE DESIGN

In stark contrast to biopharmaceutical discovery, medical device and diagnostic designers tend to know they will end up with a design that works. There is little questioning of whether or not the basic technology is feasible. Instead, development uncertainties center on the application of technology to answer five questions:

1. How effective will the device be?
2. How reliable and safe will it be?

3. How easily can it be made and maintained?
4. How much can the device be sold for?
5. Will doctors and patients like it?

Early stage design, then, is focused on resolving technical hurdles to achieve a working prototype against which these uncertainties can start to be measured.

Technologies such as computer aided design (CAD) systems and three-dimensional printers have only sped up this early stage and given companies the luxury of exploring minor design innovations to later assess in preclinical testing and clinical trials.

Whereas drug and biologic early-stage discovery is about reducing fundamental "does it even work" uncertainties, device and diagnostic early stage design is about demonstrating how the basic model works.

This, however, belies the increasing complexity of factors that go into device design. Biomedical engineers, and garage-space innovators for that matter, can no longer go it alone. New fields of knowledge now crowd the stage—materials science, computer science, bioinformatics and virtual modeling—along with new technologies such as microprocessors, ceramics, diodes, space-age metals, and nanotechnology. As a result, early stage design has slowed while increasing in cost.

Despite this costly slow down, device firms have a significant lead on drug and biologics firms in terms of getting out of basic R&D and into preclinical testing. Early stage device design typically takes less than 2-3 years and can easily cost as little as $40,000, in sharp contrast to drugs which can cost $20-50 million before entering clinical trials.[46] Given the reduced time and cost burden relative to drugs, it is little wonder that device and diagnostics companies have been the fastest growing medicine makers over the past decade, a movement that shows little sign of slowing.

CONVERGENCE TRENDS

There are three trends that emerge from these changes in the early stage development phase:

1. Explosive expansion of drug and device possibilities that must be processed by any firm
2. Increasing levels of complexity inherent in the new

scientific and engineering techniques and methods
3.   The growing inter-relationship or convergence of these
     new bodies of knowledge and technology

The first two trends overlap, building upon one another to grow into an ever-widening field of possibilities. Firms must sample, compare, and process more and more potential possibilities just to achieve a functional prototype device or an optimized drug candidate for preclinical testing. The result: an early stage discovery phase that takes longer, costs more, and has increasingly poorer odds. In other words, the mouth of our new product development funnel continues to widen at the same time that the funnel itself grows longer and the outlet shrinks.

The third trend—exemplified by the combination of device and drug or biologic medicine—is one that will continue to grow. From drug-eluting stents to bone fusion growth titanium implants, combination devices are indicative of the need for convergence between devices and therapies in the 21st century. Another example is the use of genetic tests and other diagnostics to determine which genetic subgroup responds best to which new therapeutic compound. Because this type of convergent development can help to quickly refine viable disease, molecular, and physical targets, convergence can help speed the development of new medicines. We will learn more about taking advantage of convergent development later in chapters four and five.

Despite advantages of convergence in the early development stages, which can quickly synthesize and screen potential medicines, getting better candidates into clinical trials faster, skepticism continues under the traditional development mindset. Executives continue to be leery of anything that might shrink potential market size or impede realization of their dream of a one-size-fits-all blockbuster[47]

However, there are signs that this is changing. In August 2009, Abbot Laboratories and Pfizer announced they would work together to develop a diagnostic test to assess a prospective patient's genetic status and ability to effectively respond to a new Pfizer drug candidate.[48] The drug candidate, PF-02341066, is currently entering preclinical development testing. The genetic test will be used to select patients for future clinical trials. Assuming the drug is approved for market launch, Abbot's test will be used by doctors to identify which patients will best respond to Pfizer treatment.

NONCLINICAL DEVELOPMENT

Following selection of good drug candidates or good device prototypes, the potential therapy moves from fundamental research into nonclinical testing.

Nonclinical testing involves laboratory testing and animal studies. Nonclinical testing is typically performed until the new medicine is submitted for FDA approval and—aside from its preclinical components—runs concurrently with clinical trials. Examples of nonclinical testing include analytical chemistry analyses, formulation testing, bioimaging cell assays, animal studies, molecular modeling, materials stress testing, final prototype testing, and hundreds of others.

There used to be a "do them all" mentality for nonclinical testing, but the growth in knowledge and techniques over the past thirty years has forced companies to be selective in deciding which tests to undertake and which tests to forgo. This selectivity introduces a level of heightened risk very early in the development process, and it is one reason that the FDA becomes involved at this stage of the new drug and device development process. Information from these tests is used to determine initial dosing limits and treatment ranges for humans. As a result, the agency requires companies to apply for approval to start clinical trials. This gives the agency an opportunity to examine test results to ensure that such tests were conducted under controlled conditions and that all the test results were used to justify entry into clinical trials, not just the most appealing test results selectively presented by executives with a vested interest in getting a new medicine to market.

Both nonclinical and preclinical development are covered by the FDA's Good Laboratory Practices (GLP) regulations, which I will discuss more in the next chapter. For now, though, I will continue to walkthrough the traditional development model so it can serve as a common reference point throughout the rest of the book.

Preclinical

Before a company proceeds into clinical testing of its new medicine on humans it must submit an application based on nonclinical and preclinical testing. Preclinical testing is conducted to further optimize and identify the single drug or prototype device which will enter clinical trials. Tests are performed to demonstrate that a new medicine is safe to use on humans in clinical trials, and to provide early indicators of, and preliminary dosage ranges for, potential effectiveness.

As a result, the FDA has a significant interest in ensuring the information gathered in nonclinical and preclinical studies is reliable and has integrity. The agency has worked with its counterparts in the International Conference on Harmonization (ICH) to publish a slate of guidelines listing preclinical and nonclinical expectations, including the adoption of quality by design as early as possible. We will discuss how to take advantage of these publications in chapter six.

While preclinical testing may last up to six years, the usual timeframe is less than 24 months. The goal of preclinical testing is to determine which new medicine candidate looks like it could be the one in 6,000 winner to make it all the way through the development funnel, and enter the marketplace. Toward the end of the preclinical phase, three activities occur:

1. Filing of patent applications
2. Selection of a trademark name (*e.g.*, the name under which the new medicine may be sold)
3. Application to the FDA to start human testing in clinical trials

During the preclinical phase, the newly developing intellectual property is at significant risk for loss due to corporate espionage. Later, in chapter five, I will discuss several specific tactics that compliance executives and professionals should take to help prevent corporate espionage. You can also read more about ways to protect against corporate espionage in a previous work, in the chapter I wrote for the book *Best Practices in Biotechnology Business Development*, "Protecting Intellectual Property from the Inside Out."[49]

Nonclinical Trends

Since the late 1990s, several challenges in the nonclinical development space have arisen. As noted above, it is no longer possible to "test them all" and companies need to be selective when determining which tests to perform. This introduces increasingly greater risk when it comes to selecting the right new medicine candidate for further development. A wrong choice in which tests to perform can easily lead a company down a costly dead-end.

There are three trends occurring as a result:

1. Increased reliance on development partnerships
2. Increased outsourcing to cut costs
3. Increased emphasis by the FDA on risk-based quality by design in preclinical decision-making

The latter trend is helping drive compliance professionals deeper into early stage product development, less to enforce rules and regulations, and more to transfer skills of risk-based decision making, joint clinical and regulatory planning, and to implement a quality-centric mindset. As we will see later in chapter six, firms can advance their reimbursement and product supplier strategies through early involvement of regulatory affairs and quality personnel. Thus, any new medicine's product development plan can have well-defined "go/no-go" decisions built into the overall funnel.

In addition, because of the complexity of medicine development, cross-functional coordination and planning is critical. This is a key bridging role that regulatory affairs management can play. Because so much of product development work from the preclinical and later stages supports regulatory strategy, it is common sense for regulatory affairs executives to play a coordinating role in product development. Regulatory affairs groups can also help business management teams understand why financial milestones cannot be the sole drivers of development and market launch.

Finally, it is important to note that in a review of pre-Investigative New Drug (pre-IND) meeting notes, I have been consistently surprised to see how often it is FDA officials—not company personnel—who question how companies plan to assess patient population preferences such as dosage formats (*e.g.*, liquid, pill, intravenous, etc.). In a client's pre-IND meeting in August 2006, FDA officials specifically suggested that the client investigate orally disintegrating tablets if the company was serious about pediatric usage. Given the broad view of the industry, and the many pre-IND meetings that FDA officials attend, it makes sense that they would raise such suggestions and questions from one meeting to the next. In the 21st century, however, these are perfect questions for regulatory affairs professionals to be asking their development colleagues long before a pre-IND meeting with the FDA is arranged. Companies should be ending their preclinical work by updating their clinical strategies with plans for assessing patient population and sub-population preferences. Indeed, as I will discuss in chapters five, six, and eight, the preclinical stage is the time to assess such customer preferences, using clinical trials for verification.

A recurring theme in this book is that while compliance issues are important, striking a balance between compliance concerns and business realities is one of the biggest challenges facing FDA-regulated firms in the 21st century. Increasingly, medicine development must be made in a challenging environment of limited information. At the same time, we are constantly expanding the edges of new science and new technologies. As a result, more and more firms are turning to outside development partners.

Among the top fifty biopharmaceutical firms, 48% of their new medicines have been developed in conjunction with outside partners, increasing from 108 collaborations in 1988 to 569 collaborations in 2002.[50] While the examples of convergence cited earlier in this chapter are one form of development partnership, increasingly biopharmaceutical firms are seeking collaborations with university research labs. Such labs are expected to do the necessary fundamental R&D work and even some of the preclinical work, thus giving rise to the growing number of university technology transfer offices to handle intellectual property licensing and discovery sharing. Whether university labs are consistently compliant with the FDA's Good Laboratory Practices (GLP) regulations is questionable, but economic pressures combined with access to the cutting-edge technologies frequently found in universities increasingly force firms to rely upon academic laboratories. Treating these labs as suppliers to be controlled and monitored is difficult for compliance teams, and is one of the reasons for the third trend: increased outsourcing of development work to other companies.

Companies that conduct research and design work for biopharmaceutical and device makers are known as contract research organizations (CROs). Increasingly competitive, the worldwide CRO market is currently valued at over $18 billion, and is forecast to grow to more than $35 billion by 2014.[51] Firms that use CROs do not need to build an infrastructure or organization for those aspects of development which they outsource. Additional supplier oversight is required to ensure compliance with FDA requirements, but this cost is paltry compared to the tens of millions of dollars required for preclinical development. CROs also tend to have experience in submitting applications to enter into clinical trials, and can thereby contribute their expertise to help a client firm move from preclinical development into clinical trials.

CLINICAL DEVELOPMENT

Once potential efficacy and safety information is gathered and the final prototype / formulation selected, a firm submits an investigational new drug (IND) or investigative device exemption (IDE) application to the FDA to begin human testing. While the vast number of devices today do not require IDEs, as the number of drug and device or drug and diagnostic combinations continues to grow, the distribution is likely to change. Unless your company's device is a simple one such as a sterile wound dressing or a non-computerized non-implantable device, it is wise to expect to have to submit an IDE to enter clinical trials.

In the 20th century model of new medicine development, clinical trials are divided into three distinct stages: Phase I, Phase II and Phase III.

PHASE I TRIALS

In Phase I clinical trials, a drug or device is first tested on humans. The focus is on establishing safe dosing levels (for a drug) and safe usage levels (for a device). Other information such as pharmacokinetics, bio-markers, and toxicity types are also gathered. Ideally, efficacy indications may be captured, but this has not typically been the case. Given the relationship between efficacy and regulatory approval I discussed in chapter one, failure to gather efficacy data in Phase I trials can hamper a new medicine's chances of eventual marketplace success.

And, as I noted in the book's introduction, executives need to consistently prowl for ways to improve the odds of marketplace launch. While the average rate of success in Phase I trials is 58%, only 7.3% of those medicines in Phase I actually end up gaining marketing approval.[52]

With an average cost of $10 million, Phase I clinical trials typically take one year.[53] And that is without gathering pharmacogenomics and pricing data. Pricing data can be gathered using efficacy as a surrogate for cost-effectiveness. Gathering pharmacogenomics data is more complicated, but ultimately, very beneficial, as illustrated in these examples:

- Pharmaco-metabonomics is the prediction of outcomes

such as efficacy or toxicity in any given person based on mathematical models. Early validation studies have shown the ability of pharmaco-metabonomics to accurately predict patient response to new drugs and biologics simply by analyzing data from urine samples.[54]

- Genentech, the National Cancer Institute (NCI), and Curis entered into a collaborative agreement in early 2009 to advance a new biologic, GDC-0449, through clinical trials involving patients who have a genetic mutation in the Hedgehog pathway. While the Phase I trial was moderately successful (55% patients responded positively), use of molecular pharmacogenetic data in planning the trial allowed Genentech to prepare for, and to have the mechanisms to capture, the surprisingly few side effects the new drug generated.[55]

I should also note that with the increasing capabilities of databases and data mining, all the information gathered during a Phase I clinical trial can be retained and leveraged later on with different new drugs or devices, helping reduce the risks, timelines, and costs of those new medicines. I will discuss more aspects of how to apply this strategy, called "bookshelving", in chapter six.

Phase II Trials

Phase II trials are considered to be the weak link in the development process: potential medicines have only a 45% chance of progressing beyond Phase II trials. Multiple Phase II trials are often necessary for drug approval. Each Phase II trial lasts approximately 2 years at a cost between $20-30 million.[56] In the 20th century development model, Phase II trials focus on safety and toxicity, with increasing emphasis on efficacy from trial to trial.

Phase II trials are starting to be broken apart into various "arms" (Phase IIA, IIB, IIC, and so on) to clarify different aspects. These so-called "adaptive arm" trials, first accepted by FDA in its Critical Path initiative in 2004, can be used to optimize formulations, dosing, usage, or even ideal patient profiles. Biostatistics and modeling are very important components of Phase II trials, as is the selection of the future manufacturing site for the finished and approved medicine. Because Phase

II trials are intended to demonstrate how the drug/device performs in actual patients (as opposed to Phase I trials which are usually conducted on healthy volunteers), Phase II data undergo greater scrutiny by the FDA and by reimbursement agencies.

PHASE III TRIALS

In the 20th century development model, Phase III trials represent the final testing step before FDA approval and market launch. Involving 2,000 – 5,000 patients worldwide, Phase III trials can last up to 5 years and cost between $50 to $500 million.[57] Even though all this effort and planning has come together in Phase III, there is still only a 58% chance of approval.[58]

Phase III studies are designed to show regulators, healthcare providers, prospective patients, and investors what the new medicine can do. In the 20th century development model, during Phase III trials marketing plans are designed and reimbursement strategies are hatched. From a compliance standpoint, Phase III trials not only confirm all the earlier work; they also validate the manufacturing site and distribution network. Following a successful set of one or more Phase III clinical trials, the new medicine is submitted for approval.

CLINICAL TRENDS

A lack of information and knowledge to make informed decisions has been undermining traditional clinical development. Difficulties in understanding the increasing complexity of diseases "has resulted in an increasing number of clinical failures and overall development costs."[59]

The inability of firms to predict which chemical compounds will be successful in humans, and which of the millions of device software, hardware, and chemical interactions will be problematic in patients and the environment also contributes to poor clinical success rates and rising development costs. These uncertainties also contribute to a growing compliance burden.

In the 1970s and 1980s, approximately 100 clinical trials were held in the US during an average year. Today, 4,000 – 6,000 clinical trials occur annually in the US.[60] As we increasingly segment the prospective patient population from a one-for-all to one based on genetic or other personalization aspects, the number of clinical trials is predicted to at least double by 2020, commiserate with the doubling in size of the CRO industry.

Some proponents of personalized medicine argue that as our understanding of genetics grows, we will conduct smaller trials that produce more reliable data. The FDA recently indicated that companies need to gather genomics information during all clinical trials and should try to start collecting and analyzing such information even during the preclinical phase for submission in the request to start clinical trials. FDA commissioner Dr. Margaret Hamburg told an American Association for the Advancement of Science forum that while most clinical trials are structured to determine if a drug is safe and effective, few trials delve into the reasons why. By using companion biomarker tests, firms can learn about how and why a new medicine works, lending more scientific certainty to a new medicine's application for market approval.[61]

Unfortunately, smaller trials do not proportionately decrease the effort required to oversee a trial and analyze its data. Whereas executives might have only had to oversee one trial during a particular year, now they will be forced to supervise three or four, and trials are increasingly moving overseas. Imagine having to audit sites, plan, supervise, analyze, and prove compliance for a half-dozen clinical trials all conducted in the same year but in different countries on multiple continents.

With personalized medicine development, the amount of compliance work involved will go up, not down, as firms must manage an increasing amount of risk.

A further challenge in current clinical trial trends is the increase of data intensity: more tests, more procedures, more controls, more documentation, more third-party scrutiny, and more ways to track, coordinate, and follow-up with patients, clinical investigators, and adverse events. The amount of information gathered is growing exponentially, and it is expected to meet FDA expectations for data integrity and regulatory record retention requirements. Ten years ago the average regulatory submission was the equivalent of approximately 100,000 pages of information. Today, the average submission contains approximately 500,000 pages of information.

POSTMARKET DEVELOPMENT

A fairly recent phase of new medicine development, introduced in the 2007 Food and Drug Administration Amendments Act, calls for companies to conduct postmarket development studies and clinical trials.

In the 20th century model of new medicine development, the final act of development is submitting a request for marketing approval to the FDA. The FDA then reviews the application and its reams of data proving product safety, efficacy, and quality, and aims to respond within one year. To get a priority review of 3 months or less, a new medicine must be deemed an "orphan" medicine –a drug addressing a unique medical need affecting fewer than 200,000 patients in the United States. The FDA publishes a list of potential orphan medicines on its website (see the book's website for a link to the specific page on the FDA's website).

Approval by the FDA not only allows the drug, device or biologic to be marketed in the US, but it also determines which claims a company can make in the medicine's advertising and marketing. Thus, the more marketing-relevant data you can test for and gather during development, the greater your opportunities in marketing your device. This expansion of claims can translate into greater profit potential.

Increasingly, however, a new drug application (NDA), biologics application (BLA), or other premarket application is not the end of development, but only another gate through which the medicine must pass in its lifecycle. Since 2007, the FDA has increasingly called upon firms to extend their development cycle into the postmarket with Phase IV clinical trials and postmarket nonclinical studies.[62] Postmarket studies, trials, and monitoring will be just as important within the next five to ten years as the pivotal Phase II clinical trials are now.

MANUFACTURING

Although approved product manufacturing is not traditionally considered part of development, because postmarket monitoring is now part of the new medicine development lifecycle, some aspects of manufacturing need to be considered when taking a holistic view of product development and compliance. In this case, the new medicine development funnel might look like Figure 2.

Medicinal product manufacturing is a topic beyond the scope of this book. However, there are several points relevant to our discussion of compliance and bringing a new medicine to market in the 21st century.

In 2006, the FDA revised its Good Manufacturing Practices (GMP) regulations with the publication of its guidance entitled *Quality Systems Approach to Pharmaceutical CGMP Regulations*. In conjunction with the 2004 guidance *Current Good Manufacturing Practice for Combination*

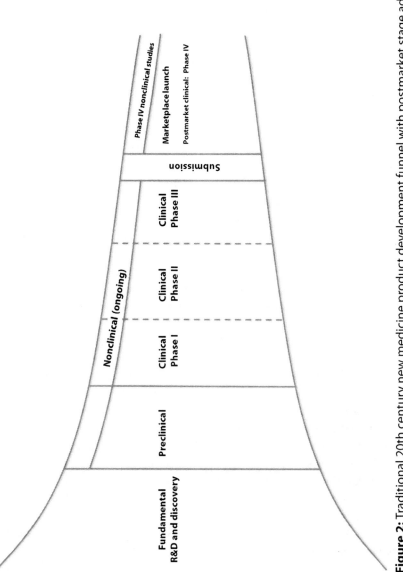

Figure 2: Traditional 20th century new medicine product development funnel with postmarket stage added

Products, this revision laid out a regulatory schema consistent with the device Quality Systems Regulations (QSRs).[63]

As noted in these guidance documents and in the ICH and the Global Harmonization Task Force (GHTF) guidelines that the FDA has promoted, manufacturing methods and processes are expected to be defined during preclinical and clinical development. Under a fully integrated quality by design strategy, a drug's manufacturing processes and methods should be as completely defined and as similar to the approved drug's manufacturing processes as possible by the time a firm is manufacturing its drug, biologic, or device for Phase II clinical trials.[64] In other words, design of finished product manufacturing needs to move from its current position in the 20th century development model, where this design takes place during Phase II and Phase III clinical trials, further up the funnel to take place during preclinical and Phase I clinical trials. Optimization of production processes then occurs in Phase III clinical trials. This is a significant change from the traditional approach where such optimization was often left until after marketplace launch.

As a result of these changes, compliance with GMPs is advanced considerably in the new product development pipeline to Phase I clinical trials.[65] For executives expecting to deal with GMPs after market approval—or to contract a finished medicine manufacturer to deal with the GMPs—the 21st century will require significant adjustment.

SUMMARY

Evolution in regulations, from revised GMPs to international harmonization, has been matched by the accelerating pace of scientific knowledge and engineering capabilities. From proteonomics to nanotechnology, every new realization gives us a glimpse of how much more we must discover and understand.

Companies are increasingly collaborating to handle the complexities of development in the 21st century. The trend of biopharmaceutical companies partnering with medical device and diagnostic firms will continue.

Taken together, there are nine trends shaping the medicinal development landscape in the 21st century:

4. Explosion in scientific and engineering knowledge
5. Increasing complexity of technical and scientific

equipment

6. Growing convergence across fields of knowledge to produce a functional medicine
7. Increase in combination devices
8. Increased rise in the risk of intellectual property theft from all the outsourcing and development collaborations
9. Increasing demand for compliance executives to ensure development meets regulatory expectations
10. Increased outsourcing of development work
11. Segmentation of clinical trials—especially Phase II trials—into adaptive arms
12. Increased expectation of Phase IV trials and other postmarketing studies

Given the traditional model's reliance upon 20th century know-how and regulatory expectations, it is little wonder that medical product innovation in the 21st century is declining while its costs rise. Executives need to adapt their mindset and their company to the new realities of product development and regulatory expectations. Sadly, as we shall see in the next chapter, this is made all the more difficult by the black-and-white quality systems and compliance infrastructures we have inherited from last century.

EXECUTIVE'S CHECKLIST FOR CHAPTER TWO

The second step toward medicinal product development success is determining how your organization is impacted by the trends affecting new drug, biologic, and device development. Here's a step-by-step to-do list:

☐ Build a cross-discipline development team that includes members dedicated to regulatory affairs and quality management

☐ Using the development funnel model, assess where your compliance team needs to start enforcing FDA regulatory compliance, quality by design expectations, and your quality policy

☐ Design your development strategy to optimize cost-efficiency and product efficacy by Phase II clinical trials

☐ Decide which marketing claims you will pursue upon market launch, and plan to start gathering supportive data in Phase II clinical trials, at the latest

☐ Outline your postmarketing surveillance strategies and risk mitigation controls by the end of Phase III trials (and preferably by the end of Phase II trials)

☐ Read the section on Phase 0 clinical trials in Chapter 8, "Ensuring Lean Regulatory Affairs"

☐ Read the sections in Chapter 6, "Building in Quality and Flexibility from Day One," on incorporating quality by design and product development "bookshelving" in your preclinical and clinical development efforts

☐ Review Chapter 5, "Improving Innovation," on steps compliance executives can take to prevent intellectual property theft during medical product development

☐ Download and read the GAO report 07-49 *New Drug Development* and summarize relevant takeaways for your organization (a copy of this report can be downloaded from the GAO or the book's website at http://www.Get2MarketNow.com)

☐ Download and review the FDA guidance documents *CGMP for Phase 1 Investigational Drugs* and *Current Good Manufacturing Practice for Combination Products*, and summarize relevant takeaways for your organization (copies of these documents can be downloaded from the FDA or the book's website)

☐ Review the ICH *E*-series guidelines on clinical trial topics and the *S*-series guidelines on preclinical study topics (see the links to ICH in appendix two and on the book's website)

☐ Download and read the ICH Q8 guideline *Pharmaceutical Development* (a copy is available on the book's website) and other ICH *Q*-series guidelines relevant to clinical and nonclinical testing

☐ Download and review the ICH M3 Guideline *Nonclinical Safety Studies for the Conduct of Human Clinical Trials and Marketing Authorization for Pharmaceuticals* (a copy is available on the book's website)

☐ Review the GHTF *SG1-Premarket Evaluation* and the

SG5-Clinical Safety/Performance guidelines, plus the *SG2-Postmarket Surveillance/Vigilance* guidelines (links to the GHTF are in appendix two and on the book's website at http://www.Get2MarketNow.com)

☐ Ask your colleagues to assess their level of comfort with new product development terms such as "stage gates" and "open innovation"—I will discuss these more in-depth, including how to apply them to your environment, in Chapters 5 and 6

3 — Today's Quality Systems and Regulatory Compliance Landscape

In response to regulatory oversight of medical development, companies have adopted "compliance" programs. These programs are most often split into those groups responsible for operational aspects (quality) and the team that regularly interfaces with the FDA and other regulatory health agencies (regulatory affairs).

Until the 1990s, regulatory affairs departments were relatively small, involved only in regulatory submissions and tracking communications and commitments with the FDA. Since the 1990s, the scope of regulatory affairs professionals has expanded to include regulatory strategies and operational aspects of R&D; clinical, reimbursement, and postmarket surveillance; product distribution and recalls; advertising and promotions; labeling; and manufacturing. All of this has been driven by the need for companies to adapt to some of the conclusions we arrived at in chapters one and two—the explosion of scientific and engineering knowledge and complexity plus the increasing "product lifecycle" view espoused by regulatory authorities around the globe.

Quality has also undergone its own diversification. While it was originally conceived of as quality control and only involved at the end of any process, over time quality control has morphed into quality assurance, then quality management, then quality unit, and most recently, simply quality. Quality departments are increasingly seen as not just relevant to adherence with industry standards such as those maintained by the International Standards Organization (ISO), but relevant to the regulatory requirements of the FDA and other regulatory health agencies.

Just as the FDA has evolved in its approach to oversight of the industry since the 1990s, regulatory affairs and quality departments have expanded their involvement. Unfortunately, the command and control philosophy of many quality and regulatory affairs departments has not kept pace with either the evolution of product development practices or the FDA's regulatory expectations. Since 2007, FDA officials have energetically espoused a refrain similar to Dr. Barry Rothman's from an August 2009 conference: "Do not conceive of the GMPs as they were before 2006 [when the agency published its guidance *Quality Systems Approach to Pharmaceutical CGMP Regulations*] or you'll find yourself in trouble."[66]

In my own experiences, and those of my clients and colleagues who contributed insights to this book, companies are increasingly struggling internally with a compliance mindset rooted in last century's all-or-nothing attitude—processes and/or business results are either compliant or non-compliant. This polarized view mistakenly reduces an entire spectrum of possibilities down to the two extremes. As a result, internal organizational disagreements become exacerbated at a time when firms face business conditions such as increased globalization and the rapid gain of competitors using newer scientific and engineering knowledge and technologies. When 21st century business realities require compromises, agility, and constant adaptability, compliance professionals who insist upon a dichotomous system of compliance/non-compliance cannot contribute in a meaningful way to business decisions.

As a result, company competitiveness is being inadvertently undermined by last century's compliance structures. These 20th century structures present five weaknesses in the 21st century landscape:

1. Risk aversion
2. All-or-nothing mentalities
3. Operational silos
4. Cost inefficiencies
5. Customer exclusions

In this chapter, I will touch upon each of these within the context of the four formal FDA requirements of today's quality and compliance landscape:

1. Good Laboratory Practices (GLPs)
2. Good Clinical Practices (GCPs)

3. Good Manufacturing Practices (GMPs)
4. Quality Systems Regulations (QSRs)

I will also touch upon a fifth aspect that, while not yet fully required by regulatory health agencies, is increasingly necessary: compliance with the harmonized regulatory standards put out by the ICH and GHTF.

GOOD LABORATORY PRACTICES

Good Laboratory Practices (GLPs) are a set of FDA regulations encapsulated in 21 CFR 58, first published in 1979 and then slightly updated in 1987. In late 2008, the FDA announced an initiative to begin to update the GLPs to better align with international harmonization efforts and the revised GMP regulations.

GLPs apply to all laboratory studies that produce results intended for submission to the FDA, intended to support an FDA submission, or intended to support requirements of good manufacturing and good clinical practice regulations. GLPs apply to any laboratory conducting such studies. Thus, GLPs apply to the nonclinical studies mentioned in the previous chapter. And accordingly, this is where we begin our analysis of some the strengths and weaknesses in drawing 20th century practices into the 21st century.

USE OF STANDARD OPERATING PROCEDURES

In order to ensure a consistent compliance approach, compliance teams—whether in labs or offices or manufacturing environs—write standard operating procedures (SOPs) to document standard processes. Both US and international regulators require companies to have effective policies and procedures. The creation, use, and maintenance of SOPs has become the *de facto* industry strategy to ensure effective procedures and maintain consistent control over operations. In other words, SOPs document a process to achieve uniformity of adherence. In this way, control is achieved. And through control we can proclaim compliance.

Templates for SOPs abound in industry literature and on the Internet, and it is beyond the scope of this book to analyze and discuss in detail the merits and drawbacks of any one type of template. For the purposes of our discussion on compliance programs and the challenges they face, it is sufficient to note that most SOP templates are fairly similar and cover:

- What the process is (including any dependencies and ordering of steps)
- Who is accountable for what parts of the process
- What tools and equipment are used in the process

For a sample SOP template, see the book's website http://www. Get2MarketNow.com. The discussion below focuses on the usage of SOPs in the context of compliance, and specifically when it comes to GLPs. Drafting SOPs will be discussed in chapters seven and eight.

An SOP typically includes a summary of the purpose of the process as well as the logic dictating said process. For instance, "This SOP is intended to describe the process for evaluation, selection, approval, contracting, and monitoring of suppliers providing components, materials, and services used to support the development, testing, and manufacture of the Company's products and its Quality Management System to ensure that suppliers are qualified and appropriately monitored to assure the Company of a consistent level of quality in the components, materials, and services received as per 21 CFR Part 820.50."

Rather than clarifying anything, this SOP's "purpose" section only begs more questions. Here are the questions I asked of one of my clients:

- Is the purpose of this SOP to ensure that suppliers are "qualified and appropriately monitored" to deliver what the company needs?
- Or is the purpose of this SOP to describe a separate process that should be followed when a company needs qualified suppliers?
- Are these processes only required when dealing with "21 CFR Part 820.50"? Does that mean this does not apply to laboratory suppliers?
- And does this SOP meet with the rules spelled out in 21 Code of Federal Regulations Part 820.50, including any revisions applicable from recent statute changes?

A properly written SOP should provide answers; not introduce more questions.

This level of poor guidance in an SOP's purpose section is typical, and given that the purpose section is usually found in the first third of most SOP templates, it is no surprise then that firms with this type of poorly written SOP run into problems when expecting compliance from busy, constantly multi-tasking employees. As I discuss in my process mapping workshops, with SOPs (or almost anything else you want followed) simplicity, brevity, and clarity are critical. The typical SOP is missing at least two of those characteristics—simplicity and brevity—and as a result, comprehension, and more importantly, compliance, is weakened.

Compounding the poor structure of SOPs, guidelines are perpetually changing as there is a constant disagreement throughout the industry over how detailed an SOP should be. As non-compliance increases, the tendency is to make the written procedure so explicit that, as one quality executive claimed, "a trained monkey could follow it." Ironically, the more explicit a process explanation is, the less likely it is to be read and thus, the less likely it is to be followed.

In addition, because documenting a process takes effort—and effort is required for more detailed documentation—I have also discovered that firms with extremely stringent SOPs tend to see at least one of three problems develop:

- The SOP enshrines a process which is out of date with current realities
- The people who are supposed to follow the SOP routinely ignore it due to practical time limitations
- The compliance organization is ignored when it complains of non-compliance

In most product development laboratories flexibility and agility go hand in hand with innovation. SOPs that attempt to document every single process with excessive precision– or as my friend Clinton Hallman, a counsel at Kraft Foods points out, "SOPs that start with 'open door, turn 48 degrees to the southeast, take three 14-inch spaced steps...' are not going to succeed in ensuring consistent compliance in the laboratory or other knowledge-intensive environments. In one fashion or another, such SOPs will inevitably fail."

HIDDEN COST OF STANDARD OPERATING PROCEDURES

Creating a good SOP is no easy task. On average, I have found that it takes at least 20 to 40 man-hours from start to finish. While investments in developing SOPs may seem like wasted time and money, the cost of creating an SOP is low compared to the costs of trying to comply with poorly crafted SOPs.

Think about SOPs as photographs. Each SOP is a digital snapshot of a process. As time passes and business realities change, that snapshot becomes out of date. An out of date SOP increases noncompliance and costs.

Costs are incurred in changing an SOP and then retraining people on the revised SOP. The more detailed your SOP is, the more frequently you will need to change your SOP and retrain your people. And the more frequently you have to do this revising and retraining, the greater the cost of compliance. Unfortunately, the cost is not just in compliance or in dollars, time is also consumed. For instance, if having scientists and engineers spend 2-3 hours a month in SOP training is an acceptable cost of doing business in FDA-regulated industry, that "cost of doing business" doubles if scientists and engineers are also spending an additional 2-3 hours away from their labs and designs getting retrained on revised SOPs every month. The more detailed SOPs are, the higher the productivity loss incurred trying to keep the SOP current. Rather than SOP training causing a 2-3 hours loss in monthly productivity, SOP training and SOP-revision retraining have caused a loss of 4-6 hours in monthly productivity. In other words, the way in which compliance has been addressed (*e.g.*, detailed SOPs) has inadvertently driven down productivity.

The second way in which the traditional approach to SOPs adds cost and lowers productivity is through reducing flexibility. This is especially important when it comes to knowledge workers such as scientists and engineers.

The more detailed SOPs and policies are, the less flexibility exists. While the intent to ensure uniformity of performance is good, the practical result is an unplanned decrease in flexibility. Detailed SOPs lock in how processes are to be performed at the exclusion of other, perhaps better, ways. And any other manner of performing the process then results in a deviation, generating a report of noncompliance, which then results in retraining, *ad nauseum*. While many assume that these wasteful practices are simply a cost of doing business in a regulated industry, they can be avoided with properly-written SOPs.

The hidden costs of SOPs are most significant in knowledge-intensive environments like laboratories and offices because SOPs are so-often based on practices from manual labor-intensive manufacturing environs.

SOP specificity is essential for manufacturing to address its discrete, step-by-step processing. Poorly documented processes can result in operator harm or an unsafe finished product. Because historical emphasis by regulatory health agencies has been on manufacturing, compliance expertise has largely developed around process control in this area. Translating this level of command and control from factory floors to laboratory benches, or from warehouse shelves to office desks, is not, as I have noted, a simple matter. Not only does poor translation run the risk of slowing productivity, but if a rigid mindset is transferred from manufacturing to a dynamic knowledge-based environ, conflict is sure to ensue.

As we will see in chapter seven, there are ways to strike a balance, achieving flexibility and control in SOPs. For now, though, recognize that executives with a 20th century view of the use of SOPs frequently hamstring themselves and their colleagues in the labs, offices, and design spaces of the 21st century.

CUSTOMER EXCLUSION

Another example of where out of date compliance practices accidentally placed firms at a disadvantage is in exclusion of the customer—especially at an early stage in product development—because of worries about compliance.

A common citation in FDA enforcement actions such as warning letters is for marketing an unapproved product. Indeed, a search for the phrase "marketing an approved product" in the FDA's warning letter library turned up 305 specific warning letters over the past seven years; approximately 1-3 every month. Compliance executives know that the FDA is aggressively vigilant in finding and acting against firms for marketing unapproved products. As a result, compliance professionals tend to be conservative when considering anything that might be seen as marketing an unapproved drug or device.

An unintended consequence of this awareness and anxiety is an innate risk aversion when it comes to involving the customer in helping define and drive product development. To sit in a medicinal product development meeting and ask about introducing a focus group of potential customers would likely cause serious consternation. In one such example, when I suggested to a client that we conduct a survey of prospective patients on product characteristics the prospective patients would like to see in a new medicine then under preclinical development, my client's regulatory affairs manager stated that the firm could not survey prospective patients as, "We are not yet ready for clinical testing."

Biopharmaceutical and medical device companies have retarded themselves by at least two to three decades by not regularly incorporating customer involvement in medicinal development. Such customer involvement and feedback at an early, conceptual stage of product development has become *de rigueur* for other products as diverse as automobiles and laundry detergent.

It is also important to understand, in terms of product development, the term "customer." The customer is not simply the end patient of a medicine. Clearly we all understand the role of the healthcare provider as a customer of medicine as well; they play important roles in determining which treatments a patient will receive. But does your firm also recognize the hospital administrator who purchases and stocks your medicine as a customer? What about the reimbursement specialist who makes decisions on reimbursement approvals for the vast majority of your intended patient population? And what about the spouses of those for whom the medicine is intended? Did product development executives think of asking patient spouses what they would ideally like in a medicine's packaging, product inserts, or application? Perhaps the patient's spouse would like a "quick start" guide to giving a complicated dosing regimen? And if a new medicine's target patient population is the elderly or children, getting input from their caregivers—not just healthcare providers—would seem to be a crucial guiding step for further development.

Not one of these "customers" will be in a clinical trial. And thus we have unintentionally blinded ourselves. We do not seek out information which, as I noted previously, will help differentiate our medicine to the marketplace and to the regulators.

In chapter five, I will specifically discuss ways in which you can incorporate these "voices of the customer" in your development efforts without running afoul of regulations. For now, though let us continue to look at ways in which a 20th century approach to complying with the regulations has unintentionally hampered our ability to innovate, driven up costs, and reduced our chances of medicinal product success.

GOOD CLINICAL PRACTICES

Good Clinical Practices (GCPs) apply to clinical trial design, conduct, recording, and reporting. They are a collection of regulations that have grown since 1938 to now cover protection of human beings as biomedical subjects, disclosure of financial conflicts of interest, independent scientific and safety review boards, plus rules on the sponsorship of the trials and control of the actual medicine to be tested. The FDA has eight different regulations comprising GCPs—21 CFRs 50, 54, 56, 312, 314, 601, 812, and 814.

Two compliance aspects GCPs reveal as the underlying weaknesses inherent in continuing to apply 20th century controls to the 21st century personalized medicine landscape are:

1. Institutional Review Boards (IRBs)
2. Data Monitoring Committees (DMCs)

INSTITUTIONAL REVIEW BOARDS

Covered specifically by 21 CFR 54, the Institutional Review Board's (IRB) primary purpose is to ensure the protection of human subjects in clinical trials. Historically, IRBs have been bound to a not-for-profit research institution or university. The emergence of independent for-profit IRBs is of concern to the compliance of clinical trials, and to the eventual success of a new medicine's approval and market launch.

In April 2009, a private for-profit IRB, Colorado-based Coast IRB, was accused by the FDA of improper behavior, conflicts of interest, and compromises in conduct and results of clinical trials. And in August 2009, Coast IRB went out of business. Hundreds of clinical trials— and the fortunes of many biopharmaceutical and device firms that had used Coast IRB—were thrown into jeopardy. There is little doubt that the sponsors who had hired Coast IRB now wish their due diligence of Coast IRB was more thorough. The problem, of course, is that at the time, most executives thought they had been thorough in their evaluation of Coast IRB—after all, they were following their own due diligence

SOPs.

A common weakness of many compliance programs is the difficulty of taking stock of external factors and adapting to them. From an insular "not invented here" philosophy to a reticence to alter what has always worked in the past, compliance programs that are not amenable to better ways to do things are often those programs that end up costing their companies more than they should. As we saw in chapter two, clinical development takes years and costs millions of dollars. In the case of Coast IRB, companies that followed their compliance programs in a rote fashion—using a quality system due diligence review which often does not consider financial records or public records—lost tens of millions of dollars and years of clinical development time. It remains to be seen whether any of the new drugs tested by Coast IRB will ever be launched, or even approved by the FDA.

When firms take a "set it up and leave it" approach to their compliance programs, compliance too often becomes a routine checklist to complete rather than living controls designed to reduce risk. In a competitive environment the attitude can easily become 'let me just fill out this checklist and the due diligence will be complete.' Rather than critically thinking about one's mission, the unspoken assumption is that if something was an important consideration, a part of the checklist would be devoted to it.

Lest we lay the blame on routine compliance checklists blinding firms to the risks associated with Coast IRB, there were undoubtedly compliance professionals whose recommendation not to use Coast IRB was overruled by senior executives more concerned with meeting timelines and the financial bottom line. This is a common calculation especially among firms whose funding is not driven by sales of product already on the market (*e.g.*, development-stage companies). Whether implicit or tacit, the pressure put on management by investors, shareholders and venture capitalists is incidental. As I noted in chapter one, firms as diverse as Sanofi-Aventis, Upjohn, KV Pharma, and InterMune have discovered that the desire to improve bottom line perceptions at the cost of compliance comes with significant negative financial and publicity risks.

DATA MONITORING COMMITTEES

One means by which companies have tried to control their risk in clinical trials and limit the ability of unscrupulous executives to influence trials is through the use of Data Monitoring Committees (DMCs).

First used in the 1960s, DMCs are responsible for monitoring clinical trial safety, including the overall conduct of the trial and review of interim data. Appointed by sponsors of clinical trials—biopharmaceutical and device firms—the DMC can help ensure the scientific validity of the trial and act as a third-party to oversee the safety of human participants. In a March 2006 guidance document, *Guidance for Clinical Trial Sponsors: Establishment and Operation of Clinical Trial Data Monitoring Committees*, the FDA began to encourage sponsors to have their DMCs also evaluate comparative effectiveness.[67]

In a 2009 speech to pharmaceutical and device clinical and regulatory affairs executives, I made the case that without including comparative effectiveness information, a DMC will only benefit interactions with the FDA by demonstrating that clinical trials have scientific integrity. But safety data alone will not get a new product to market. In July 2009, King Pharmaceuticals brought an impressive array of safety data to an FDA advisory panel but was unable to obtain approval for its new drug CorVue; panel members felt there was not a strong enough case for efficacy, particularly in relationship to drugs already on the market.[68] As I covered in chapter one, there is an increasing emphasis by regulatory health agencies on medicinal effectiveness as well as safety and quality. DMCs that operate in the traditional 20th century manner and do not tackle comparative effectiveness, now represent only a partial solution to clinical trial compliance.

This also brings to light a larger theme that quality and regulatory affairs departments have struggled with over the past decade: ensuring data integrity. To guarantee the scientific validity of a clinical trial, the data generated in that trial must be guaranteed to be trustworthy. In our digital age, where computer problems, password sharing, and privacy losses are rampant, how secure, how accurate, and how authentic are the clinical trial data? Considering that most clinical trials build one upon the other as the medicine develops, is there a risk of an unscrupulous employee or contractor tweaking the data from an earlier trial to better justify decisions around the new trial? What about the risk of unethical employees or contractors deleting datapoints that throws off the expected averages? To the FDA, the answer to the above questions is simple: yes, there is a risk, a very significant risk.

MISSING DATA INTEGRITY

One-third of all pre-approval inspections by the FDA are undertaken due solely to concerns about the integrity of the information submitted by the sponsor of the clinical trial.[69] Fraudulent data is not the only issue that throws data integrity into question. FDA reviewers ask hundreds of questions of the submitting company's data, analyses, and conclusions:

- How has the company represented adverse events?
- Are errors in trials explained away by pat phrases like "not attributable to the investigative drug / device?" when they might be better explained by …
- Which statistical methods were selected by the sponsor and why?
- Did the sponsor's inclusion or exclusion of outliers negatively skew the data?
- Did the members of the DMC and the IRB faithfully disclose all potential conflicts of interest prior to their selection to serve on those groups?
- Do charts and analyses incorporate all source documents? Are such source documents referenced?
- Did the sponsor review patient logs? If 100% of the logs were not reviewed, what was the justification? Was this consistent in all studies?

You can get a list of more than 120 questions FDA reviewers ask of clinical and nonclinical data integrity in one of the recorded compliance seminars accessible through the book's website.

In any FDA inspection, just as in a pre-approval inspection, the agency's inspectors will spend approximately 80% of their time examining records and your data, looking for incongruities.[70] Given the other activities of inspectors such as meeting and interviewing employees at the firm and receiving a tour of the various site facilities, most people are consistently surprised at how little review time is spent by inspectors on the company's SOPs. The assumption is that by virtue of having SOPs, the company will be in compliance. However, as demonstrated by pre-approval inspections and all other FDA inspections, the emphasis is on records and data. A company's records are the result of the SOP and stand as proof of intent to comply.

Standing in the crosshairs of the FDA's skepticism of clinical and nonclinical data integrity are a company's compliance executives. It is the job of quality and regulatory affairs executives and other compliance professionals to guarantee that medicinal product safety, efficacy, and quality measures exist. It is the responsibility of compliance executives to ensure a firm is compliant with both regulations and agency expectations. And proof of success in these areas lies in records. Specifically in records that are accurate, legible, complete, contemporaneous, original, and attributable.

So how well prepared are executives and their staffs? Judging by warning letters and new medicine application rejections, the answer is "poorly." Over the past few years, CDRH analyses consistently have shown that 7-out-of-10 submission problems arise from record integrity issues. The magnitude of this ratio for devices makes one wonder about the typically more complex drug and biologics submissions. Off-the-record conversations with biostatisticians and other colleagues in CBER and CDER have cited ratios in the range of 9-out-of-10 submission problems due to record integrity issues, but neither center has published formal analyses. These problems affect large and small firms equally. At the end of 2009, the FDA rejected a joint marketing approval submission of international giant Johnson & Johnson and a small Swiss drug firm, Basilea, because data from 10 out of 49 clinical sites was deemed unreliable.[71]

Data integrity mistakes are costly. An independent analysis of delay costs over an 18 month period determined a cost of $11,000 to $30,000 *per day*.[72] To avoid that expense, firms would be wise to consider hiring a person solely tasked with ensuring data integrity in applications, reports, amendments, and all other submissions to regulatory health agencies.

As we continue to move away from paper records to digital data, questions and concerns about information integrity will persist; not only under the GLPs and GCPs and the FDA's Bioresearch Monitoring Program (BIMO) inspectors, but also under the Good Manufacturing Practices and Quality System Regulations. Not only must firms developing new medicines comply with the GLPs and GCPs, the investigative products they make for those clinical trials must also be compliant with the manufacturing regulations governing their production.[73]

GOOD MANUFACTURING PRACTICES

GMPs are nominally comprised of three regulations: 21 CFR 210, 211, and 606. As discussed in chapter one, the FDA has now revised these regulations through a mix of guidance documents and passages within the Food and Drug Administration Amendment Act (FDAAA) of 2007. It is also within the context of the Good Manufacturing Practices (GMPs) that the FDA has begun enforcing harmonized regulatory guidelines from the International Conference on Harmonization (ICH).

The GMPs cover ten broad areas of drug and biologics manufacturing:

- Personnel
- Facilities
- Equipment
- Components, containers, and closures
- Production processes and sampling
- Packaging and labeling
- Inventory, warehousing, and distribution
- Laboratory controls
- Records and documentation
- Returned product, recalls, and postmarket safety

While the rules are fairly generic—setting basic standards to ensure a minimum level of medicine safety, efficacy, and quality—the industry has, over time, dissected these broad areas in detail to try and gain better control over the operating environment. As a result, a number of subspecialty job functions have developed to handle different aspects of a broad requirement. For instance, the category "equipment" might include specialist activities such as the cleaning process, cleaning process validation, equipment calibration and maintenance, equipment qualification, and so on. Each specialty has industry conferences devoted to best practices and sharing experiences, along with dedicated industry journals, magazines, websites, and outside consulting firms. Hand in hand with such excessive specialization comes organizational turf wars, miscommunications, and coordination constraints.

OPERATIONAL SILOS

In his 2004 bestseller, *The Fiefdom Syndrome*, Robert Herbold noted that these types of organizational specializations can quickly lead to operational silos or "fiefdoms" and cause:

- Reduced profitability
- Stunted innovation
- Insular "not invented here" mentalities
- Organizational mediocrity[74]

When helping compliance executives deal with operational silos, I often use an image of the many-handed Indian goddess, Kali. Kali's many hands are associated with energy and change. She also brings about destruction, for if one hand does not know what the others are doing, then energy and change become negative.

A weakness of many GMP compliance efforts is this excessive specialization, wherein many hands are responsible for some aspect of compliance. As we discussed in chapter one, the FDA and other regulatory health agencies are increasingly pushing firms to adopt a holistic, integrated risk-based approach to compliance and to ensuring medicinal product safety, efficacy, and quality. Agency officials I have spoken with continue to be concerned about the lack of cohesion between departments and groups in companies, allowing finger-pointing and gaps to develop and widen. Departments often/frequently claim aspects of compliance that are not normally their responsibility, and for which they have neither the background nor the expertise, putting their companies and executives into an inappropriate level of risk.

In one recent mock FDA audit and compliance gap analysis I performed for a client, I discovered that the quality department of a pharmaceutical firm was writing its own contracts with outside suppliers and vendors. The vendors were happy to sign such contracts knowing that a contract between a legal entity (the vendor company) and a non-legal entity (the pharmaceutical firm's internal department) was unenforceable.

Departments trying to independently prepare legal contracts with outside legal entities is typical of a sub-group trying to make itself vital to the larger company and trying to gain as much control as possible. It is a downside of specialization. The resulting unenforceable contracts not only jeopardize regulatory compliance and medicinal product safety, efficacy, and quality, but place executives at risk. Until I presented my preliminary findings, the officers of the company had no idea that one of their departments had been writing and signing contracts with outside firms. In the event of a lawsuit or government investigation, the company would have had a hard time convincing anyone that it was operating in a state of control.

Records Retention and Control

Another area in which firms are increasingly failing is in their control of records and information. Beyond those aspects already discussed, scant attention to records retention is paid by quality, regulatory affairs and other regulatory health agency-focused compliance professions. In a survey of industry literature from 2000 through 2009 on regulatory affairs and quality systems, I found a total of twelve sentences on keeping the records that FDA requires. That translates to less than 250 words on the single activity which firms must handle correctly in order to get a new product approved and onto the market, in order to meet and maintain regulatory compliance, and in order to minimize the risk of penalties from product liability and other lawsuits: retention of the right records.

In chapter nine, I will layout precisely how to implement an FDA-compliant records retention program as part of an overall compliance effort. In the discussion below I detail the impacts of this weakness on getting a new medicine to market.

The first piece of information to keep in mind is that since 2006, when the FDA issued its update to the GMP regulations through the *Quality Systems Approach to the Pharmaceutical CGMP Regulations* guidance document, 90% of FDA warning letters have cited records-related issues.[75] This includes missing records and documents, incomplete records, and fraudulent records. During the same period, only 30% of warning letters cited SOP-related problems.[76] In February 2009 the FDA's Jan Welch noted that for the regulation requiring process validation alone, 72% of violations were failures to document or retain the appropriate documentation while only 12% were related to lack of SOPs.[77] All the efforts that companies are expending on getting "the right" SOPs are not paying off. Simply put, having an SOP means nothing without the records to prove the SOP has been followed.

In 2008 Deborah Autor, director of compliance at the FDA's Center for Drug Evaluation and Research, offered companies three suggestions: "Train your employees on proper record handling, assure the reliability of the data reported in records, and emphasize that everyone in the company is responsible."[78] Poor controls over data integrity not only jeopardize one's chances of new medicine approval, but put marketplace success at risk by not retaining the right records.

So is the answer to retain everything? Before you think "yes," remember that the average new medicine application to a regulatory health agency contains approximately half a million sheets of paper. Storing such applications, at $0.08 per page, works out to almost $40,000 a year. Without question, storing it all electronically reduces that cost to a fraction of the $40,000, but it also dramatically raises the chances of complete loss.

A 2008 study by Interactive Data Corporation (IDC) found that inadvertent failures in archived storage—backup tapes, computer hard drives, compact discs (CDs), and so on—occur every 15 seconds, resulting in near complete loss of the data in most cases (computer hard drives can still have a chance at data restoration at a very hefty price tag).[79] Carnegie Mellon University published a study at the 5th USENIX Conference on File and Storage Technologies citing annual failure rates of archived digital storage between 2-13%.[80] In other words, switching from paper storage of your regulatory submission to digital format, can end up running a 2-13% risk every year of completely losing your submission records and all the supporting data without proper auditing and other controls (something I address in chapter nine).

A third reason to avoid keeping all the records and documents and emails and so on has to do with your liability in the event of product-related litigation or government-sponsored investigations of your company. As Eli Lilly & Co. found in June 2009, keeping records far beyond their required retention period can be an asset to opponents in litigation proceedings. Internal marketing department records from 1999 were used against Eli Lilly in 2009 in multiple product liability lawsuits over its dementia drug Zyprexa.[81] More than 10,000 of Eli Lilly's internal documents relating to Zyprexa were released to the public. A release made not voluntarily by Eli Lilly and its lawyers, but ordered by the court and plaintiff's attorneys. These disclosures caused Eli Lilly significant damage in the public's eye and, so far, resulted in costs of more than $1.2 billion (USD) to settle patient claims.

GlaxoSmithKline suffered a similar fate when a 29-year old internal summary report came to light in a product liability lawsuit; in the report, a company scientist had written that information in rat studies indicated that the newly acquired drug Paxil "could be" a cause of birth defects.[82] Accused of misrepresenting the safety of its drug, GlaxoSmithKline now faces hundreds of multi-million dollar product liability lawsuits.

There should be little doubt that as we move forward in the era of personalized medicines, product liability lawsuits will increase. The more information and knowledge we gain about genetics and various biomarkers, the greater the ability to question what a company should have known, should have tested for, or otherwise should have addressed. As firms such as Eli Lilly, GlaxoSmithKline, Merck, Sanofi-Aventis, Johnson & Johnson, Boston Scientific, and others have found, keeping all your records can be a liability when it comes to defending yourself against lawsuits.

Unfortunately, this is an insidious problem. When firms have tried to tackle this on their own, they have uncovered all sorts of difficult problems in the realm of FDA compliance records. Records problems are not easy to solve. I have helped many companies through these problems—and will show you how to avoid these problems in chapter nine. For now, though, let's look at a fairly straightforward example of how quickly, how easily, and how subtly these records control problems develop.

The quality department in a typical FDA-regulated firm usually views training records as part of "personnel qualification" and thus coming under 21 CFR 211.25 (for drugs and biologics) or 21 CFR 820.25 (for devices and diagnostics). Records under 21 CFR 211 are typically retained for one year after the finished drug's expiration date; records under 21 CFR 820 should be retained for two years after the date of the device release or the device design's life expectancy. Thus, if a quality department were in charge of retaining employee training records, such records might be disposed of within a few years of training. Yet FDA regulations are only one consideration. 29 CFR 1627.3 requires employee training records to be retained for at least one year after an employee's departure. For a long-term employee, this could easily be decades. Not keeping the training records puts a company at risk, especially in the event of a discrimination or wrongful termination lawsuit.

When I hold records requirement overviews for my clients, I ask questions such as:

- What are the record retention requirements for employee training?
- How are departments notified of an employee's departure date?
- How are the training records of independent contractors handled?

When it comes to independent contractors in the US, according to Uniform Commercial Code 2-725, contractor training records are to be retained as supporting documentation of a contract and retained through contract termination plus at least five years. And finally, even the FDA, especially in its Quality System Regulations governing medical devices and diagnostics, requires that a two year retention time applies only if the life of the device is less than two years. 21 CFR 820.180 specifies that training records are to be kept at least for two years after the product is released for sale or for the life of the device or its design, *whichever is longer*. In other words, even for the retention of training records, there is no simple all-or-nothing rule.

Retention of training records is just one of myriad examples demonstrating a greater point: compliance groups that do not acknowledge and address the overall scope of regulatory compliance jeopardize the companies and the executives for whom they work. There is little doubt that excessive specialization and the view of *compliance* through discrete professional interpretations—quality assurance, regulatory affairs, records management, and so on—contributes to this lack of a global, strategic perspective.

Let us now highlight the remaining themes of 20th century compliance weaknesses in light of today's 21st century compliance landscape by looking at the FDA regulations that govern medical device and diagnostic production and distribution, the Quality System Regulations.

QUALITY SYSTEM REGULATIONS

As I noted in chapter one, FDA's Quality System Regulations (QSRs) are structured to require an integrated quality management system. The QSRs promote the incorporation of risk-based decision-making and risk-management controls, a framework on which the FDA and other members of the ICH have been harmonizing the biopharmaceutical GMPs.

Such a framework also dovetails with the harmonization efforts underway for device and diagnostic regulations, the Global Harmonization Task Force (GHTF).

For combination products—those that involve both device and drug—compliance with the QSRs, the GMPs, ICH, and GHTF can become a nightmare. Depending on how the product is made and marketed, and even packaged, the facilities that prepare the product may be subject to all of these regulations and rules, or just those that govern the specific component which the facility contributes (*e.g.*, a factory that makes the drug element of a combination device might need only comply with the regulations governing manufacturing and not the regulations governing laboratory testing).

When it comes to diagnostic devices, particularly those which provide a genetic test or a personal biomarker evaluation that then influences which drug is prescribed, the implementation of QSRs is murky. At the time of writing, conversations with FDA officials have revealed significant uncertainty over whether the diagnostic device and the drug should be treated as one combination product or not. Eric Lawson has coordinated an Association of Medical Device Manufacturers working group of industry representatives and officials from the FDA and Health Canada to discuss these specifics. Over the next ten years, the FDA is planning to release a series of guidance documents addressing how to handle development of diagnostic equipment in tandem with biopharmaceutical clinical trials. Asking medical device and diagnostic makers to create unique diagnostic equipment for each new drug or biologic is clearly not in the interest of either device makers—many of which are small entities and cannot afford such repeated development and submission efforts—or in the interest of healthcare cost containment. It is, however, in the interest of the drug-makers who can then use the exclusive diagnostic device to help protect their drug exclusivity and stave off lower-cost generics; combination products have extremely low generic competition and low price sensitivity.

Even in the era of personalized medicine, with a growing emphasis around the world on healthcare cost containment, competing interests make compliance decisions and product development decisions difficult. This is the case even with a set of regulations, the QSRs, that FDA officials have cited as recently as 2007 as examples of rules wherein they "got it right" with the incorporation of risk management and product design that builds in risk control and quality from day one.[83]

Risk Elimination

In theory, the incorporation of risk management early in development is appropriate for any new medicine. In reality, though, risk management has turned into a quest for risk elimination, with dedicated risk management departments divorced from day-to-day realities and complexities. Risk elimination may be an attainable goal with older well-understood technologies, but employing the same risk averse, risk elimination mindset with newer, cutting edge scientific and engineering innovations such as nanotechnology and gene-based manipulation may result in failure to deliver worthy new medicines to market.

Whenever I consult with companies on how to streamline and simplify their compliance and quality programs, I often have to set aside some time to have a serious discussion of how risk management does not equal risk elimination. Risk elimination is a quixotic goal. Risk-based decisions need to focus on controlling risk, grounded in the level of confidence we want in those controls with on-going monitoring and improvements. In chapter seven, I will provide the plan and the template needed to strike a healthy balance of control and risk. In this section, it is enough to state that although risk-based decision-making can be a strength, given the all-or-nothing compliance mentalities and heightened anxiety over risk elimination, risk management can be a never-ending, costly, and ultimately futile, quest for perfection.

In the manufacturing environ, for executives who face real day-to-day pressure to produce products (as opposed to those who face the perceived pressure of an eventual FDA inspection), there comes a time when they are no longer willing to suffer demands from either their supervisors or from shareholders and investors to ignore concerns raised in a risk evaluation. When the risk evaluation is reasonable, and based on agreed-upon confidence levels in risk control, the decision to approve the product's release is invariably a good one. When risk management is assumed to mean risk elimination, the decision to ignore concerns raised in a risk evaluation and move the product into distribution is more problematic. Sadly, in my experiences and those of my colleagues and clients, the (short-term) business rewards—bonuses, promotions, etc.—go to those who tend to ignore compliance concerns and get the product out the door the quickest.

When it comes to product development, it is too frequent that intelligent and capable scientists and engineers proclaim, "We don't need to

do that [risk control step]. This just works—I know. That's all we need."
It's very common when working with the scientists and engineers who
created the product in the first place; their comfort with their innovation or product is so extensive that it is often difficult for them to view
a potential non-compliance with objectivity. It is a natural human tendency, but one that gets in the way of good risk control.

LOST IN BUSINESS TRANSLATION

Compliance professionals often do not know how to speak in a language
understandable to senior management. To grab the attention of senior executives, compliance professionals, and lawyers FDA officials frequently resort to directly warning of dire consequences for non-compliance.
Senior decision makers are the individuals cited in warning letters and
other regulatory enforcement actions. Warning letters are addressed to
company presidents and officers. But then, having grabbed the spotlight,
the message of what to do becomes lost in a list of activities and actions
all relating to various specific citations in regulations and rules. In other
words, the opportunity to effect change and improve compliance is squan-
dered by not speaking in terms of financial implications.

Compliance and quality cost money and time. Money and time are
certainties—they will be spent this year. Being named in an enforcement
action is not a certainty; it is a matter of the odds of getting caught. The
likelihood of FDA inspection for a Class I exempt device maker, even
though it should occur once every two years, are likely only once every
nine years. The FDA will never have enough money, time, or resources
to inspect all the firms that exist and all the new firms that are continually created by entrepreneurs. I have heard CEOs state "Assuming
nothing bad happens to a patient, getting an inspection by the FDA is
a numbers game." In other words, compliance professionals and managers need to recognize that getting everything on the compliance list
budgeted and completed is simply not realistic. Instead, priorities need
to be established. Perhaps the firm can focus on better preparation for
an inspection and so the priority is on implementing controls that will
lower the likelihood of an FDA inspection. The cost of these controls—
both their implementation and their maintenance—need to be factored
into any discussion between compliance executives and business teams.
How much do those particular steps cost?

Discussing compliance improvements brings forth the divergence in communication. Compliance professionals talk in terms of absolutes: "To be in compliance, we must do all these things—otherwise we will not be compliant." The subtext is simple: compliance at any cost.

For a business to exist, however, it must be profitable. Quality departments and regulatory affairs and other compliance roles are not, in and of themselves, profit centers. Like any support function, compliance only enables the rest of the business to make money. As a result, compromise is necessary. A natural human reaction, when faced with someone who is strident and unwavering in their single-minded approach, is to simply tune them out.

Because we are discussing developing medicines and issues of safety and health—not colors or other aesthetics—when a company tunes out its compliance groups, the chances of making it to market are low. For regulatory affairs, quality, and other compliance groups to help their company's new medicine get to market as quickly as possible—and as safely and efficaciously as possible—compliance executives need to learn to speak in terms that their business listeners understand: compromise and money.

VALUE PROPOSITIONS

Compromise is measured in cost. I have noticed a consistent refrain at industry conferences on FDA compliance: "this is what you have to do." I clearly remember the quality director of a large *Fortune 1000* device maker standing up and declaring, in response to a speaker's question on supplier control, "If we have to station our quality control inspectors at every mine in China to make sure we get the right metal for our implant, then we will."

Clearly, not only would this company have bankrupted itself had it followed their quality director's advice, but it would hardly have improved its product's safety, quality or efficacy to have stationed medical device quality control inspectors at raw ore mines in a foreign country. Ultimately, if you cannot speak in terms of compromise and cost, you cannot effectively contribute the compliance advice your company needs.

To consistently ensure product safety, quality and efficacy, and to further ensure your new product gets to market, quality executives and CEOs must speak the same language. In business, that language is all about profit and loss.

When I counsel quality department and regulatory affairs executives on how to speak in terms of money, I propose ways to use their quality system or regulatory management review as an opportunity to translate compliance components into costs. In chapter seven, when we discuss processing mapping and SOPs, I will review some means to translate compliance components into financial implications.

As we close this chapter on how the weaknesses of traditional compliance efforts from the 20th century are hampering us in the 21st, keep in mind the words of a colleague of mine at Johnson & Johnson:

> *"For years, we'd just been doing what it said to do in the regulations. So when we had an activity we needed to do, we'd just write an SOP for it. Well, now we know that just following the regulations doesn't work if you also want to run a business. Following all the regulations results in just one department having over 200 SOPs. How can you stay compliant with that? We've learned that we need to look at compliance from a business perspective too. How can we get to a manageable structure that's compliant, flexible enough especially at the local level, and still produce a good, safe, product?"*

SUMMARY

Executives at large global firms are beginning the process of simplifying and streamlining their compliance infrastructures. The harmonization of regulations and quality systems expectations across political boundaries has reinforced how ill-prepared their compliance programs are for the era of personalized medicines. The weaknesses were always there, and most often evident at the local, operational level, but not apparent until they began to impact the ability of the overall company to achieve its strategic objectives—when compliance began hindering basic business operations.

For companies to succeed in the 21st century, the weaknesses of the 20th century model of compliance must be addressed:

- All-or-nothing mentalities
- Risk aversion
- Operational silos
- Cost inefficiencies
- Customer exclusions
- Poor records integrity and controls

As I noted earlier, we cannot lay the blame for these failings on quality assurance, regulatory affairs, records managers, and other compliance professionals. We have arrived here unintentionally. The compliance initiatives undertaken in response to the many new and strict regulations coming out in the 1900s were appropriate to those times. The philosophies and underlying assumptions driving quality assurance, quality control, quality management, and regulatory affairs were completely in line with FDA expectations. Indeed a review of regulatory enforcement actions and historical court cases between the FDA and company executives over the past fifty years demonstrates the good intent of compliance professionals.

As we have seen through examination of the trends impacting the global regulatory landscape and the medicinal product development landscape, the tactics and strategies of 20th century compliance programs are not serving us well. Compliance executives are bound to be disappointed and are not helping their companies—or prospective patients—by being slow to modernize, simplify, and streamline. Because business realities are intimately intertwined with product development and compliance, quality and regulatory affairs teams can no longer stand apart from the rest of their business colleagues. Cross-functional coordination and communication is crucial when trying to get a complex new medical product through the approval process and onto the market.

As a result, compliance executives and their companies are poised to make a choice: continue as they have always done things, or choose to adopt elements of compliance as a competitive edge.

Determining how best to make this choice requires taking look at the larger context in which companies will bring a new medicine to market over the next decade, a view revealed in the next chapter.

EXECUTIVE'S CHECKLIST FOR CHAPTER THREE

Understanding the major limitations inherent in companies' compliance infrastructures today that have been brought over from the 20th century will allow you to take aim at improvements for the 21st century. Here's a step-by-step to-do list:

☐   If you have not done so already, read the FDA's 2006 final guidance, *Quality Systems Approach to Pharmaceutical*

CGMP Regulations (a copy of this be obtained from the FDA or can be downloaded from the book's website at http://www.Get2MarketNow.com)

☐ Assess the average length (in number of pages and total word count) of your SOPs

☐ Download the SOP template from the book's website

☐ Read Chapter 7, "Designing the Lean Quality System," to learn how to put in place a global framework of SOPs based on process mapping, risk management, and readability that encourage compliance and business flexibility

☐ Ensure that you have an inclusive definition of "customer" that goes beyond just the patient and/or healthcare provider in your product development (design control, preclinical, nonclinical, clinical) and postmarket monitoring SOPs

☐ Read Chapter 5, "Improving Innovation," to learn how to incorporate the "voice of the customer" in your medicinal development efforts

☐ Assess your supplier / vendor due diligence process and ensure it includes financial and public records reviews (if need be, use services such as Dun & Bradstreet and KnowX to conduct these reviews)

☐ Verify that your Data Monitoring Committee procedures incorporate ensuring that the DMC is also responsible for reviewing comparative effectiveness data as per the FDA *Guidance for Clinical Trial Sponsors: Establishment and Operation of Clinical Trial Data Monitoring Committees* (2006)

☐ Obtain and review the recorded seminar, *How to Improve Data Quality & Record Integrity in Your NDA, 510(k) or BLA*, through this book's website

☐ Ensure that someone in your company is focused on compliance-related records management

☐ Read Chapter 9, "Driving a Holistic Compliance Framework," to learn how to put in place a compliant records retention and data integrity program

4 — Larger Landscape Trends

The ways in which we develop medicines and structure compliance have only modestly changed over the past half century. By contrast, our scientific and technical know-how—with the Internet, virtualization technology, genomics, pharmacodynamics, nanotechnology, and other fields of discovery—are drastically altering the greater landscape around us. The significance of these shifts is why focusing just on compliance or just on medicine development alone is insufficient. By looking at key factors influencing the marketplace around the biopharmaceutical and device industries, we can better see how to adapt our product development and compliance infrastructures in the era of personalized medicine.

The starting point for this larger landscape view is the growth of scientific and technical knowledge, and its convergence to create new opportunities.

MORE SCIENTIFIC AND TECHNICAL TRENDS

The easiest way to understand scientific and technical evolutions and their convergence is by continuing our discussion of the merging of diagnostic devices and new drugs that we began in the previous chapter.

DIAGNOSTICS AND DRUGS

In July 2009, the neuroscience research department at the Centre for Addiction and Mental Health in Toronto, Canada announced that it would begin treating patients based on a combination of genetic testing and brain imaging.[84] This first in the world approach will use genetic testing to look for the presence of genes that raise the likelihood of side effects or reduced efficacy in patients. Several genes affect how quickly drugs are broken down in the liver. For instance, with the drug Paxil, approximately 7% of people metabolize it so slowly that under normal dosing regimens, too much of the drug exists at one time in a person's bloodstream, dramatically increasing the severity of the side effects. The hospital will then use the brain scans to assess how well a drug is delivered to a patient's brain.

According to Dr. James Kennedy, the center's director, "It adds new kinds of information that in conjunction with the genetics information allows a much better decision about which drugs at which dose to give the patient."[85] The end result will be better, more personalized treatments for patients plus more information and knowledge about neurochemical changes produced by drug therapies.

When we think of personalized medicine, we too often imagine a genetic profile being run and then voila, we know what medicines and what dosages will work best for us. This may be the case in the long-term, but over the next decade personalized medicine will first consist of individual convergences of diagnostics and sensor technologies to tailor treatment. As biopharmaceutical and device firms slowly alter the way in which they produce new medicines, treatment options will shift from one-size-fits-all questions to different varieties of the same drug or device. A large part of that tailoring today—both in treatment and in new drug or device development—can be seen in the use of biomarkers such as blood pressure and protein generation rates.

US Navy researchers have uncovered biomarkers that can predict if recent amputees will develop painful bone spurs or other abnormal bone growth. Such abnormal reactions then interfere with prosthetic devices and often require further surgery. Navy researchers have also uncovered biomarkers in blood and body tissue that predict how a person's immune system will react to wounds such as a cut or scraped knee. The Navy published its findings in 2009 to encourage pharmaceutical firms to develop drugs that can counteract the identified elements of the immune system that generate harmful bone growths or prevent proper wound closure.[86]

Combining predictive biomarkers and molecular imagery not only improves treatment, but also improves research of new and developing drugs. Computer software algorithms can rapidly screen each molecule from an image, and allow the researcher to quickly assess the effectiveness of a new drug or biologic agent. Today, researchers use animal models for predictive research, but over the next decade, as technology continues to improve, more of these basic predictive studies will be conducted in humans in what has been termed "Phase 0" trials (chapter eight will explain how to plan for and incorporate this in your development efforts).

The Massachusetts Institute of Technology (MIT) has developed an implantable sensor, approximately 5-mm in diameter (less than ¼"), designed to remain in cancer patients and continuously monitor the disease's progression and its reaction to treatment.[87] Expected to be commercially available by 2012 or 2013, scientists could use this sensor in Phase 0 trials simply to collect information about patient responses to drugs, and potentially identify patient subpopulations, to then aid in the development of new drugs and biologics.

Predictive methods can also help select patients for specific trials. Researchers at the University of California, San Francisco, developed a risk index that can predict the likelihood of people 65 and older developing Alzheimer's disease.[88] At its current stage, the index has only been correct 88% of the time. Companies seeking an edge in their new drug development targeting Alzheimer's disease will clearly be interested in using the risk index to identify patients for various adaptive arm trials. Not only will this provide better scientific measurements of Alzheimer's patient responses (or prospective Alzheimer's patient responses), but by quickly eliminating people not at risk for developing Alzheimer's, companies can save money and time during clinical trials.

USE OF ALGORITHMS AND DATA MINING IN RESEARCH

New drug and biologic therapies, not to mention device design variations, are also getting a boost from computer-based technologies such as complex software algorithms and database indexing.

A software algorithm is essentially a flowchart for processing data and making calculations based on those data. A simple algorithm might ask if a patient has the KRAS gene mutation? If the answer is yes, one dataset is analyzed; if the answer is no, a different dataset is examined. As such, software algorithms are reliant upon libraries of information— they are not much good without data (*e.g.*, if a new biomarker is discovered tomorrow, existing algorithms will not be able to process the new biomarker—a new version of the software algorithm must be written).

A number of firms exist solely to provide researchers with specific predictive analyses based on large databases. DDI Predict software focuses on drug-to-drug interactions, which can prevent FDA approval or cause drugs to be pulled from the market. The DDI Predict system draws on a library of over 25,000 known compounds and nearly 400,000 biological data points.[89] Researchers using predictive algorithms can quickly identify any potential drug-to-drug interaction risks for a new biopharmaceutical under development.

Lest we think of such algorithms as useful for drug researchers alone, Imagination Engines used their Creativity Machine algorithm to sort through thousands of possible designs for the original Oral-B CrossAction Toothbrush.[90] Thinking back to the new product development funnel I described in chapter two, this algorithm went from the broadest part of the funnel to the narrowest end in a matter of hours, a significant shift that allowed very rapid device development. Despite this speed, all the various design characteristics had to be manually input into database format for the algorithm to be able to process, sift, and select the winning design.

One database used by many of the predictive algorithms is the ClinicalTrials.gov clinical trial registry maintained by the US National Institutes of Health (NIH) at http://www.clinicaltrials.gov. ClinicalTrials. gov provides information about a clinical trial's purpose, the trial sponsor, trial site locations, contact information, general patient profile information such as gender, ethnicity, etc., the medical condition targeted by the trial, and other details. Participation in ClinicalTrials.gov is voluntary, and so not all information is available to researchers.

Traditional technology firms like IBM, Cisco, and Hewlett-Packard are bringing their expertise to the biopharmaceutical research industry with massive enterprise-level databases and meta-databases. IBM and the University of North Carolina (UNC) Health Care signed an agreement in 2009 to build a meta-database that integrates information from public databases (like ClinicalTrials.gov) and UNC's hospital and outpatient centers, insurance records, and other clinical sources.[91] The intent is to provide researchers an incredibly broad and deep source of information on genetic profiles, demographics, biomarkers, and other predictive risk factors associated with diseases such as cancer, diabetes, and cystic fibrosis. In addition, the meta-database is expected to be searched by preclinical researchers who are seeking specific information to help plan clinical trials and obtain approval from the FDA to initiate human testing.

Researchers and executives may also want to analyze this information in order to determine patterns and relationships that might allow segmentation of physician and healthcare practitioners by specialty, by patient subpopulation, and other factors. This information could then be used to identify physicians who are "early adopters" of new therapies. These physicians might be good candidates to help produce literature and participate in clinical investigative review boards or data monitoring committees. In their 2008 e-book, *BioStory*, authors Peter Abramo and Michael Edmondson encourage biotech founders to undertake such physician research and segmentation as part of the build-up to requesting funding and interesting venture capitalists.[92]

NANOMEDICINES

Another larger landscape trend is the emerging field of nanomedicines. Nanotechnology refers to the manipulation of particles smaller than 100 nm (nanometers), which cannot be seen without a specially designed microscope. Products incorporating nanoparticles contribute more than $200 billion to today's global marketplace, and by 2015, are expected to contribute to $3.1 trillion worth of products globally.[93]

When it comes to nanomedicine, the Massachusetts Institute of Technology (MIT) has several nanotechnology-based biomedical research projects underway, including:

- Microscopic batteries constructed with nano-scale wiring and components which would then allow vastly smaller device implants
- Nanoparticle guides for stem cells that would direct the stem cell to specific damaged cells in internal organs like the heart or kidney, allowing regeneration to occur
- Microscopic arrays of nano-sized drug reservoirs. This "pharmacy on a chip" technology could allow doctors and patients the ability to control the release of drugs on an immediate basis in response to changes in biomarkers
- Synthetic nanoparticles that carry a tiny amount of toxins directly to cancer cells

In the latter project, preclinical testing showed the nanoparticle-carried toxin to be as effective as traditional cancer treatments like chemotherapy, but with drastically reduced side effects. The project will enter Phase I clinical trials early this decade with market launch anticipated in 2018.[94]

To help companies and universities develop nanomedicines, the US enacted the Twenty-First Century Nanotechnology Research and Development Act of 2003 and the NIH published a roadmap to guide nanomedicine research over the next few decades.[95] As part of any research into new medicines that involve nanotechnology, it is crucial that safety data be extremely well-grounded, be reliable, and have integrity. This is one area where the FDA, along with the US Environmental Protection Agency (EPA), has increased its scrutiny and review levels. For the EPA, responsible for minimizing environment impacts, companies may want to assess what quantities of nanoparticles are released into the environment under worst-case conditions. FDA and EPA officials have both stated that factual assessments and testing are necessary to support any claims.[96] For the FDA, such evidence needs to be gathered in preclinical and nonclinical studies (especially toxicology testing) prior to requesting permission to enter clinical trials with a nanomedicine.

From a reimbursement standpoint, executives should be aware of two factors:

- Investors are less likely to be swayed by "nanotech" hype and more insistent on hard data
- Private insurers associate nanomedicines with a high degree of risk because it is such a developing field

As I discussed in chapter one, reimbursement and funding play an increasing role in driving new medicine development. Lloyd's of London, Swiss Re, Allianz Gruppe International, and Continental Western Insurance Group are examples of health and life insurers who are extremely reluctant to grant coverage and reimbursement for nanomedicines. Wise investors and venture capitalists are well aware of this reluctance and will seek to understand the actual data that support any claims of safety in a new nanomedicine.

For executives in compliance, further caution is merited when developing nanomedicines: regulatory health agencies around the world are drafting regulations covering nanomedicines. The FDA has so far not published specific regulations, but does have several task forces at work on outlining potential guidance documents. In a January 2007 Parenteral Drug Association meeting, Dr. Nakissa Sadrieh of the FDA's Center for Drug Evaluation and Research (CDER) gave a presentation entitled "FDA Regulatory Considerations for Nanotechnology Products" in which a number of specific design and development questions for consideration were laid out. A copy of Dr. Sadrieh's presentation is available at the book's website.

Expect any FDA guidance publications to include significant contributions from regulatory health agency members of the International Conference on Harmonization (ICH) and the Global Task Force on Harmonization (GHTF). In chapter eight I will specifically discuss the steps you can take to build a regulatory intelligence gathering mechanism so you are not caught unaware as these new regulations and guidance documents emerge over the next decade.

ADDITIONAL SCIENTIFIC TRENDS

While many advances in science, engineering, and technology will contribute to personalized medicine and the compliance structures in which we must operate, there are two advances that merit special mention:

- Stem cells
- Automation of synthetic cell production

Along with nanoparticles, stem cells are furthering regenerative medicine. Stem cells target specific areas in the body to treat or cure diseases and injuries. A number of stem-cell based medicinal treatments are entering the marketplace today, such as BioHeart's stem cell treatment for heart failure that completed positive Phase III clinical trials in 2009.[97] Most of these experimental therapies are autologous; they use a patient's own stem cells.

Over the coming decades, research will continue to find a one-size-fits-all type of stem cell that is not autologous and is able to be translated into infinite medical treatments. Compliance executives will want to watch such research for signs of safety and efficacy challenges, especially given any of the impacts of genetic profile variability between subpopulations. In the nearer term, I expect to see new startup companies designed to help each of us be able to "bank" a set of stem cells that can then be used not only to research better drugs for the subpopulation to which we belong, but also to provide replacement organs, tissues, or cells.

One organization, Germany's Fraunhofer Institute for Interfacial Engineering and Biotechnology, is tackling just such a prospect by developing an assembly-line approach to artificial skin and cartilage creation. The goal is to create an automated system capable of easily and inexpensively creating artificial skin tailored to patients in various subpopulations. Today, such synthetic tissue engineering is a pain-staking, costly process. Fraunhofer scientists and engineers are slowly elucidating the process and automating individual segments, with a goal of combining all the various automated segments –similar to the assembly-line processes by which automobiles and appliances are assembled.[98]

RISE OF THE PRE-INFORMED PATIENT

All of these scientific and engineering advances have had impact beyond biopharmaceutical and device firms. Even twenty years ago, such advances would only be shared among a small group of specialists via research conferences. Physicians and patients would only learn about the advances through reading medical journals. Today, however, the Internet has brought specialized knowledge out of the conference room and the lab and into the domain of Internet forums and wikis. As I noted in the introduction to this book, the millions of "future patients" who make up Generation Y look to the Internet to conduct basic research on physicians, treatment options, and even new medicines in development.

Those firms who can take advantage of this tremendous thirst for knowledge and insight, and leverage it as part of their new medicine development pipeline process, will craft themselves a sharper competitive edge. The key is to figure out some of the characteristics of what I term the "pre-informed patient" and how best to take advantage of this growing trend.

INFORMED CONSUMER

In 2009, the Pew Internet & American Life Project, a non-profit research organization, released an updated version of a study on how adults obtain health information. Executives, researchers, and compliance professionals—and also the marketing and sales teams who target healthcare providers—should find the results eye-opening. Instead of seeking out the opinion of their doctors, 60% of adults turn to the Internet first. In just three years time, this number has nearly doubled from 31% in 2006 to 60% in 2009.[99] As Generation Y moves into the adult consumer marketplace over the next decade, Internet research will dominate all other forms of health information.

The survey also found that half of all health information research conducted by consumers is conducted on behalf of family and friends. It turns out, we are not just visiting websites like the Mayo Clinic or pharmaceutical company web pages on their medicines and the diseases they treat; 59% of us are visiting third-party blogs, wikis, and online comments as well.[100]

Concurrent with this rise in Internet-based health research has been the growing number of patient-support groups, disease organizations, and private companies that provide websites and forums for information and online discussions. Internet websites such as WebMD (www.webmd.com), RateADrug (www.rateadrug.com), Drug Recall (www.adrugrecall.com), and DrugWatch (www.drugwatch.com) offer constantly updated information on biopharmaceuticals and devices in the marketplace, medicines under development, medicines that have been recalled, and even user reviews of medications. Using the vast reach of the Internet, consumers are becoming advocates for a particular treatment, not just a particular disease or condition.

Companies such as Novartis and Genentech (now a division of Roche Holding AG) have used these sites, and in particular, the patient-support groups' online forums, to help gather information on side effects and drug interactions for already marketed medicines. Firms have not, however, successfully reached out through these forums to grab the "voice of the customer" to inform product development decisions for new medicines still in the pipeline.

This is an ideal opportunity for executives willing to step outside the traditional medicine development route. Such executives must stop following just the science and, instead learn how they might best differentiate their new medicines to future consumers. As I noted in the introduction, only a few executives—Sanofi-Aventis's CEO Chris Viehbacher, for example—have recognized the need to base business decisions on what patients want versus where the science leads. In chapter five, I will lay out some specific steps you should be taking right now to start incorporating the voice of your customer; more informed consumers means more people willing to help you bring a better medicine to market faster.

TRANSPARENT DATA

Government efforts around the world are also helping the rise of the pre-informed patient. In the US, in addition to the NIH's ClinicalTrials. gov, the FDA has increased its level of transparency in communicating risk to consumers. The agency is also studying ways in which it can disclose confidential information about drugs and devices under study to help better inform the public and limit the criticism of the agency as too cozy with the industries it regulates.

A 2008 study published in the *Journal of the American Medical Association* (JAMA) found that five different companies, unaware of the dangerous side effects each firm's clinical trials were revealing, continued to develop and test blood substitute products, assuming that the observed side effects were unique to their product and not a general characteristic of the blood substitute product category. The FDA had the collective information but did not act or make it public due to fears about disclosing confidential information about medicines in development, leading critics to charge that by keeping such information private the FDA contributed to clinical trial deaths.[101]

The US Congress has also been considering various bills to create device registries and databases open to the public, similar to those found in Australia, Sweden, and the U.K. Device industry groups, such as the American Academy of Orthopaedic Surgeons (AAOS), have also tried, with limited success, to create such public registries. The databases would collect and analyze data on patients, devices, side effects, long-term quality of life, and the need for implant replacement surgeries based on wear-and-tear of artificial joints. Physicians, consumers, and healthcare insurers support such public registries because the databases improve safety and lower costs. In 2008 the Durom Cup, a hip replacement component, began failing at a high enough rate for physicians all over the US to warn the manufacturer, Zimmer Holdings. While Zimmer eventually halted Durom Cup sales after several months of review, registry advocates and patient-support groups argued that public registries would have increased the health information availability and would have revealed the issue sooner, and also would have helped individual patients—as they conducted their online research—avoid receiving the implant until the device quality issues were resolved.[102]

SOCIAL NETWORKING AND GENETIC PROFILES

In addition to device registries and drug watch sites, there is a growing public awareness of the importance of genetic profiles in medicinal effectiveness. As a result, several small companies have emerged to tap into the consumer genetic testing market, aiming to provide DNA testing and genetic profiling to the average person.

Reminiscent of the television crime drama, CSI, but without the actual crime, people purchase a personal DNA collection kit, swab themselves or spit in a tube, then drop the kit in the mail. A few weeks later, the person's full DNA profile arrives along with a genetic risk profile that estimates chances of getting a particular disease compared with the overall population and the most common genetic profile of individuals who have that disease. Despite the lack of a direct, one-to-one correlation between a person's genetic profile and the diseases from which he or she will suffer, the direct-to-consumer genetic testing market is expected to continue to grow over the next decade.[103]

Personal genetics company 23andMe has taken this a step further, and lets customers create a public profile and share their genetic data through a social networking site. The National Human Genome Research Institute is sponsoring several anthropological studies of the social networks that people form based on their genetic identities. The studies hope to assess the ethical implications of posting such information online, including the risks inherent in defining a subset of people solely based on their genetic makeup. It is unknown whether such genetics-based social networking will lead to discrimination in medicine and healthcare.

BENEFITTING FROM THE PRE-INFORMED PATIENT

Executives in new drug and device development organizations and their compliance colleagues can make tremendous use of these informed consumers. Pre-informed patients actively seek out the best treatment for themselves, their family members, and their friends. Firms that can demonstrate a superior product can gain a strong market position and avoid the fate of most medicines that go off patent—the loss of 80% of sales within 12 months.[104]

To makes use of the pre-informed patient requires going beyond the requisite demonstration of safety, efficacy, and quality. It requires building in quality and the voice of the prospective customer from day one.

These are common new product development tactics outside of drug, biologic, and device industries, and need to become more common in medicine development. And I will give you a suggested path to follow in the second half of this book, starting with chapter five.

The key, however, is to understand that pre-informed patients want you to succeed. They operate from their own self-interests. Who does not want a better medicine that is more efficacious, with fewer side effects, and maybe even costs less? Pre-informed patients can be partners to help channel development efforts, and even raise funds and help firms overcome development obstacles.

And while all of this sounds wonderfully helpful when it comes to developing new medicines, we also need to be cognizant of the downsides to pre-informed patients. Specifically, there is a higher burden placed on risk communication—gone are the days when a "dear doctor" letter might have sufficed. On the Internet, if firms do not present risk information, then someone else will. Thus, compliance executives need to see the rise of the pre-informed patient as something that has both favorable and unfavorable consequences: helpful when things look promising, downright dangerous when frustrated and feeling misled.

INCREASING EXECUTIVE LIABILITY

Pre-informed patients, comfortable with using the Internet for health research, also tend to be investors, equally familiar with financial websites as they are with health websites. As a result, when anonymous blog posters wrote at the end of 2007 that a pivotal clinical trial of the drug Vytorin was "a bust" and "heard it crashed and burned," the lawsuits against Vytorin's makers, Schering-Plough and Merck soon followed. Investors sued, saying they were misled by company executives who in news conferences continued to tout the preliminary results of the trial even though company officials were already aware of the trial's failure.[105]

ANGRY SHAREHOLDERS

As I have noted in my newsletter over the past few years, this type of case is increasingly common. Shareholders, investors, and financial backers are suing pharmaceutical and device firms and their executives for failure to accurately disclose risks, development setbacks, and regulatory compliance mistakes. Genzyme and its management were hit with a shareholder lawsuit in July 2009, alleging that regulatory compliance and quality systems failures were "material information" that should have been disclosed to investors.[106] And in October 2008, angry investors sued Biovail and its executives claiming that the firm and its management "materially delayed" a new drug from coming to market by failing to disclose that the new drug did not meet all the FDA approval criteria.[107] KV Pharmaceutical and its executives suffered a similar shareholder lawsuit in December 2008.

The US Food and Drug Administration has also stepped up its enforcement actions on individual executives. The former chief executive officer of InterMune was convicted in September 2009 of wire fraud for allowing a press release that contained misleading information on the drug Actimmune to be published and distributed by his company.[108]

FDA's Drive for Management Accountability

In the past few years, FDA officials have repeatedly stressed that previous case law and Supreme Court decisions uphold individual executive accountability and responsibility. To the agency, company executives are ultimately responsible for any misdeeds, intentional or otherwise, because executives hold positions with great impact to the public. As the FDA's deputy chief counsel, Eric Blumberg, has pointed out, "Executives who did nothing still broke the law. The law requires executives to know *and* prevent."[109]

The agency relies heavily upon a company's current and former employees, contractors and vendors to help provide whistleblower details and spark investigations. According to the FDA's Edwin Rivera-Martinez of CDER, "The greatest source, by far, of information to initiate inspections is a company's former and current employees."[110]

The FDA will continue its push to pursue individual executives and business owners over the next decade. An 18-month review of warning letters coupled with interviews I conducted of current and former FDA inspectors indicates this trend to "ensure accountability at the top" will strengthen, playing directly into the hands of frustrated shareholders and patients.

Patient frustration has also started to erupt over medicine costs and misleading effectiveness claims. Multiple consumer class action lawsuits were filed in US federal courts in an individual states alleging that Merck and Schering-Plough misled patients into believing that the pharmaceutical firms' branded drugs were more effective than new generics. Lawyers in the trials have estimated that in just two years since the generics came on the market, Merck and Schering-Plough were able to gain $3.5 billion simply by issuing misleading marketing and advertising copy.[111]

Whether any of these consumer complaint or shareholder-driven lawsuits will succeed remains to be seen (the appeals process can drag out for years). The key point is that product development decisions, safety and efficacy claims, compliance and quality systems actions—or inactions—do not occur in isolation. Executives need to expect and plan for their decisions to be second-guessed by inspectors, investigators, and plaintiffs.

And when it comes to containing healthcare costs, insurers and reimbursement agencies are joining the fray, blaming pharmaceutical and device firms for unnecessarily causing high prices.

THE DRIVE FOR COST CONTAINMENT

In October 2009, Medco, a pharmacy benefits management company, announced it would conduct its own comparative effectiveness clinical trial of two drugs, Plavix and Effient. Plavix is close to going off patent protection and being available generically while Effient is new to the marketplace. To Medco, this begs the question: what justifies Effient's higher price over the Plavix generics? One answer lies in personalized medicine. Approximately 25% of patients, those with specific genetic profiles, cannot metabolize Plavix very well, so for that 25% of the population, the higher cost of Effient may be justified.

The overall implication for drug and device executives is clear: If they are not already including comparative effectiveness testing in their clinical trials, especially among subsets of patient populations, they should be prepared for others to do this testing—without their input. And the third-party's emphasis will be on cost-effectiveness. As I laid out in chapter one, reimbursement organizations are increasingly equating a medicine's effectiveness with its cost-effectiveness. The greater a new drug or device's efficacy, the greater its chances of higher reimbursement rates are.

A firm's ability to obtain positive reimbursement rates and generate profits from new drugs and devices is also subject to three trends in the greater landscape:

1. Rise of generics and low-cost competitors
2. Growth of telemedicine
3. Cost-sharing as an approval condition

How well a company can capitalize on these trends will dictate the direction of its new medicine's market debut.

COST-SHARING AS AN APPROVAL CONDITION

In 2006, the UK's National Institute for Clinical Excellence (NICE) rejected a new bone marrow cancer drug from Johnson & Johnson called Velcade. And yet, one year later, NICE reversed course and approved the drug for reimbursement in Britain.[112] What changed?

After an appeal by patient-support groups and cancer charities, NICE and Johnson & Johnson developed a "money-back guarantee" for the drug. Prescriptions for patients who respond to the drug will be fully reimbursed by the UK's health service. For patients who show only minimal response or none at all, Johnson & Johnson will refund the cost of the treatment to the UK's health service. As Andrew Dillon, then chief executive officer of NICE stated, "If the drug's manufacturer accepts the proposal … it will mean that when the drug works well, the National Health Service pays but when the drug doesn't, the manufacturer should bear the cost."[113]

In other words, drugs and devices are like any other consumer product and should be treated as such by the consumer (in this case, NICE). This stands in stark contrast with last century's view of drugs and devices as beyond the traditional bounds of products—as necessary for life and thus not accountable to "consumer rights." There should be no doubt that healthcare cost-sharing is the path for how new medicines will eventually be approved for reimbursement in nearly all markets.

Johnson & Johnson's deal with NICE was just the first. In 2008, GlaxoSmithKline arranged to pay for part of the costs of treatment with its new drug, Tykerb, and Pfizer's Stutent was approved solely on the basis of Pfizer's agreement to pay for the first round of treatment for all patients.[114] In studying medicine labels, Dartmouth College researchers noted that "just because a drug is approved, doesn't mean it works very well. You really need to know more to see whether it's worth the cost."[115]

The self-interests of patients, healthcare providers, reimbursers, and insurers typically work against drug and device companies. As a result, cost-sharing as a compromise to get a firm's new medicine to market is an inevitable part of doing business in the 21st century. And this means that it is incumbent upon executives to develop their new medicines and run their compliance organizations as lean as possible. For if cost-sharing doesn't erode profits, generics and low-cost overseas competitors will.

RISE OF GENERICS AND LOW COST COMPETITORS

On average, a generic drug costs $85 less than the brand name version.[116] This is the main reason that once a drug or biologic goes off patent protection and loses its exclusive market access, sales and revenues from the drug plunge 80% in less than twelve months.

In response, drug makers have tried multiple tactics such as bundling branded medications together as one. To date, bundling has not been particularly successful. In the case of bundling, insurers are seeing through the ploy and refusing to pay for bundled brand name medicines when generic versions—even if sold separately—are available. GlaxoSmithKline's migraine medicine, Treximet, combines GlaxoSmithKline's branded Imitrex with the anti-inflammatory naproxen, has met fierce resistance from both insurers and physicians. The branded bundle costs $18 per pill, while the two generics together cost $5.[117]

But what about devices? Do they need to worry about generics or so-called "copycat" devices? Yes, there is the risk that once a patent on a design runs out, a copycat device will come along, but given the shorter design and development timeframes of devices, device makers have a longer span of exclusivity. A duplicate device by a competitor may not arrive on the market for 14 years or more and by then, presumably, the device company will have developed different, more improved designs or even other devices. So where does the risk come into play? With low cost competitors—those with *extremely* low costs—who make a variant of the device such that it is not a direct copy or a direct derivative, but a comparable device. Device makers in India are starting to seek FDA approval for medical devices that cost one-tenth of comparable devices in the US and Canada. Few device firms are equipped to cut costs by 90%

just to stay competitive.

Consider the marketplace success of low cost generic drugs in the US. Figure 3 shows the increasing market share of generics over the past decade. There is little doubt that this trend will continue.

Now, picture a hypothetical graph showing the market share increase of low-cost devices from countries where an increasing amount of research and development, and manufacturing expertise, has been outsourced (*e.g.*, China and India). If we factor in contributions from small companies in emerging market regions like Latin America, Africa, Eastern Europe, and Southeast Asia, it would be fair to assume that the influx of low-cost devices into the US market will be similar to the rise of generics in the US back in the early 1980s and 1990s.

In light of the mounting low-cost competition, biopharmaceutical and device firms that have built themselves—and designed and developed their products—on traditional models are finding it tough to keep doing the same things in the 21st century that they were doing last century. As former employees of US steel, textile, and television manufacturing industries will agree, simply counting on cost cutting, mergers, and acquisitions to save your marketplace position will only prolong challenges. In order to flourish, much less stay afloat, pharmaceutical, biotechnology, and medical device makers need to do more than cut costs, file suit against competition, and push for higher reimbursement. Executives responsible for new product development, quality systems,

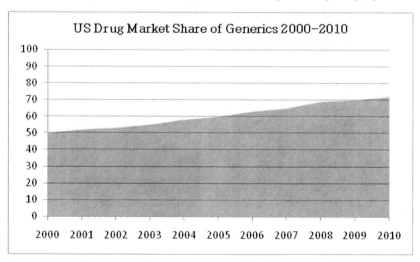

Figure 3: US drug market share of generics.
Source: Author's analysis

and regulatory affairs will need to adapt their strategies and tactics to 21st century realities, for it is from these executives and their teams that new products emerge, are produced, and bring in profits.

As a simple example of how executives can adopt to the new realities, in a July 2009 article[118] I suggested that compliance executives could save tens of thousands of dollars a year and still get the same level of outside expert advice and insight by employing a page from physicians and healthcare services—telemedicine.

EXPANSION OF TELEMEDICINE

Telemedicine is the use of technologies to remotely monitor and treat patients anywhere in the world. Studies conducted over the past several years by Harvard Medical School have found that doctors who use telemedicine technologies such as videoconferencing and teleconferencing to diagnose patients can have just as great an impact as if the doctor were physically present.[119] In July 2009, UnitedHealth, the US' second largest private insurer, and Cisco Systems, the world's largest computer networking company, announced plans to build a telemedicine network across the US, connecting thousands of doctor's offices and hospitals in rural and urban areas with high-speed network links. By 2012, when the network is set to be completed, the telemedicine market is expected to be providing more than $6 billion of healthcare to patients in the US alone.[120] The wave of telemedicine has just begun, and its impact on device and drug development will be felt for decades to come.

Because we are in the early stages of this trend, there are only a few recommendations that I can suggest starting, in the areas of:

- Device data formats and security
- Usability factors
- Marketing activities

Insurers and physicians must be selective about the use of data formats and security encryption in order to ensure compliance with US rules on patient privacy.[121] When it comes to telemedicine, insurance groups are liable for privacy regulations such as the Health Insurance Portability and Accountability Act (HIPAA). Device or diagnostic executives, or companies that have partnered with device firms to create a combination product (including a diagnostic and drug combination as noted in the previous chapter), should consider working with the insurers of their target patient population. It is imperative to find out what data formats and security technologies the insurer is requiring to meet HIPAA regulations and still be able to ensure the remote digital diagnoses are legitimate. The next step should be to build those formats and security technologies into any remote, networked capability of devices—including in clinical trials (an area where I also see telemedicine expanding). It may be beneficial to review the FDA guidance, *Radio-Frequency Wireless Technology in Medical Devices*.[122]

When it comes to remote diagnoses and treatment, both devices and drugs need to better incorporate design elements for patient usability. Usability is a measure of how easy it is for a person to use a particular tool (including a computer software program) in order to achieve a particular goal. Usability is a design component widely tested for in industries producing goods as diverse as automobiles, computers, construction tools, software programs, and video games (an exemplary case is Nintendo's Wii game console), digital cameras, and other products that are internally complex, but need to be very intuitive for consumers to feel comfortable owning and using them. ISO standards 16982 and 9241 address designing for usability.

On its surface, usability seeks to answer fairly straightforward questions that can then drive design and development of a new product:

- What is the context in which the consumer will use the product?
- What can the consumer do versus what can be left to the machine or tool?
- How quickly will the tool need to be used?
- What special capabilities need to be built in to accommodate a consumer with a limited range of motion?

Think of automatic defibrillators, those now-ubiquitous devices, designed to be used rapidly by the average person. The firms that designed these devices incorporated an incredible amount of usability testing during their development. Firms that make devices, diagnostics, monitoring tools, automatic drug dispensers, and so on, need to place a similar emphasis on usability testing into their design and development processes for their new medicine to remain effective and relevant as telemedicine expands.

Usability is a discipline that dovetails nicely with drug and biologics development as well, especially when it comes to incorporating the voice of the customer in preclinical and clinical activities. At a minimum, drug and biologics makers will want to consider questions such as dosage formats and frequency (*e.g.*, how will the target patient population be impacted if they need to take a drug three times a day versus once a day), packaging (compare the brand version packaging of Zyrtec versus its generic competitors: the branded drug's packaging is more difficult to open and nearly 80% of the packaging ends up in the garbage, leaving the consumer with the impression that they paid a price premium for trash), and labeling. In a speech on the FDA's Safe Use Initiative, a program designed to minimize patient harm from poor usage of medication, the FDA's Dr. Janet Woodcock noted, "Many accidental overdoses result from confusion about exactly how much of a drug to take."[123] And FDA commissioner, Dr. Margaret Hamburg, said the agency estimates that nearly half of all drug-related injuries and severe side effects could be prevented with labeling and drug inserts better designed for patient comprehension.[124]

With the rise of the pre-informed patient, medicines with greater usability are far more likely to see better adoption—and thus better marketplace success—than their counterparts without patient-friendly features.

SUMMARY

As should be clear from the above—increased executive liability, the rise of the pre-informed patient, and the drive for cost containment—each of these trends is based on someone's self-interests. Device and drug makers are only slowly recognizing the need to adapt and capitalize on these trends, rather than the less-effective responses of lobbying against or ignoring them.

The sooner executives can motivate their teams and their company to take a proactive role in capitalizing on these trends and all the others I have mentioned in the previous chapters, the sooner their new medicine will be able to get to market and the more profit their new medicine will achieve.

EXECUTIVE'S CHECKLIST FOR CHAPTER FOUR

Understanding the major trends surrounding and influencing the compliance and product development landscape allows you to assess all the various opportunities. This is a crucial fourth step in designing your strategy and tactics for marketplace success in the 21st century. Here's a step-by-step to-do list:

- ☐ Verify that your development labs are taking advantage of at least one of the many predictive software algorithms such as those available through ap-algorithms.com or specs.net; remember to screen for drug-drug interactions; not just for specific biomarkers or chemical compounds
- ☐ Review the Collaborative Drug Discovery website and the Open Source Drug Discovery website (links to these are in appendix two and on the book's website at http://www.Get2MarketNow.com) to see if access to their preclinical research databases will help you speed your preclinical efforts (see "Bookshelving" in chapter six for ways to take advantage of these databases)
- ☐ Visit the NIH nanomedicine website to review the NIH roadmap and identify where your new products may fit (links to this are in appendix two and on the book's website)
- ☐ Download the presentation of Dr. Nakissa Sadrieh of the FDA's CDER development considerations for nanomedicines (available from the book's website)
- ☐ Obtain and read the *2009 Pew Internet & American Life Project* report on trends in health research among adults (links to this are in appendix two and on the book's website)
- ☐ Survey drug and device monitoring sites such as WebMD.com and RateADrug.com to see how your medicines—current and in development—are reviewed by these sites (links to these are in appendix two and on the book's website)
- ☐ Read Chapter 5, "Improving Innovation," to learn ways to incorporate the voice of the customer in your

medicinal development efforts

- [ ] Read my free report, *FDA Enforcement Trends 2008-2009*, available on the book's website http://www.Get2MarketNow.com
- [ ] Make sure your regulatory affairs department reviews all press releases and other forms of publicity that cite specific product claims or product data or product risks
- [ ] Visit the US Department of Health & Human Services' Office of Inspector General website and review their suggestions on what goes into a corporate integrity agreement—these elements need to be built into your compliance and quality system programs (links to this are in appendix two and on the book's website)
- [ ] Verify that your quality system management review includes a summary certification letter similar to the one in use by blood banks in the United Kingdom (you can obtain a template based on FDA suggested improvements to the UK letter in the recorded seminar, *Best Practices for Your Quality System Management Review*, through the book's website)
- [ ] Read my free report, *Ten Ways to Control Your Compliance Costs*, available on the book's website
- [ ] Visit the NICE website to review guidelines on how NICE conducts its technology appraisals of new drugs, diagnostics, and devices, including how it evaluates cost effectiveness (links to this are in appendix two and on the book's website)
- [ ] Download and read my July 2009 article, "Virtual Consultants—Are They for You?" available on the book's website
- [ ] Have your marketing and reimbursement teams determine the main insurers of your target patient populations for new drugs and devices you have in development
- [ ] Review the FDA guidance *Radio-Frequency Wireless Technology in Medical Devices*; a copy of the most current version is available through the FDA or on the book's website
- [ ] Ask your development teams how familiar they are with

the term "design for usability"

☐ Obtain a copy of *ISO 16982: Ergonomics of Human-System Interaction—Usability Methods Supporting Human-Centered Design* (a link to ISO is available in appendix two and on the book's website)

☐ Craft a checklist of consumer-oriented product usability components that can be tested by the quality department as part of design control or as part of your clinical trial efforts

☐ Read the FDA report *Safe Use Initiative: Collaborating to Reduce Preventable Harm from Medications*; (a copy is available on the FDA website or on the book's website http://www.Get2MarketNow.com)

Summary of Part One

Over the last four chapters (1-4), I have presented my analyses of current trends in medicinal product development, regulatory expectations, and compliance—including quality systems and regulatory affairs. I have also reviewed the larger contextual trends in which product development, regulatory rules, and compliance programs must operate.

Here is a summary of the conclusions:

☐ Medicinal development costs will continue to rise due to the continuing explosive growth in scientific knowledge, engineering technology, and all the various combinatorial options and development paths that continue to open up.

☐ Development and design—once comprised of "everything before FDA approval"—now extends to the post-market; FDA approval for marketplace launch has become just another gate in the development cycle.

☐ Pre-informed patients and rising consumer expectations of new devices, drugs, and the accountability of executives in the firms who make these products will lead to smaller economic niches of targeted therapies.

☐ As a result of the above factors, the development of new drugs, biologics, and devices will increasingly be influenced by reimbursement considerations and potential marketplace acceptance (i.e., how much will payers be willing to pay).

☐ Potential medicines expected to fare poorly when it comes to coverage by reimbursement agencies such as

NICE, CHMP, and CMS will increasingly be dropped from the pipeline; product development funding for new medicines expected to be poorly reimbursed will be more and more difficult to obtain.

☐ Reimbursement and marketplace potential is increasingly evaluated through cost-effectiveness, which assesses medicinal efficacy, safety, and the medicine's price.

☐ To accurately measure cost-effectiveness, and determine as soon as possible if a potential new medicine will get a high reimbursement level, executives need to drive quality and compliance components further up the new product development funnel as far as possible. This will shift, as a result, developmental failures upstream, toward the wide mouth of the new product development funnel, where failures are less costly.

☐ Most companies will *not* implement this shift of quality and compliance components very well. They will attempt (unwittingly or otherwise) to apply rigorous command and control methodologies designed for single-item manufacturing environments to the far more knowledge-intensive, non-standardized new medicine R&D and administrative support function environments that require flexibility and low overhead.

☐ Failure to appropriately shift quality and compliance components up the new product development funnel will further erode those companies' ability to innovate and compete in the global marketplace.

☐ In contrast, companies that *are* able to provide flexible, low-overhead compliance and quality structures in their new medicine design and development activities will have a significant competitive edge for the foreseeable future.

☐ Executives who can master compliance as a competitive edge will get their new medicines to market faster, for less money, and with less risk; theirs are the companies that will dominate the era of personalized medicines.

The rest of this book will now provide you many of the strategies and tactics to achieve this competitive edge. I will answer five critical questions:

1. Within the confines of the GLPs, GCPs, and design control, how can innovation and R&D productivity be improved?
2. How to can quality and compliance be driven upstream into product development without wrecking development processes?
3. How can flexibility be structured in FDA-driven quality systems and regulatory compliance programs?
4. How can cost-efficiencies be achieved in FDA quality systems and regulatory compliance programs?
5. How do all of these strategies and tactics tie together to bring new medicines to market faster, for less cost and less risk, while encouraging and strengthening compliance?

5 — Improving Innovation

Exactly how to improve new medicine research and development productivity is a difficult question. When tackling complex questions, I always suggest my clients begin with the end in mind. Who stands at the end of the new medicine product development process? The customer of the new medicine is the endpoint of any effort to improve research and development productivity. It is in his or her voice that the first answers to improving new medicine innovation can be found.

With so much emphasis on the testing, production, and marketing of new drugs, biologics, and devices, it is easy to forget that the customer is the true target of the product. Potential or current customers are a wonderful, far too-often overlooked source of product insight. Executives striving for innovation must learn to seek help from their best, and ultimately most important partner: their customers.

To capture the advice of medicinal product customers, businesses must go beyond traditional mechanisms such as complaint forms and informal feedback given to sales and marketing representatives. Executives must go beyond skimming online opinion forums. To build in the voice of the customer in product development, executives must envision a co-creative environment.

First, a workable definition of a medicinal product customer is needed. As I alluded to in chapter three, the customer of a drug or device firm is not only the patient (or in the case of a firm without something already on the market, the prospective patient); other customers include physicians, nurses, hospital administrators, healthcare office managers, reimbursement specialists, and the primary caregivers of patients (parents of children, adult children of their elderly parents, etc.).

To help refine product development and design control policies and standard operating procedures (SOPs), I offer a definition of customer easily adopted into any SOP format:

> *Customer:* an individual who purchases and/or uses a medicinal product. A customer may be actual or prospective, and may be, but is not limited to, a patient, physician, nurse, hospital administrator, healthcare office manager, reimbursement specialist, or primary caregiver.

There are four key concepts important in using this definition with product design and development:

1. A customer may be current or prospective
2. A customer is an individual, not an organization
3. A customer is not, by definition, limited to a patient
4. A customer may or may not be the one actually using your drug or device

These concepts allow executives to take the greatest advantage of customers to dramatically enhance innovation and bring new medicines to market faster, easier, and for less. They allow the definition of customer to include people in and out of a company with whom the firm collaborates to create and bring new medicines to market.

As an example, I had an experience many years ago working with a combination device firm. As we were discussing upcoming forecasts and needs at a budget meeting, we wandered off topic and instead began discussing a new device we had designed that was headed into Phase II clinical trials with a drug partner. Our concept was for the device to serve as a reservoir for any drug that could be made in liquid form. The patient would get the prescription from his or her physician, have the reservoir filled by the pharmacist, and then take the appropriate dose using the device. Our development partner was focused on strong pain-relief narcotics and their lead engineer was discussing how they would need money in the upcoming financial quarter to help further refine a dosage calibration system to prevent accidental overdose (thus the budget meeting context). As he discussed this, I pictured my children—they were very young at the time—discovering this very attractive-looking device, full of a powerful pain-relief drug, lying on the bathroom counter. "How," I piped up, "are we building in child-proofing?"

For several minutes, as everyone considered their own visions of what could ensue without a child-proof control, the room was deadly silent. Then, pandemonium broke out with everyone talking at once. Ideas were discussed, and we ended with a new side project to design a child-proof control. Because the device was so far along (we were close to selecting a final contract manufacturer), and we now needed to "re-open" design control, the clinical trial was delayed by eight months at a cost of nearly $1.5 million.

This is the cost of not including the voice of the customer. And it was this experience that taught me a simple lesson: the sooner the voice of the customer is included in research and development (R&D), the lower the R&D costs and risks. Or, to put it in product development parlance, collaborating with customers allows firms to fail early, fail fast, and fail cheaply. As I discussed earlier, the faster a firm identifies and develops a new medicine with the best efficacy, safety, and quality, the faster it gets to market.

In this light, innovation and R&D productivity can be improved by:

- Capturing the voice of the customer
- Collaborating with open innovation
- Caring for developing intellectual property

And I will begin by showing how to capture the voice of the customer.

CAPTURING THE VOICE OF THE CUSTOMER

Chances are, most firms already capture some customer voices. With a product on the market, customer complaints and healthcare provider feedback is recorded. Clinical trials obtain the biologic voice of the customer along with clinician feedback. And in the discovery or preclinical phase, executives undoubtedly picture their eventual product being put to use, compare it to competing products, or even receive a neighbor's feedback on what he or she wants to see in a new medicine. These simplistic methods do not generate consistent results. A more systematic, repeatable, means to gather and incorporate the voice of the customer is sorely needed.

Using the new product development funnel I discussed in chapter two, visualize where—at each point in the development process—a connection can be made with customers to get their input (see Figure 5). Activities within these phases are likely to resonate with different types of customers. A reimbursement specialist might have a lot of insights early on in the clinical stages, relating to efficacy targets to strike, but very few insights for packaging or labeling. A primary caregiver—especially a harried parent of a sick child—may have a lot of advice on packaging and labeling, but very few suggestions on comparative efficacy targets. The key is to consider your position in development efforts and then decide with whom to talk.

FUNDAMENTAL R&D AND DISCOVERY VOICE OF THE CUSTOMER

In the discovery, or basic research and development phase, prior to the initiation of preclinical and nonclinical work, use the voice of the customer to:

- Identify which needs are currently unfulfilled
- Eliminate unneeded features
- Validate the target market

Because the front-end portion of the new product development funnel tends to be dynamic and amorphous, executives should use the voice of the customer to quickly refine where best to focus research, development, and design efforts. The techniques executives can use in this early phase are geared to provide fast access to the customer's voice.

To start gathering the voice of the customer data, make sure to answer the following:

- What disease or condition will the product diagnose or treat?
- What causes the disease or condition?
- What are the most common symptoms?
- Is the disease or condition predominant in a gender or age range?
- Is the disease or condition predominant in an ethnic group or geographic region?
- Is the disease or condition dependent on a particular

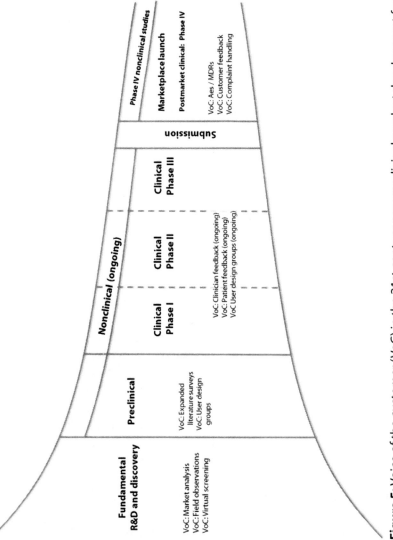

Figure 5: Voice of the customer (VoC) in the 21st century new medicinal product development funnel

gene or mutation?

- What is the typical impact of the disease or condition on a person's daily life?
- What is the typical impact on the affected person's family?
- What is the typical impact on the affected person's employment capabilities?
- What is the typical timeline or progression (if any) of this disease or condition?

Assuming executives already have basic answers to the above questions, it is time to hear the customer's voice and collect customer data. Three of the most effective methods of collecting customer data during the discovery phase are:

1. Market analysis
2. Field observation
3. Virtual screening

Market analysis includes the common elements of any market intelligence and estimate effort: reviewing investment firm reports and trade journals, identifying key competitors and their products, identifying adjacent products, and so on. The focus of a market analysis is on assembling an overall picture of the potential market, its size, and the possible avenues of growth for a new medicine to target.

Field research should also be done, preferably through observation. The key is to view potential customers in their own setting, to watch how they use existing products, and to determine if and how they compensate for the "gaps" that a new medicinal product can exploit. For instance, several years ago, Hewlett Packard sent its medical device engineers to gather ideas for new products from customers. One of the engineers met with customers—patients, physicians, nurses, and so on—at a hospital and watched a surgical operation. During the operation, the engineer noticed that the surgeon's ability to see the micro tools inside the patient was interrupted every time a nurse walked between the surgeon and the video screen display. This observation was taken back to the product development team and Hewlett Packard developed a small screen that could be worn by surgeons, giving them an uninterrupted view.[125]

The third technique, virtual screening, takes advantage of the communication capabilities of the Internet to quickly gather customer input using the following tools:

- Conjoint analysis
- Information pump

The Information Pump is a computer-facilitated simulation that offers researchers the unedited voice of the customer. Invented by Drazen Prelec, a marketing professor at the Massachusetts Institute of Technology (MIT) Sloan School of Management, the Information Pump allows developers to understand how customers think about drugs, biologics and devices, how customers understand the terminology, and what would make a new drug or device appealing, beyond just the science. Participants interact over the Internet and describe product concepts in their own words as to what is appealing about a product, what is confusing, what are the highly desired features, and so on. Dr. Prelec has made two self-study papers on his Information Pump—*The Information Pump* and *Readings Packet on the Information Pump*—available for download over the Internet. Search for these items on the Internet, or go to this book's website where I have included copies for readers to download.[126]

Conjoint analysis is used to assess how customers make tradeoffs between competing characteristics of a potential new product. Think of these tradeoffs in developing a new drug. Which would be better: a drug which must be taken intravenously but has no side effects, or a drug that can be taken in pill form with side effects? Is one pill a day that makes you queasy 2 hours after you have it better than having to take two pills a day with no queasiness? Is it better to take a drug at the doctor's office or at home? Is it better to take a drug on an empty stomach or with food? Those are simple questions, but they are examples of tradeoffs potential customers are in a unique position to answer. The result is a ranked set of product features developers can then use to further prioritize design and development efforts as the new medicine leaves the discovery phase for the preclinical stage.

Product Concept Summary

To help capture and document all of this information in an easy-to-grasp, straightforward manner, I suggest creating a simple high-level overview. This overview can then be used as a guiding set of principles throughout development. It is also a good basis for seeking funding for a new medicinal product development effort. I call this overview a "product concept summary."

Craft the overview around the disease or condition the product will address, inputting relevant information gathered from the voice of the customer. For executives familiar with the pharmaceutical target product profile, the overview I am suggesting is much simpler and geared to the layperson (see Figure 6).[127]

The SmarterCompliance™ Toolkit

[INSERT YOUR COMPANY NAME]
PRODUCT CONCEPT SUMMARY

PRODUCT CONCEPT NAME: *[insert the proposed product name or your project name]*

OVERVIEW
[craft a very brief summary of your new product concept addressing what specific need / gap is being addressed; think of what you might say at a cocktail party or to friends who ask what you're working on]

INTENDED MARKET / CUSTOMER
[what is the size of the market?]
[what are the adoption rates of similar medicines in this customer population?]
[what are the specific types of customers who would use and/or buy this product?]
[why those specific customers?]

CUSTOMER BENEFITS
[explain the specific customer benefits]
[what exists in the marketplace now?]

INTENDED USE
[what does the medicinal product do?]
[are there any known side effects - beneficial or detrimental?]
[what are the various functions and/or means of delivery?]

DISTINGUISHING / DESIRED FEATURES
[what are the distinguishing features of your product that set it apart from potential or current competition?]
[why should each type of customer choose your product over something else?]
[are there any specific ease-of-use, ergonomic, or reimbursement features that will set your product apart?]

DEVELOPMENT CONSIDERATIONS
[what are the key technologies for this product and are they available?]
[do you hold, or are you in the process of applying for, all necessary patents? if not, can they be licensed or designed around?]
[do you have sufficient resources for designing and making this product? what might you want to outsource?]
[what is its current development stage?]

Page 1 of 1   info@cerulean.com
www.cerulean.com

Figure 6: Product concept summary template

There are seven simple headings in the document:

1. Product concept name
2. Overview
3. Intended market / customer
4. Customer benefits
5. Intended use
6. Distinguishing / desired features
7. Development considerations

A completed product concept summary should be one to two pages in length. For my clients, the creation of a product concept summary ends the fundamental research stage and signifies the start of design control and preclinical development. In terms of required regulatory records, the product concept summary is the start of a medical device's design history file or the start of a new molecular entity's drug history file.

PRECLINICAL VOICE OF THE CUSTOMER

With the product concept summary in hand, executives enter the preclinical stage ready to aggressively court the voice of the customer. Information gathered here will help shape clinical trials and provide the initial outlines of the eventual marketing strategy. While there are a lot of potential product characteristics that can be determined in the preclinical stage, use the voice of the customer to define:

- Reimbursement considerations
- Usability preferences

When it comes to medicinal product reimbursement, the primary concern is comparative effectiveness. The preclinical stage is the time to clarify answers to questions such as: What are the ideal efficacy targets from the viewpoint of health insurers, the Centers for Medicare and Medicaid (CMS), the National Institute for Clinical Excellence (NICE), and others? What is the lowest efficacy range reimbursers are willing to consider as reasonable? If the new medicine is only able to achieve the low efficacy range, what other benefits and features would it need to have in order to have a good chance of marketplace acceptance? Specific answers to these types of questions are what to drive for in assessing reimbursement considerations and incorporating them into preclinical development.

Customer usability preferences need to be assessed in the preclinical stage as well. Expect to use clinical trials to confirm these preferences, allowing further refinement and personalization of any new medicine. In the preclinical stage, the tasks are gathering and synthesizing enough of the voice of the customer to allow the identification of usability preferences.

Keeping in mind the multiple customer segments—nurses and doctors, patients, primary caregivers, hospital administrators, and so on—each of these groups can be queried to determine usability preferences. Before delving into ways to assess usability, I will provide a definition of usability which can be adapted into design and development SOPs and work instructions:

> *Usability:* denotes, at minimum, the ease and effi-
> ciency with which customers can learn, use, become
> proficient, and stay satisfied with a medicinal product
> and its features or functionality; also known as "user
> friendliness."

Given this definition, designers might want to, for example, query nurses to ascertain preferences when it comes to integrating a new device with remote monitoring and the hospital's network. What are the most common problems that nurses face when devices are linked together? What is the one characteristic that defines a "must have" connectivity feature from the nurses' viewpoint? What does a good user manual or set of instructions look like from the nurses' perspective? Can the firm provide prototype devices to the nurses and get specific feedback on ease-of-use?

In the context of a combination device where a partner is providing one element (say the drug) and you are providing the other (the device), your partner may also represent an important customer voice to help drive preclinical design considerations. For instance, if a combination device is intended for use in a hospital operating room, sterility is a top concern for operating room physicians and nurses. By knowing this, executives can then focus on how best to ensure an appropriate degree of sterility. This can have serious design ramifications to be resolved as early as possible. Traditional device sterilization techniques are often incompatible with drugs, leaving the partners to look at processes like gamma irradiation. But what if there are components in the device that degrade rapidly upon exposure to gamma rays? Is that component in the device a required engineering part or something that was rated as a "nice-to-have" in the voice of the customer feedback? How should the design be changed and what impact will that have upon both its medicinal function and usability?

For a drug or biologic, executives might ask nurses if, given the other medications taken by the new medicine's intended patient, there is a visible formulation characteristic—color or consistency—that might help reduce medication errors. If executives are developing a drug typically used in emergency situations, is there a particular color-coding of the formula and its strength that might help the caregiver quickly distinguish between the one used for a child versus the one for an adult?

It sounds so simple, but in my experience answers to these questions can give a new product a marketplace advantage and can help convince skeptical reviewers of the product's value over and above current products on the market. Years ago, I helped design a device that emitted vaporized molecules of various chemical formulations so clinicians could study vapor disbursement and absorption. The clinician clicked a green button on the computer screen which then initiated a sequence in the device that emitted the vapor. Everything was proceeding along wonderfully as we prepared for our first clinical trial until the day the clinicians were testing a colorless chemical vapor. Very quickly, the clinicians and their laboratory assistants began complaining that the device was not working properly. After a number of days of troubleshooting and calming frustrated technicians and clinicians, we all stumbled upon the real culprit: the device had no independent indicator of operation. In other words, the clinicians had been depending upon the color of the vapor as a cue to start analyzing disbursement. Without a visible vapor, the clinician had no way of knowing whether the vapor was coming out of the device. All along, the scientists had assumed that the device was producing an auditory clue; they had just never paid any attention. And the device development team had assumed that a silent device was a nice touch, undoubtedly helping the clinicians concentrate. That is the kind of usability characteristic—a noticeable cue that the device is working properly—that executives should make sure to ask about. It's often the simple things that are the most important and the ones most overlooked.

There are two techniques best used in the preclinical stage to gather the voice of the customer:

1. Expanded literature survey
2. User design groups

A literature survey is a common project in the preclinical phase. But to capture the voice of the customer, executives need to go beyond traditional, scientific and medical journals, websites, and conference papers. Executives need to engage the pre-informed patient, the consumer who has done his or her own research, head-on. An expanded literature survey includes reviewing blog and wiki postings, patient-support group forums, and even proceedings from primary caregiver and hospital-centered conferences on the disease or condition the firm's new medicine is targeting. This expanded literature survey relies upon the same Internet sites used by the pre-informed patient.

I suggest creating a simple table (see Figure 7) and inputting the information gathered. A table can help identify patterns, themes, and connections. Any commercial spreadsheet application like Microsoft Office Excel can sort the data to further help spot trends or significant outliers. Gathering and analyzing this information can also help in the second phase of gathering the customer's voice: user design groups.

There are two types of user design groups: focus groups and virtual user design groups. The more traditional focus group gathers potential customers in a room and provides them with prototypes or questionnaires in an effort to assess product characteristics most valued by customers. Virtual user design groups take advantage of the Internet to harness the input and opinions from customers all over the world.

Imagine going to an Internet site that provides a picture of the basic shell of a medical device, perhaps an implantable pacemaker or a newborn baby warming station. Visitors are then presented with icons representing various features such as monitoring, size, battery life, whether

Source	Author / Presenter	Date	Key Concerns

Figure 7: Voice of the customer literature survey matrix

the device is combined with a particular type of drug, and so on. Visitors can drag and drop these icons onto the picture of the device shell and the image is updated to show the customization. Car companies have a similar system, allowing visitors to customize a proposed car purchase with desired features. The benefit to drug and device firms is that as pre-informed patients drag and drop features on the device, estimates on efficacy and pricing are also updated. By gathering an aggregate of these pre-informed patient decisions, executives now know the precise premium prospective patients are willing to pay for a particular product characteristic.

This type of virtual user group website can also gather this information based on a visitor's geographic location, so executives may, for example, learn what prospective customers in Provo, Utah, are willing to pay a premium for over prospective customers in Gdansk, Poland. And, of course, because of the broad definition of customer, executives can further segment this information by physician type, insurer, primary caregiver, and so on. And all this is gathered before a company has spent a single penny on clinical trials.

Voice of the customer information is also a very powerful inclusion in an investigative new drug (IND) or investigative device exemption (IDE) submission. Such information can also give firms an edge when seeking funding for a new product's clinical development. To get an idea of the success one client was able to achieve with this approach, read my 2009 case study, "Can Compliance Help Marketing and Business Development?" (a copy is available on this book's website). This is an example of the competitive edge that the voice of the customer can provide.

End the preclinical stage by inputting insights from the voice of the customer collection efforts into a clinical regulatory integrated strategic plan (CRISP). I will discuss the CRISP, its various inputs, format, and usage later in chapter eight. For now, though, it should be clear how much stronger clinical strategies and regulatory plans can be simply by gathering input from customers as early as possible in the development funnel.

Clinical Voice of the Customer

Having used voice of the customer data to refine product characteristics to those most agreeable to the two groups that increasingly influence market acceptance (pre-informed patients and reimbursers), it is time to confront the remaining group standing in the way of the marketplace launch, the regulatory health agency (*i.e.*, the FDA).

The clinical voice of the customer is—as I mentioned earlier in the chapter—largely predicated on biologic input from clinical patients and feedback from clinicians. There are, however, five additional areas where executives should seek out the voice of the customer as a new medicinal product proceeds through clinical trials:

1. Safety priorities
2. Product characteristic refinements
3. Process characteristics
4. Packaging and labeling preferences
5. Marketing messages and materials

Gathering clinical voice of the customer information is the point at which to develop a dedicated devotion to the top 3-5 aspects of safety important to customers and to the regulators. Executives unsure of how to divine regulatory opinion when it comes to safety considerations may want to review questions suggested in the 2009 FDA guidance, *End-of-Phase 2A Meetings*.[128]

Draw upon the same voice of the customer techniques discussed earlier to clarify the safety features and side effect tradeoffs most important to intended customers. Allowing survey takers to choose between just two alternatives will help force ranking and prioritizations. Use Phase I and Phase II clinical trials to validate this voice of the customer information and drive further product characteristic refinements.

During clinical trials, as executives define production processes such as design space and process analytical technologies (see chapter six), use the voice of the customer data to prioritize process conflicts. Thinking back to the previous example of a combination device destined for the operating room, at what point in a product process should gamma irradiation be used to sterilize the device and drug? How might this impact assembly of a highly desired customer feature? Perhaps the dose meter—critical to physicians and nurses—degrades rapidly after exposure to irradiation. Can the production processes be revised so that the dose meter is sterilized with ethylene oxide gas while the rest of the device and drug undergoes irradiation? In the next chapter, when I discuss production processes and building-in quality by design in the development funnel, the relationship between the voice of the customer, quality by design, and production process design will become even clearer.

By the end of Phase II clinical trials, executives should be at the point where only minimal tweaks to the new product and its production processes are being made. It is now time to focus the voice of the customer on product packaging and labeling, as well as on shaping a marketing message.

Customers get their first real, hands-on impression of how tailored a new medicine is to their preferences with a product's packaging and labeling. This is a make or break point in the world of customized drugs and devices. Ultimately, patients cannot discern the chemical or efficacy difference between a branded pill and its generic, but they do know what they like in terms of packaging, labeling, and inserts. So it is this design of information that executives must seek out using voice of the customer techniques.

The FDA has also become increasingly concerned about the user-friendliness of packaging and labeling when it comes to presenting risk information (see the FDA's guidance, *Label Comprehension Studies for Nonprescription Drug Products*). How might packaging look if a firm used virtual user design groups to assess customer preferences for the placing of risk and dosage information? How much weight would the voice of customers lend executives in presenting their designs to the FDA? The FDA has provided a partial answer to that question by taking the time and effort to craft a guidance document on patient-reported outcome measures, *Patient-Reported Outcome Measures: Use in Medical Product Development to Support Labeling Claims*.[129] While this guidance is specific to supporting labeling claims, the document does provide insight into the value that FDA reviewers place on one aspect of the voice of the customer.

Just as firms can draw upon voice of the customer information to help design packaging and labeling, firms can use customer insights to shape marketing messages. And with an increasingly cluttered landscape of product marketing and advertising, the better a firm can choose messages that resonate with various customers, the better the market success.

While a detailed discussion of marketing message development is beyond the scope of this book, it is important to recognize that some type of consistent marketing theme should be crafted prior to Phase II clinical trials to allow time for refinements based on customer feedback prior to product launch. Given the broad definition of customer—including physicians and nurses, for instance—even something as simple as the naming of clinical trials and how the new medicine is referred to in scientific presentations offers executives the opportunity to demonstrate how they have heard and made a partner of the customer to customize a new drug or device.[130] Executives can also use the voice of the customer to tailor multi-media marketing efforts, from cell phone applications to computer desktop widgets.

As a final note on incorporating the voice of the customer in the clinical stage to help speed product development and approval, voice of the customer can be used to help define requests for FDA fast-track or orphan drug designation. In these cases, executives may want to summarize voice of the customer studies undertaken that show customers have a clear preference for having the firm's new drug or device now rather than, as an example, having the drug or device some years down the road when it has undergone more comprehensive testing and long-term review.

POSTMARKET VOICE OF THE CUSTOMER

Most firms already incorporate some level of the voice of the customer in their postmarket monitoring by collecting customer feedback, adverse events, medical device reports, complaints, and other information. Consider incorporating some types of voice of the customer studies into the postmarket when getting ready to submit product or process changes. I have spoken with several FDA reviewers, who have told me how favorably-disposed they and their colleagues would be to approving postmarket changes generated as the result of postmarket customer feedback studies. Given the increasing trend of regulatory health agencies relying on postmarketing studies and so-called Phase IV clinical trials (see chapter two), staying on top of the voice of the customer in the postmarket stage of the product development funnel is a prudent philosophy.

VOICE OF THE CUSTOMER RESPONSIBILITY

Gathering and implanting the voice of the customer begs two questions:

1. Who is to be accountable for this work?
2. How long will this take?

To answer the latter, in my experience, overall efforts to incorporate voice of the customer into product development take approximately 4-6 weeks from the discovery phase all the way through medicinal product approval. As an example, the Information Pump technique can gather actionable voice of the customer input in about 30 minutes. So while gathering voice of the customer information may initially seem to be a great deal of work, it can be accomplished very quickly. Most of these techniques are relatively fast-paced because they are designed to gather input from busy customers.

The first time a firm puts these components in place will probably take longer than 4-6 weeks to implement, but at least 80% of the components—surveys, field research questionnaires, Internet site, permission letters, etc.—are all reusable, so executives can quickly implement them in a manageable 4-6 man-weeks per new product. I have also added the product concept template, referred to above, on the book's website to help streamline implementing the voice of the customer in development efforts.

To conduct and oversee the adoption of the voice of the customer in design and development efforts, consider a small team; preferably with no more than three to four members. Because so much of voice of the customer efforts involve aspects of customer communication common to marketing, business development, and sales personnel, it only makes sense to staff a voice of the customer team with members from these three groups.

One of the key challenges in any product development effort, irrespective of industry, is figuring out how best to involve marketing and business development expertise and help. The goal is to have these business professionals take care of the commercial aspects, as opposed to the science, engineering, and compliance aspects, of new product development. Gathering, analyzing, and incorporating voice of the customer information in drug and device development programs affords executives the opportunity to easily jump this traditional hurdle while producing a more personalized medicinal product.

Firms also need to involve their regulatory affairs departments in any voice of the customer efforts. For example, the regulatory affairs department needs to review all of the material—surveys, websites, etc.—

that will be used to gather the voice of the customer to ensure there is no inadvertent promotion of medicinal products in development. This review should abide by rules similar to those regulatory affairs used when it reviews scientific and medical papers and presentations on developing products. For instance, the review should ensure that statements of safety, efficacy, and risk are supported by good laboratory and good clinical practices-compliant data, that questions asked in a survey do not lead potential customers to think that this experimental medicine is approved or that it will work, and so on (some of these are discussed in the *Patient-Reported Outcome Measures* guidance referenced earlier).

For executives in a small company, assembling a three to four person team to focus on the voice of the customer may not be feasible. Fortunately, there are good alternatives. Firms with sufficient resources can hire an outside marketing firm experienced in gathering and analyzing voice of the customer data. A less expensive approach might be to employ the collaborative approach I described earlier and use outside development partners. Even big pharmaceutical firms such as GlaxoSmithKline, Johnson & Johnson, and Eli Lilly are embracing a collaborative innovation model as a means to incorporate some voice of the customer aspects and improve their research and development (R&D) productivity.

COLLABORATING WITH OPEN INNOVATION

Open innovation, defined as taking advantage of the capabilities and expertise of others outside your company to help with new product development, has been popular in other industries for the past two decades. Just as Toyota is synonymous with the business concept of *lean* and GE is synonymous with *Six Sigma*, so Procter & Gamble is synonymous with *open innovation*. At Procter & Gamble, open innovation is known by its operational format, "connect and develop." Since 2006, Procter & Gamble's open innovation model has been producing more than 35% of the company's new products, representing nearly $24.5 billion a year.[131]

There are multiple techniques to tackle open innovation. To date, the most common approach has been for one company to partner with another and jointly develop the intellectual property, such as the partnership between GlaxoSmithKline and Oratech, LLC to develop and launch a teeth whitening product. Only recently has the biopharmaceutical industry considered open innovation strategies reminiscent of Proctor &

Gamble's connect and develop model. The leader in this area has been Eli Lilly. In 2001, Eli Lilly developed an external network of 75,000 contract scientists and engineers around the world operating under a subsidiary, InnoCentive (now an independent company), to identify solutions to very narrow scientific problems (*i.e.*, can a five-step chemical reaction be shortened to three steps?).[132] And in 2002, Eli Lilly created an independent R&D unit known as Chorus to "quickly and cost-effectively advance candidate molecules from discovery through clinical proof-of-concept."[133] Chorus operates on an open innovation outsourced model in which work is completed through a mix of consultants, internal employees, and more than 200 contract research organizations. Chorus' open innovation approach has been able to cut the costs of preclinical development from the industry average of $30 million to $4.5 million, reduce the preclinical period by 1.5 years, and still maintain a candidate proof-of-concept success rate consistent with industry averages.[134]

The success of Eli Lilly's Chorus has helped encourage a growing number of pharmaceutical, biotechnology, and device firms to adopt similar open innovation strategies and outsource complex product development aspects of their overall product development funnel, from nonclinical animal studies to entire clinical trials from start to finish. Biotechnology venture capitalists foresee nearly 75% of development work being done on an outsourced, virtual basis by 2020.[135] As I noted in the introduction, virtual organizations operate with a skeleton crew, outsourcing as many functions and projects as possible. However, outsourcing of R&D tasks should be done with care. Not only does increased outsourcing lower direct oversight, but risks of nascent intellectual property loss increase.

A fourth approach to open innovation—after virtual companies, one-to-one partnerships, and connect-and-develop opportunity-driven frameworks—is to collaborate with universities and nonprofit organizations in public-private partnerships. Sixty three public-private partnerships are on track to deliver as many new drugs over the next decade.[136] One such public-private partnership, between the Institute for One World Health, the University of California-Berkeley, and Amyris Biotechnologies, is working on developing large-scale, low-cost production processes for key ingredients in anti-malarial drugs and vaccines.

A fifth approach to open innovation takes the virtual organization to an extreme and has no direct employees. The Pink Army Cooperative is one such example: it is a biotechnology venture made up completely of volunteers trying to create individualized therapies for breast cancer.[137] In theory, by creating an individualized treatment, the whole panoply of new drug development process costs is drastically eliminated: clinical trials are reduced to one person.

Detailing the myriad open innovation options is considerably beyond the scope of this book. However, keeping with the theme of balancing innovation productivity with lean compliance, I will explore one means to leverage open innovation while developing new personalized medicines: collaborating with universities.

University Open Collaborations

Incumbent in leveraging universities is being able to use any university-generated study results in submissions to the FDA, a challenge made more difficult given that most university labs do not operate in compliance with Good Laboratory Practices (GLP) and therefore are apt to produce results that the agency has historically looked upon with a great degree of skepticism. Tackling this skepticism requires a two pronged approach. First, I will look at innovative ways to mine the knowledge in universities, and then (in chapter seven), I will explore how to ensure such open innovation results can be used—either directly or in support of—any regulatory submission.

The simplest way to identify what universities can offer in a knowledge-sharing collaboration is to classify options based on the three main stages of product development and commercialization:

1. Preclinical
2. Clinical trials
3. Postmarket surveillance

Preclinical - University Open Collaborations

When discussing the preclinical and feasibility stage, I am referring to medicines at least 7-10 years away from any approval to market. These are perfect pipeline candidates to be able to get the most benefit from university collaborations, so make sure to put in place appropriate GLP compliance components as soon as possible (tactics I will cover in chapter seven).

At this feasibility and preclinical stage, universities can provide six collaborative opportunities:

1. Literature surveys
2. Compound optimization
3. Formulation sampling
4. Personalization target profiling
5. Pharmacometrics modeling
6. Preliminary adaptive trial design

Literature Surveys

The scientific literature survey is a familiar tool to provide broad understanding upon which firms then conduct development, determine which toxicology tests to pursue, identify potential molecular characteristics to investigate, and so on.

When developing personalized medicines, literature surveys need to go one step further. An ideal survey lays out all the components of a development program in such a manner that any actual work undertaken is simply confirmatory in nature. While actual results will not be so straightforward, with luck, a lot of a firm's testing can end up validating survey results and safety and efficacy decisions. For instance, if a firm plans to use propylene glycol as one of its excipients in its new drug, but needs to heat the propylene glycol as part of the formulation process, a literature survey might be undertaken to review risks associated with propylene glycol. Such a review would then reveal that heating propylene glycol produces a toxic by-product, formaldehyde. The firm would then need to figure out how to deal with this; the university might be asked to expand its literature survey to see how organizations have gotten rid of or avoided this toxic by-product. The firm could then test any uncovered methods in its own laboratories.

As another example, if a literature survey finds and documents that nonclinical studies previously undertaken by another organization are similar to a firm's proposed nonclinical studies, how would that inform the firm's decision-making? If the firm could obtain the results of these earlier studies by the other organization, the firm might not need to repeat such testing. The firm could simply limit its efforts to confirming the study results.

This "end result" validation is one way firms can overcome any non-GLP compliance of individual components. It is a subtle point, but one well worth noting both here and in any regulatory submission. If validation is about overall systemic integrity, rather than just piecemeal projects, then make sure to draw any FDA reviewer's attention to confirmatory testing success.

Expanded, predictive literature surveys take significant time, and paying your staff for this type of survey represents a significant cost. Providing a university grant money to perform the same work is substantially less expensive because the skill level required to conduct a literature survey is common among university graduate students. To verify the quality of such survey efforts, consider reviewing the survey source materials and assessing if anything was missed.

Compound Optimization

Work can also begin in university labs for compound optimization. Admittedly, much of this work will be integrated with other activities (such as formulation development and sampling), but firms can get much of the base optimization work underway as soon as possible, particularly in graduate student level laboratories.

Set aside worries about conducting this optimization under GLPs. Once the university labs have identified the most promising optimizations, a firm's GLP-compliant laboratories can conduct confirmatory studies, making sure to include upper and lower-limit boundary testing.

As development progresses, executives will want to continue this collaborative effort to identify, optimize, and confirm a product's critical quality attributes (CQAs) and critical process parameters (CPPs) as part of your quality by design efforts (something I will discuss further in the next chapter).

This will also help ease adoption of process analytical technologies (PAT) and real-time quality control and product release—activities that will be crucial with the smaller batch sizes and more frequent changeovers inherent in producing personalized medicines.

Formulation Sampling

At a bench-top level, universities can develop and test various formulations alongside their attempts to optimize your compound. Focus first on formulations that support findings in the literature survey. For instance, a developer may have found that a certain subsection of patients in need of the firm's new drug or biologic are also on heartburn medication. While the new compound itself is not known to react adversely to the various heartburn medicines, the literature survey reveals that formulation scientists need to be cautious about several chemicals initially planned to be used in the overall formulation. Workarounds will need to be found, something that is costly and time-consuming, and, again, a perfect candidate for a university to tackle.

Personalized medicine brings the potential for hundreds of time-consuming miscibility challenges; executives need to consider where their monies will be better spent—sleuthing and solving with graduate students or costly professional staff? Graduate student work is inevitably less expensive, and professional staff can be used to verify the quality of such work. Furthermore, in my experiences, as I will discuss later in this chapter and in chapter six, universities provide considerable advantages to product development that go beyond cost.

Personalization Target Profiling
Consideration of poor drug-drug interactions is also important given many of the genetic underpinnings of personalized medicines. This brings up one of the newer challenges inherent in personalized medicine development: the identification and characterization of individual target patient profiles.

While I do not assume each prospective patient will get a branded medicine unique to only him or her, just as consumer goods are personalized to appeal to different sets of overall consumer profiles, personalized medicines will likewise be targeted at groups, not individuals. This tailoring of medicines will require firms to aggregate similar prospective patient profiles to obtain some level of cost-efficiency.

Rather than trial and error or delegating the entire patient profile endeavor to the marketing department, a better approach is to mix quantitative analyses and qualitative surveys. While blending can involve an expensive learning curve for any organization, universities have the capability to be a low-cost, collaborative ally.

The scientific literature survey can include a search for relevant patient population information, genetic or otherwise. Online discussion forums of patients suffering from similar diseases can be mined. Schools of medicine can play host to focus groups of nurses and physicians-in-training to offer feedback on potential delivery methods or unusual patient complications to pinpoint in clinical trials.

Some of these results can go into preclinical new medicine design; some of it will need to be studied further in clinical trials. The sooner executives develop this information, the better a new medicine, the better the clinical trials, and thus the greater a new medicine's chances for approval and marketplace success.

Pharmacometrics Modeling

To make the most of development resources, take advantage of the rapidly evolving field of pharmacometrics. Pharmacometrics quantifies and models drug, disease and trial information to aid drug development and regulatory agency reviews. Subcomponents of pharmacometrics include pharmacokinetics, pharmacodynamics, biomarkers and medicinal efficacy relationships, trial design, genetics, and other aspects that seek to provide quantitative analyses and predictive models. Assuming a firm has not already invested the large sums of money and time required to set up an internal pharmacometrics program, this is one university service to aggressively seek out.

The FDA's Center for Drug Evaluation and Research has posted a specific section on its website for pharmacometrics that is worth reviewing—as well as sharing with any university collaborators.[138] The site contains a mix of internal FDA goals and strategic objectives for the industry to achieve by 2020, including incorporation of a pharmacometrics section on new drug applications and leveraging cumulative knowledge to design clinical trials for pediatrics. As I discussed earlier in the book, the FDA fully expects many, if not most, new drug and biologic products on the market by 2020 to be personalized medicines.

Currently, firms take advantage of pharmacometrics for three clinical design purposes:

1. Identification of patients at risk for unexpected adverse drug reactions
2. Dosing ranges by patient profile
3. Patient therapeutic modeling

As we go forward in the 21st century, executives will also want to use these data—combined with literature surveys—to estimate effectiveness comparisons, including defining the expected therapeutic value to patients participating in any clinical trials. The latter is crucial information to ensure clinical patients are eligible for reimbursement.

While executives may decide to work with an outside reimbursement specialist as a new medicinal product gets closer to marketplace launch, using students at pharmacy schools and other university programs for initial work is smart planning. Executives in a start-up company can also use results from these studies to help support funding requests or licensing deals. In addition, given the loss of industry knowledge due to baby boomer-generation retirements, executives who work with universities have a greater chance of generating future professionals willing to work for their firms upon graduation.

Preliminary Adaptive Trial Design

All of these tactics lead to university help with preliminary clinical trial design. Under a personalized medicine schema, I expect adaptive trials to increasingly be *de rigueur* in the industry. University biostatisticians can help design and document the various checkpoints and efficacy levels for each adaptive trial.

Universities that have a relationship with the National Cancer Institute (NCI) may be of significant help in this arena. The NCI's developmental therapeutics program can work as a "broker" to arrange for clinical trials to test new cancer drugs.[139] University faculty with ties to NCI may be able to help you streamline clinical trial selection (the NCI works with hundreds of medical trial sites), but more importantly, use their expertise to set up a very small Phase 0 clinical trial with two goals: to validate that a new drug interacts with its molecular target, and to verify specific biomarkers (I will discuss Phase 0 clinical trials in greater detail in chapter eight).

CLINICAL TRIALS - UNIVERSITY OPEN COLLABORATIONS

Collaborations with universities for development of personalized medicine can extend into the clinical stage as well. Formulation and compound optimization work can continue during clinical trials, and two new opportunities also emerge:

1. Pilot manufacturing optimization
2. Labeling and packaging insert designs

Pilot Manufacturing Optimization

One of my clients undertook a joint effort with a local business school to have teams of students examine the company's manufacturing and warehousing processes and equipment, and then make recommendations for improvement. While students may not provide the level of advice obtainable from a professional consultant, students will be un-afraid to challenge assumptions and can often introduce cutting-edge manufacturing techniques. As a result, a little money spent on involving universities can yield dramatic dividends.

To undertake this type of collaboration, structure it such that the students focus on a key challenge of personalized medicine production. For example, switching from large single product batch runs to multi-product small batch production, without comprising product safety and quality or process productivity. Consider introducing the concept of process analytical technologies and the need to move from post-production quality control to real-time quality control (see chapter six for more details). A pilot plant is perfect for modeling any improvements to see what will best scale-up and transfer to finished product manufacturing.

Just as with any outside firm hired to give similar advice, provide the students with an overview of your company and its operations. Make sure to also provide a basic understanding of FDA rules and obligations, keeping such an overview at a high-level (see the five slide presentation I discuss in chapter seven as an example), digressing into details only if necessary to answer specific questions.

Labeling and Packaging Insert Designs

When it comes to designing labels, package inserts, packaging, and so on, the fresh-thinking and naivety of university students can be a real asset. Students will look at comparable products that appeal to them, and will not be afraid to question assumptions and traditional packaging or formatting.

Ask any academic contacts to assemble a team of pharmacology and marketing students (for the marketing students, try to specifically request individuals who specialize in "human interfaces" or "usability"). This inter-disciplinary team will work on creating draft labeling and packaging inserts. The pharmacology students can analyze and present the data; the marketing students can offer formatting suggestions to make it more reader-friendly (*i.e.*, When is a graph more appropriate than a table? What can be done to draw a healthcare provider's attention to XYZ data? etc.). To incorporate potential customer feedback, the student team can also test out various draft labeling and packaging inserts with physicians and nurses in a local school of medicine.

As I will discuss in the next chapter, all of this information is admissible in regulatory submissions under a quality by design approach that begs for incorporation of cumulative knowledge.

POSTMARKET MONITORING - UNIVERSITY OPEN COLLABORATIONS

When it comes to knowledge-based collaborations with universities, opportunities do not end with clinical trials. For personalized medicine, expect the FDA to increasingly ask for risk evaluation and mitigation strategies (REMS) that involve a combination of postmarket monitoring plus Phase IV clinical trials, nonclinical studies, and product and process refinements.

Take advantage of a university partnership in two ways:

1. Conduct continuous postmarket monitoring studies
2. Assemble quality by design-inspired "lessons learned" reports

Continuous Monitoring Studies

In continuous monitoring studies, patients monitor themselves and/or are electronically monitored. Information on efficacy and side effects can be continuously gathered, analyzed, and reviewed for trends and outliers over a long period of time.

Such studies can be expensive to mount as a clinical trial in the traditional clinical trial model, so working with a low cost supplier (*i.e.*, a university or other academic medical facility) may be financially preferable. In addition, the outside perspectives brought by university faculty and students may provide creative solutions on enrollment and monitoring to make patients more amenable to this type of continuous monitoring and data gathering.

Not only will continuous monitoring studies generate data on a new medicine's safety and efficacy, such studies may identify unanticipated uses for which firms can then file supplemental marketing requests. Recognize that the complexity of personalized medicines means that new drugs and biologics will only be truly deemed safe and efficacious after a significant time on the market, a fact the FDA is aware of. Thus the agency is increasingly pushing postmarket monitoring programs such as its Sentinel Initiative[140] and REMS.

Lessons Learned Reports

As development on a new medicine comes to an end—or after each stage of development is completed—ask a team of students to synthesize and summarize all the work undertaken into a "lessons learned" report.

Too often, our good intentions of applying the lessons we have learned from previous efforts is superseded by busy schedules, organizational conflicts, and day-to-day tasks which overwhelm any attempts to step back and look at the big picture.

Luckily, however, university students will eagerly grasp this type of project as something akin to their schoolwork, except that it represents a valuable real-world case study. The student team can review project documents, interview staff and managers, highlight decisions that might have turned out differently, and so on. Executives can also coordinate with faculty to ensure that such a lessons learned report is the "big project" for the school year.

This report can be a class presentation to a firm's management or development team, and the report itself can be saved in the new product's development records. As quality by design gains adoption in life science companies, lessons learned reports will help executives define a better chance of success with their future new medicines.

Working with a university in an open innovation model can provide firms the same benefits other industries have seen:

- Increased innovation
- Faster development times
- Higher productivity
- Improved creativity
- Lower costs

In any open innovation, however, there is an area of risk which we must address: nascent intellectual property leakage.

CARING FOR DEVELOPING INTELLECTUAL PROPERTY

Open innovation and voice of the customer activities require firms to reveal some bits and pieces of their developing intellectual property; note the key qualifier: *developing* intellectual property. Employing open innovation and the voice of the customer involve varying degrees of external access to intellectual property before a firm has obtained or even applied for a patent, trademark, registration, or other legal mark of ownership.

Contracts with open innovation collaborators and partners can be crafted to carefully spell out who has ownership of which elements of the collaboration. But when it comes to gathering voice of the customer input, intellectual property protection contracts are not realistic.

To prevent the leakage of nascent intellectual property during voice of the customer gathering activities, work with legal counsel to establish appropriate terms and conditions for any activities to be conducted over the Internet. Prior to accessing a virtual device shell onto which consumers drag and drop features, website visitors might first have to input their email address and agree to a set of terms and conditions; these terms would then be emailed to the visitor.

There are a number of good reference materials available—Nolo Press publishes several—about crafting terms and conditions. Executives may also want to take a look at the terms and conditions employed by innovation marketplace and technology transfer websites such as Yet2.com.

BENEFIT OF THE PRODUCT CONCEPT SUMMARY

Terms and conditions, contracts, and non-disclosure agreements are ultimately means to enforce penalties against someone who has already shared information. Ideally, a firm should never need to resort to contract clauses and legal remedies because executives have taken appropriate steps to protect their nascent intellectual property from theft and leakage.

One such step is the use of the product concept summary. Among the reasons I suggest creating a high-level product concept summary geared to the layman, and use that to guide voice of the customer efforts, is that such a non-technical overview eliminates the ability of anyone to take that information and duplicate a new device or molecule. In other words, when it comes to voice of the customer information sharing using the product concept summary document, there is very little intellectual property to leak out.

The product concept summary is also beneficial during the initial negotiation stages of any open innovation collaboration effort. The risk of intellectual property leakage is greater in such collaborations than in consumer communications, however, as there is more access to nascent intellectual property by outside entities.

Fortunately, drug, biologic, and device makers have an advantage over companies in non-heavily regulated industries, namely the quality and regulatory affairs departments which less-regulated industries lack.

Compliance Team Activities

Because developing a new medicine involves quality and regulatory affairs departments, compliance teams are perfectly poised within the new product development funnel to easily incorporate intellectual property controls into typical FDA compliance-related activities. Two simple ways to add intellectual property controls into compliance programs are:

1. Asking intellectual property-related security questions in any quality or due diligence audit of suppliers
2. Removing intellectual property details from standard operating procedures and work instructions

In due diligence audits and qualifications of collaborative partners and suppliers, compliance executives can add a handful of questions designed to assess how carefully the partner or supplier protects confidential information:

- Are facility visitors required to sign-in with specific information such as citizenship, whom they are visiting, provide photo identification, etc.? Are the logs ever reviewed?
- Does the partner have a "clear desk" policy to lock up confidential papers when not in use? How is this enforced?
- Are there policies and procedures on marking documents "confidential" or is this left up to individuals?
- Are there rules against emailing confidential information outside the company? How is this enforced?

I have posted a two-page checklist of various questions on this book's website for readers to download; each of these questions can be easily incorporated into any quality systems audit or due diligence.

When it comes to SOPs, the greatest danger of intellectual property leakage occurs when either the firm, a collaborator, or a contracted partner (such as contract manufacturer) inadvertently places step-by-step instructions to recreating intellectual property in the SOP or work instruction. I have seen this most often in SOPs that tackle formulations, mixing, assembly (especially for medical devices), and even in-process or post-assembly quality testing.

To avoid this leakage, conduct a review of SOPs that relate specifically to intellectual property. Look for detailed processes that would give an outside engineer or scientist enough information to duplicate the described product. Eliminate any intellectual property-revealing step-by-step details. For a formulation, firms might leave out specific measurements, relying upon training and a separate ingredients list that is tightly controlled. The key is to avoid making it easy for someone to need only take one document to obtain critical intellectual property; the more records a person has to search through and assemble, the greater their chances of getting caught.

Biotechnology firms will want to be especially careful with trade secret processes. It is absolutely essential to split such processes over multiple SOPs, leaving out critical parameters whenever possible, referring a reader to other, more tightly controlled documents. For more information plus a detailed strategy on protecting developing intellectual property from theft, read "Protecting Intellectual Property from the Inside Out" in *Best Practices in Biotechnology Business Development*.[141]

SUMMARY

Compliance teams play a quiet role in ensuring the success of open innovation, from quality due diligence questions to helping protect developing intellectual property to regulatory affairs reviews of voice of the customer material. By listening to the voice of the customer and connecting and developing with different partners, open innovation collaborations improve R&D productivity. This is just one way that executives can get their new medicine to market faster, easier, and for less.

This improvement in new product development productivity presents a compelling opportunity to build in compliance and quality from day one of development. This is the challenge I resolve in the next chapter.

EXECUTIVE'S CHECKLIST FOR CHAPTER FIVE

Taking advantage of the voice of the customer is how to start personalizing a new medicine in the 21st century. Combine this with open innovation collaborations to translate and verify voice of the customer preferences into product characteristics and functionality, all while speeding time to market. Here's a step-by-step to-do list:

- ☐ Add the definition of "customer" into your product development and design control SOPs
- ☐ Conduct a preliminary market analysis during the discovery and fundamental research phase
- ☐ Download and read my case study, "Can Compliance Help Marketing and Business Development" from the book's website: http://www.Get2MarketNow.com
- ☐ Assemble a 3-4 person team from business development, marketing, and sales personnel to start gathering voice of the customer information
- ☐ Have your regulatory affairs group review all voice of the customer materials for inadvertent promotional claims
- ☐ Download and read the Information Pump papers on the book's website to see how easily you can incorporate this voice of the customer technique
- ☐ Download the product concept summary template from the book's website and complete it with your product's information
- ☐ Add the definition of "usability" to your product development and design control SOPs
- ☐ Expand your literature surveys to capture voice of the customer information
- ☐ Summarize your preclinical voice of the customer information to help your clinical and regulatory personnel develop an integrated strategic plan with voice of the customer-influenced clinical trial components
- ☐ Review the NCI's developmental therapeutics program for more ideas on how university collaborations can help you design adaptive clinical trials (a link is available in appendix two or on the book's website)
- ☐ Read Chapter 8, "Ensuring Lean Regulatory Affairs," to

learn about clinical regulatory integrated strategic plans (CRISPs), and adaptive and Phase 0 clinical trials

☐ Provide relevant voice of the customer information to your quality by design team to help guide development manufacturing processes and prioritize safety, efficacy, and quality product characteristics

☐ Read Chapter 6, "Building in Quality and Flexibility from Day One," to understand how to incorporate quality by design into your product development funnel

☐ Download and review the FDA's guidance, *Label Comprehension Studies for Nonprescription Drug Products* (from the FDA website or the book's website at http://www.Get2MarketNow.com)

☐ Download and review the FDA's guidance, *Patient-Reported Outcome Measures: Use in Medical Product Development to Support Labeling Claims* (from the FDA website or the book's website)

☐ Incorporate reliance upon voice of the customer feedback and insights into your labeling and packaging designs and SOPs

☐ Consider crafting a specific SOP on how to conduct voice of the customer studies in preclinical, clinical, and postmarket stages

☐ With your colleagues, use the examples on ways to collaborate with universities to discuss other opportunities for open innovation collaborations

☐ Have your supplier quality team qualify any collaborative partner as a supplier (see the section in Chapter 6 on qualifying university collaborative partners)

☐ Review my recorded seminars on managing supplier risk to make sure controls you select for your collaborations are appropriate to the risks involved (you can obtain copies of these compliance seminars through the book's website)

☐ Download my intellectual property security checklist from the book's website and incorporate its questions into your internal and due diligence quality audits

☐ Verify your SOPs—and those of your partners and open

innovation collaborators—do not inadvertently spell out your intellectual property or trade secrets

☐ Read "Protecting Your Intellectual Property from the Inside Out" (you can obtain a copy of this through the book's website http://www.Get2MarketNow.com)

6 — Building in Quality and Flexibility from Day One

All compliance comes at a cost. As I noted in chapter two, for firms developing medicinal products this cost translates to longer development timelines, higher overhead, and less certainty of success. Voice of the customer and open innovation collaboration strategies can help—and are particularly good for identifying aspects important for personalization and reimbursement—but ultimately the overall medicinal product development process, from preclinical to postmarket production and monitoring, needs systemic modifications to accommodate all the knowledge, regulatory revisions, and larger landscape trends I have reviewed.

In the 21st century, executives need to ensure a balance between having product quality, safety, efficacy, and personalization and having flexibility throughout research and development (R&D) and full-scale manufacturing to handle evolving knowledge and regulations. Effectively achieving this balance requires building quality into products and flexibility into processes from day one of design and development. And as this chapter describes, the tactics of a 21st century medicinal product development strategy can cut costs, speed time to market, and reduce risk, while meeting increasingly stringent regulatory expectations.

QUALITY BY DESIGN

In August 2002, the Food and Drug Administration (FDA) published a concept paper entitled *Pharmaceutical cGMPs for the 21st Century: A Risk-Based Approach.*[142] This document expressed a desire that companies build quality, safety and efficacy into their new biopharmaceutical products as early as possible. This concept became known as "quality by design."

Years later, the meaning and impact of quality by design is still not clear to many. Is it a new way to develop drugs and biologics? Can it shorten the product development cycle time? Will it provide more business flexibility? Where, when, and how should it be applied? For many executives who tried to adopt quality by design, confusion gave way to frustration.

And yet, properly conceived and executed, quality by design works. In 2008, during a presentation in Washington, D.C., I discussed the results of two clients who had adopted quality by design[143]. The first cut more than 3 years off their total time to market, reduced costs by 8%, and increased their success rate from the typical 45% at the Phase II clinical trial stage to an 85% success rate. The second saved 1 year off their time to market, reduced costs by 3%, and went from a typical 7% success rate in the Phase I clinical trial stage to a 32% success rate.

The following pages present an overview of quality by design and how, during medicinal product development and in conjunction with the rest of the advice in part two of this book, quality by design can give companies a powerful competitive edge.

BACKGROUND OF QUALITY BY DESIGN

Quality by design is not unique to FDA-regulated industries. In the 1970s, Toyota Motor Company pioneered many quality by design concepts to improve its automobiles. Toyota executives and engineers reframed the Japanese principle of *kaizen* ("continuous improvement") to help them improve fuel efficiency while still building cars that met US Department of Transportation safety regulations.

Rather than looking just at their manufacturing processes, Toyota management followed the product development funnel of automobile creation backward, to where characteristics such as fuel efficiency, safety, and so on were first identified. Toyota engineers realized that building quality, safety and efficacy into their product at the early conceptual, design stage was the most cost-efficient (here I use "efficacy" to include the concept of fuel efficiency and other features such as passenger room and so forth). This shift in thinking then freed the engineers to introduce innovations to the remaining elements such as style, handling and so on, improving both their time to market and their chance of market success.

By incorporating predefined product characteristics such as consumer preferences or fuel efficiency targets as early as possible in the product design phase, Toyota established a product vision which served as a reference to arbitrate conflicting constraints, limit late stage changes, increase product quality, and reduce overall development and manufacturing costs.

Those early attempts provided Toyota the funding and marketplace stature to build today's top-ranked Lexus automobiles. In 1970, few people could have imagined that the issues automobile executives were resisting as impediments for their industry—demands to improve product quality, safety, and efficacy—would today be espoused as competitive advantages among automobile makers.

In the 1990s, medical devices began to appear that were developed under similar design conditions to automobiles, identifying and building in quality, safety, and efficacy characteristics as early as possible—in other words, using the "quality by design" model. For device companies, quality by design drove down risk and cost while improving patient safety and product efficacy. FDA officials realized that biologics and drugs could also benefit from quality by design.

FDA coalesced its thinking on quality by design in a 2004 report entitled *Pharmaceutical cGMPs for the 21st Century—A Risk-Based Approach*[144]. This publication defined quality by design as having two parts:

1. Developing a medicinal product to meet predefined product quality, safety, and efficacy characteristics
2. Designing product manufacturing processes to ensure that the predefined medicinal product quality, safety, and efficacy characteristics are met

And it argued that adoption of quality by design will therefore provide:

- Streamlined product development and premarket reviews
- Easier regulatory compliance and flexibility
- Faster improvements to product maturity and manufacturing

Shortly after publication of the FDA's report, the International Conference on Harmonization (ICH) began publishing its own quality by design guidance documents (the Q-series of publications). Just as the rest of the regulatory health agency members of the ICH adopted the Q-series of publications, so too did the FDA. In May 2006, the FDA adopted the first of these publications in the form of a guidance document, *Pharmaceutical Development*[145]. In the 21st century, quality by design has quickly become a world-wide regulatory expectation.

While the FDA's quality by design guidance clarified the agency's philosophy, and the ICH publications explained the harmonized expectations, the documents left most practical questions unanswered. Should quality by design start at the clinical stage of medicinal product development and be focused on improving clinical testing? Or should quality by design be used to improve finished product manufacturing processes? While the agency worked with a handful of manufacturers in pilot programs, the vast majority of biopharmaceutical executives were left to answer these questions themselves.

Varied interpretations of quality by design further complicated adoption attempts. Regulatory affairs professionals and quality assurance personnel each saw differing considerations, some even questioning whether quality by design actually applied to their respective work tasks or their companies. Meanwhile, consultants pushed risk management and prioritization, and a number of industry scientists argued that by eliminating the need for some tests, quality by design risked undermining scientific rigor. The result was—and in many cases, still is—confusion and frustration. In addition, the wide variety of interpretations led to a haphazard adoption of quality by design, failing to achieve the results the FDA touted and the industry expected.

To start sorting through this confusion, consider a definition of quality by design similar to the one my clients have adopted in their internal development guidelines and standard operating procedures (SOPs):

> *Quality by Design:* everything we do to directly promote and prove the safety, efficacy, quality, and personalization of our product, from proof of concept (*e.g.,* the preclinical stage) to the point at which customers are buying and using our product on a regular

basis (*e.g.*, the postmarket stage).

While this definition is not as overtly product- and process-focused as the definition espoused by the FDA and the ICH, this definition delineates three points:

1. The stages in the new medicinal product development that quality by design comes into play (from preclinical through the postmarket)
2. The need to design and develop products and processes with a rigorous view to how they will meet and maintain safety, efficacy, quality, and personalization
3. The requirement for proof (*e.g.*, records) to be produced at each point where safety, efficacy, quality, and personalization are achieved

In Figure 8, the new medicine product development funnel illustrates several specific examples of where and how quality by design can be adopted throughout development.

At a May 2007 conference, Dr. Barry Cherney, the FDA Deputy Director of Therapeutic Proteins, stated that the goal of quality by design in biopharmaceuticals is to use scientific judgments and risk-assessments to ascertain "a reasonable level of expectation" when it comes to important product characteristics while eliminating non-value-added work to speed bringing innovative medicines to market.[146]

Key to successfully implementing quality by design is identifying those characteristics of a product that are critical to its safety, efficacy, and quality, plus those aspects of a firm's processes (typically during manufacturing) that impact those product characteristics. These are called critical quality attributes (CQA) and critical process parameters (CPP) respectively.

If a firm can prove that a product characteristic (such as an inactive ingredient like a chemical dye) has no impact on safety, efficacy, or quality, then the firm can stop testing, tracking, or controlling that product characteristic any further. Likewise, processes proven to have no impact on product safety, efficacy or quality can also receive minimal testing, tracking, and control. For most companies, this can significantly lower the costs involved in product development and production.

The challenge is *proving* a product characteristic or process has no

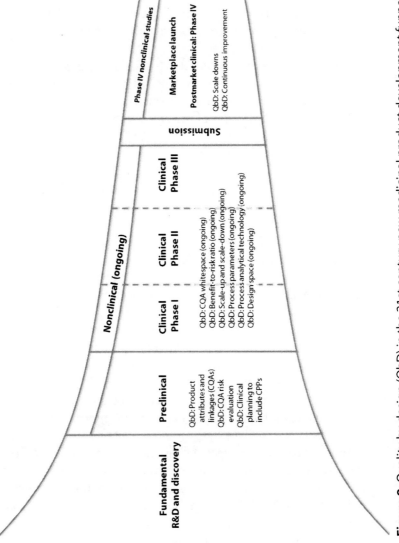

Figure 8: Quality by design (QbD) in the 21st century new medicinal product development funnel

impact on product safety, efficacy, or quality. To do that, developers and designers first need to identify the characteristics that do have an impact on product safety, efficacy, or quality. Second, a preferred range (for instance, of purity levels) for those characteristics needs to be identified. It makes sense then, that to identify such safety, efficacy, and quality targets, executives must start implementing quality by design as early as possible, preferably in the preclinical stage of product development.

Indeed, as the FDA's Dr. Cherney has noted, "Quality by design is not process capability; it's about tying new product specifications to preclinical data literature surveys, prior clinical experiences, scientific judgments, and risk assessments."[147]

PRECLINICAL QUALITY BY DESIGN

To identify the quality, safety, and efficacy specifications, designers and developers can use the same methods—literature surveys, *in vivo* and *in vitro* tests, *in serum* tests, toxicology studies, etc.—that make up the preclinical stage. Adding voice of the customer studies as discussed in chapter five provides further specifications and insights.

While capturing quality, safety, and efficacy specifications is expected under the 20th century development model, the majority of this information ends up being defined during clinical trials. The same pattern does not apply to quality by design; the sooner in preclinical trials the specifications are gathered, the better the return on R&D investment due to greater success rates during each product development stage and faster new medicinal product development. This is especially true given the ability to eliminate non value-added testing and documentation.

Identify Product Attributes and Linkages

The first step in adopting quality by design at the preclinical stage is to link product requirements to patient safety and product efficacy. Develop a matrix that lists desired patient requirements in the first column, and then match these patient requirements to product requirements that quantify the patient requirements. Both of these are then matched to actual therapeutic function. The end result looks similar to Table 1. Table 2 uses sample information from a recent client.

Once this is complete, the product components that achieve the

Table 1: Product attributes and linkages matrix

Patient Requirement	Product Requirement	Therapeutic Function(s)

Table 2: Sample product attributes and linkages

Patient Requirement	Product Requirement	Therapeutic Function(s)
Noticeably less pain	20% or greater reduction in pain when applied	Promote faster healing, consistent use of product
No (or little) scarring	50-100% level of constant hydration to burn	Promote faster healing, consistent use of product, minimize scarring

therapeutic function can then be added to the matrix. For pharmaceuticals, these product components might consist of active pharmaceutical ingredients (APIs) which can fulfill the listed requirements and therapeutic functions, while for medical devices it might consist of functional elements such as the components in a nebulizer, and so on.

With the results of this exercise, undertake two tasks:

1. Assess the risk and the impact to safety and efficacy
2. Identify product attributes that are *critical* to patient safety and product quality and efficacy

In the case of a simple pharmaceutical drug, the inert ingredients (*e.g.*, the excipients) might be important product attributes but the API and its purity would be critical product attributes. Risk and impact assessments will then provide the parameters necessary to achieve the product requirement. For example, the product requirement of 20% less pain is achieved by an API purity level between 4-8%.

In order to accurately assess risks and impacts, executives need to obtain a broad range of information. Such information can come from the voice of the customer, literature surveys, and other preclinical studies as well as information from other products in development or already on the market. As the FDA's Dr. Cherney has pointed out, "This information in and of itself does not need to be perfect, but taken together it can provide a good, reasonable level of awareness that then goes into proving the range of safety and efficacy for the intended final product."[148]

To maximize effectiveness in collecting this information, take a broad approach. Such an approach will help minimize redoing work others may have already conducted and will help avoid pursuing non-value activities (such as extensively testing and documenting a process which has no impact on product quality, safety, and efficacy). Dependent on the product, consider reviewing the following:

- Previous pre-clinical and clinical work
- Databases of adverse events
- Prior work from development partners and collaborators
- Scientific and medical literature
- Previous personal experiences with a particular type of molecule or device component
- Other platform experiences

The goal is to build an information portfolio that provides parameters of safety, efficacy, and quality. Given the need to ensure at least some level of personalization of medicines in the 21st century, make sure to add in the voice of the customer studies discussed in chapter five.

This type of undertaking usually requires at least 2-3 months, but can highlight potential trouble spots that can be resolved prior to clinical testing. Remember that in chapter five I suggested that these types of expanded literature surveys be undertaken by a university collaborator at significant cost and time savings.

Several years ago, a device and biotechnology firm I worked with discovered during its initial scientific literature surveys that the non-API delivery chemical (propylene glycol) their new combination device relied upon became toxic when heated. Under a 20th century product development methodology, such a discovery might have ended design and development efforts or at least placed the new product project on a lower priority level.

However, under a quality by design approach, this preliminary literature survey was only a first step. The company asked its university collaborator to conduct a more detailed, expansive investigation of the literature, including relevant proprietary databases the university had access to as a result of its work with other biopharmaceutical and device companies. This expanded literature survey took approximately three weeks and revealed two critical pieces of information: first, the published research had only used one method of heating; and second, once the toxicity had become apparent, no further research had been conducted.

The university collaborator then undertook laboratory tests of different methods of heating while targeting multiple thresholds of chemical purity, temperature and time. Within 18 days, a number of critical control points were identified demonstrating that toxicity could be completely avoided by controlling the heating method, temperature, and time. Further feasibility testing in humans (Phase 0 clinical trials) bore out these lab results. This is the type of proactive critical product attribute and control point identification that quality by design exemplifies.

Simply identifying such critical process attributes and critical quality attributes is not enough. As I noted earlier, the challenge is being able to prove the validity of such attributes. Validity is established through testing—either of the attribute itself (*e.g.*, a specific purity range for a chemical like propylene glycol) or the parameters around the attribute (*e.g.*, a firm can show that because of a particular downstream activity like heating, the purity of the propylene glycol is irrelevant).

Preclinical analytical testing, toxicology testing, bioassays, *in vitro* and *ex vivo* tests, bioinformatics assays and models, and others are all means to prove the validity of critical process attributes and critical quality attributes. Dr. Janet Woodcock, Chief Medical Officer of the FDA, has noted that these types of preclinical testing and modeling efforts are "perfect intermediate measures" (with clinical testing providing final confirmation) that allow companies to "put much more effort where it is really needed, as early as possible in product design and development."[149]

Dr. Peter Byron, chair of Virginia Commonwealth University's School of Pharmaceutics, has also noted the broadly applicable potential to use pharmacokinetic studies and in serum testing to clarify and verify biopharmaceutical products, particularly at the molecular level.[150] This scientific information further minimizes costs of development to a company while allowing an independent eye (such as a school of pharmacy-based data monitoring committee) to verify the critical product attributes, their impact upon safety and efficacy, and the effectiveness of any identified control points.

Clinical Trial Planning

Critical product quality attributes and process parameters defined in the preclinical stage should then tie directly to a firm's goals in the clinical trial stage. Clinical trial planning becomes a matter of prioritizing how to obtain the information needed to finalize safety, quality, and efficacy product attributes.

Given that most Phase I clinical trials are small, clinical trial planning should identify how levels of variability will be introduced to test minor changes to the product quality parameters in such a way that that these levels are statistically valid. Such variability should also provide baselines that can then be tested against in Phase II and III clinical trials and which will, presumably, provide further baselines for any postmarket Phase IV studies and clinical trials.

Appropriate levels of variability can be difficult to ascertain, and thus the preclinical work to identify ranges is absolutely crucial. For instance, if preclinical testing, literature surveys, previous clinical trial results from another product, and other observations suggest that a new product's API purity can be from between 2 – 10% and still meet the expected targets of efficacy and patient safety, then the company might consider conducting three different Phase I trials at 2% API purity, 6% API purity and 10% API purity to see if there is a statistically significant difference in safety and efficacy. Over Phase II and III clinical trials, trend analyses can be conducted to look for other unintentional variables that impact safety and efficacy, or even if the product might be safe and effective in a wider purity range.

Because quality by design allows designers and developers to draw upon a wide array of information to justify critical product parameters, a greater capacity exists for incorrect determinations to unduly bias these critical ranges. Consider a situation where multiple sets of data are gathered from a literature survey, and when the development team puts the data together, it discovers significant safety implications due to outliers in one data set. FDA investigators have uncovered such situations where company executives ordered a data set which skewed results removed from consideration, or ordered all the data averaged together so as to obscure the outliers.[151] In 2008, I was interviewed about a court case involving similar data manipulation where a company obtained ideal results from a randomized statistical analysis of collected data, then decided to hardcode (in both the archived and submitted versions) the originally random formula that generated those ideal results. In this way, any reviewer re-running the analyses would get the same ideal results.[152]

Data manipulation temptations exist under quality by design because the greater the range of the critical product attribute or the critical process parameter, the greater the flexibility the company has when it comes to controlling for safety, efficacy, and quality. Increased product and process flexibility results in lower costs and less compliance monitoring overhead, both during product development and in the postmarket stage. Given financial pressures, the temptation to manipulate results and reinterpret data beyond statistically relevant meaning can be too much for some executives.

To minimize this temptation, determine—as part of clinical planning—how clinical data will be captured, transmitted, analyzed, and stored. Just as with a manufacturing flow, this information flow—whether electronic, paper or both—can then be assessed for risk to consistency and integrity. Controls can be put in place to verify and monitor data integrity. Consider bringing in various subject matter experts from regulatory affairs, quality assurance, information technology, legal, and records management to help assess any data integrity risks and determine potential controls.

In a regulatory request to begin clinical trials, executives should identify the steps to be taken to ensure clinical trial information integrity along with the variables the firm intends to test in Phase I clinical trials and the logic behind such variables and data controls. Requests to begin clinical testing that highlight the critical product quality attributes and the critical process parameters identified during the preclinical stage provide strong support for FDA reviewers to agree not only to a firm's request to start clinical trials, but to the firms intent to test only particular variables in clinical trials. This can reduce the cost, risk, and timelines required in the clinical stage.

CLINICAL TRIAL QUALITY BY DESIGN

Under an ideal quality by design product development approach, clinical studies are confirmatory. Ideally, a firm has collected enough information on its product's critical quality attributes and critical process parameters that clinical trials simply corroborate the preclinical data. In reality, however, only some information obtained in preclinical testing will not change; there is only so much that modeling and *in vitro* studies can predict.

The key, then, is to define a product's critical quality attributes within a range rather than assigning a specific number. Design Phase I clinical trials to validate that range. The FDA defines "validation" as establishing documented, objective evidence which provides a high degree of assurance that specific processes, test methods, automation, etc. will consistently meet predetermined specifications and quality attributes, and that data produced as a result will have integrity.[153] Thus, by determining the predetermined specifications and critical quality attributes in preclinical using such "intermediate measures" as expanded literature surveys, in serum testing, voice of the customer, bioanalytical assays, toxicology tests, and so on to clarify and verify these critical quality attributes, Phase I clinical trials should simply confirm and validate the ranges.

Phase II clinical trials can then be designed to improve the ranges further and identify additional product attributes (such as dosing levels or comparative effectiveness variations). Phase III clinical trials are then conducted to provide final validation of all these additional product attributes. In this way, when reviewing clinical trial results with FDA reviewers in an end-of-Phase II meeting[154], executives can focus on ways to use Phase III clinical trials to improve—rather than prove—their new medicine's safety, quality, efficacy, and personalization.

CQA White Space

In graphic design, "white space" is an important element that serves to draw a viewer's eye to the desired focal point. In the era of personalized medicine, executives can adopt this idea of white space as a critical quality attribute for a new medicine. A new medicine that serves a target patient population with a particular gene sequence is an example of a CQA white space. Amgen's cancer drug, Vectibix, exemplifies a product with a CQA white space: the absence of a genetic mutation that otherwise makes patients resistant to the drug. As discussed in chapter one, by screening out patients with the KRAS mutation, Amgen showed dramatic drug efficacy and cost-efficiency to enable approval for the drug.

So one critical quality attribute to look for in clinical trials is the need for a particular patient genetic profile. While such a profile might ideally be identified in the preclinical phase, given the continuing expansion of knowledge around genomics, I expect that in many instances executives will often only become aware of such genetic profile-related critical quality attributes in clinical trials. One task, then, for clinical and regulatory affairs executives will be to correlate patient response data with genetic profile information to identify emerging efficacy and safety-related issues.

Benefit-to-Risk Ratio

A new product's critical quality attributes should also shape an acceptable level of treatment risk. Combined with treatment efficacy, this provides benefit-to-risk regulatory endpoints to target in Phase II clinical trials and validate in Phase III clinical trials.

This type of approach is particularly critical for drugs that may be used in escalating dosages, such as anti-depressants, or that are candidates for pediatric use. Use critical quality attributes to help determine the point at which the drug's risks will outweigh its benefits. This information can then be incorporated into labeling, product inserts, and physician awareness programs. This is the exact type of information that the FDA has stated it intends to discuss in end-of-Phase II meetings and that it considers when evaluating whether postmarket studies and risk evaluation and mitigation strategies are necessary.[155]

Pilot Scale-Up

During clinical trials, firms also need to focus on validating the critical process parameters determined during the preclinical stage. Scaling up production of a new medicine, from small, lab- or pilot plant-based production to full-scale manufacturing is an ideal opportunity to conduct this validation. Each transition, first from lab-based to pilot plant production, and then from pilot production to full-scale manufacturing, can be timed to coincide with a shift from preclinical to Phase I trials, then Phase I to Phase II and III clinical trials.

For instance, imagine that in the switches from lab to pilot production, and then pilot to full-scale manufacturing, the nozzle size on a piece of equipment needs to be made larger to accommodate to a higher spray rate. As long as the larger nozzle sizes maintain the same droplet size, then no further testing, validation and verification are required.

In this example, during the preclinical phase, the firm should determine the basic range of droplet size required. Then, during the first changeover from lab-based production to the pilot production plant, the firm should measure droplet size to ensure that it is within the required parameters. During Phase I clinical trials, as the product is produced in the pilot plant, the firm continues to measure droplet size and verify it to be in the same range as the droplet size in preclinical—even though the equipment has changed to a larger sized nozzle. In the changeover from pilot plant production to full-scale manufacturing, the firm changes equipment to a larger nozzle size. Again, the firm measures droplet size and verifies that droplet size is maintained within the critical process parameter range identified back in preclinical. In Phase II and Phase III clinical trial production, the firm measures droplet size and sees that throughout clinical trial production, droplet size is within the desired range. Thus, the firm has maintained and validated a critical process parameter. In this way, the firm has focused on the end result—the droplet size—and not had to conduct extensive testing and validation work on the various pieces of equipment involved, saving the company money and time.

Another set of processes to assess during clinical trials as new medicine production is scaled-up from lab and pilot production to full-scale manufacturing is the control of raw materials and components. Often in the early design and development stages, such as during preclinical studies and Phase I clinical trials, firms inspect 100% of the incoming raw materials and components that will go into the new medicine. As clinical trials proceed and pilot production is replaced by full-scale manufacturing, this kind of complete inspection becomes extremely difficult. The question, then, is how to ensure the consistency, stability, and quality of incoming goods. One method is to use sampling based on the level of confidence desired (*e.g.*, achieving a higher level of confidence requires higher numbers of incoming materials to be sampled). Using a similar thought process to the equipment scale-up example above, when it comes to sampling incoming goods, the critical process parameter is the end result—the achievement of the level of confidence desired. During the preclinical stage, sampling methods and appropriate ranges are determined; then during Phase I clinical trials and pilot plant production, sampling plan ranges are verified; and then during Phase II and III clinical, sampling plan ranges are validated. In this way, despite a change in personnel, facility, and amount of incoming material (and even suppliers), the end result—the critical process parameter—is achieved. More money and time are saved.

Manufacturing Scale-Down

One challenge which firms in all industries struggle with is the handoff between R&D (where scientists and engineers have developed an intimate level of knowledge around the new product) and manufacturing (where production supervisors and line workers may be encountering the new product for the first time just as they are asked to make large numbers of this new product).

When it comes to biopharmaceuticals and medical devices, after full-scale manufacturing processes and controls have been planned, firms can first test these processes and controls in the pilot production area to identify and resolve any potential problems. Full-scale processes and controls are shrunk down enough to be able to be duplicated in the pilot plant, and if need be, in the lab. AstraZeneca terms this a "scale-down."

This scale-down process can be extended to test nearly all the controls and quality systems processes planned for multiple variations of the same drug. Can two variations of a same drug or biologic be produced in the same manufacturing line without initiating a full-scale cleaning? Does the changeover require only minor cleaning of some production line parts? If this minor or partial cleaning fails, how early in the rest of the production process can this failure be detected?

Because following full-scale cleaning protocols between production runs requires production lines to be stopped, parts to be inspected, equipment to be cleaned and re-inspected, full-scale cleaning can drive up manufacturing costs. With critical quality attributes and critical process parameters in hand, executives can conduct a risk assessment to determine where and how to conduct partial cleaning between product changeovers and use the scale-down approach to identify, control, and verify potential hazards.

Executives can also use scale-downs to define and document how production personnel will be able to easily differentiate between runs of similar formulations with only minor variabilities to address patient differences. Can the different formulations be color-coded? What threshold alerts need to be defined and validated? What are the controls to be put in place throughout production, quality control, and stocking? Some of the most fundamental assumptions for how production changeovers are managed may need to be re-examined, and the handoffs from lab-based production to pilot production to manufacturing represent the appropriate places to test and verify, using Phase II and III clinical trial production to validate.

Additionally, consider this scale-down tactic when dealing with contract manufacturers (CMOs). Use scale-downs not just for the standard handoff to a CMO's manufacturing site, but also when the CMO suggests altering a production method to better match its standard processes. CMOs typically want to minimize variation—variations drive up their costs, lowering their profit margins. Use the scale-down technique to test and validate that any suggested changes do not adversely impact a product's critical quality attributes or critical process parameters (e.g., fit into what the ICH and FDA term "design space"—see below).

QUALITY BY DESIGN IN REGULATORY SUBMISSIONS

Quality by design-based submissions have more scientific information on the product, the processes involved, and the validity of the various controls on the product and processes than traditional submissions. This additional information allows the FDA to conduct faster reviews. Preliminary analyses by FDA of the few quality by design-based submissions received to date show that the agency can process such submissions 63% faster than traditional industry applications, a time savings of approximately 6-9 months in time-to-market.[156] For a drug expecting one billion dollars in sales a year, an extra 6-9 months of patent-protected drug sales can easily be worth $500-700 million.

To help expedite FDA review, executives will want to make sure any submission cites and provides evidence of:

- The critical quality attributes of the product
- The critical process parameters that impact the product and its critical quality attributes
- The postmarket monitoring and studies planned to further improve the critical quality attributes and process parameters

Preliminary FDA analyses have also shown that when a firm proactively identifies the latter—the postmarket monitoring and studies planned to further improve critical quality attributes and process parameters—in its submission, the need for the company to request FDA approval for future manufacturing changes declines by 80%, saving the company a significant amount of time, money, and compliance overhead once the product is on the market.[157]

MANUFACTURING AND POSTMARKET MONITORING QUALITY BY DESIGN

Historically, firms that wanted to make significant manufacturing modifications needed regulatory approval prior to implementing changes. Under quality by design, this review can be largely eliminated by relying on three tactics:

1. Continuous improvement
2. Process analytical technology
3. Design space

Continuous Improvement

Look back at the definition of quality by design several of my clients have adopted: "everything we do to directly promote and prove the safety, efficacy, quality, and personalization of our product." In this context, continuous improvement is a critical part of promoting and proving safety, efficacy, quality, and personalization. It allows executives the freedom to focus on efficiencies in production processes and improvements in product attributes.

Continuous improvement is demonstrated through measuring, tracking, trending, controlling and—most importantly—acting upon that information. Data comes from manufacturing processes, feedback from customers (complaint files and voice of the customer studies), and other postmarket studies and clinical trials. Central to acting upon this information is relying upon risk management techniques to make decisions. Good risk management decisions rely upon knowledge gained throughout product development, from preclinical through the postmarket stage (*e.g.*, quality by design).

As I noted in chapter one, the FDA intends to align biopharmaceutical regulations with device regulations. One of the core tenets of the device regulations is continual improvement. Firms are required to take the monitoring information they have gathered—both from customers and from internal quality systems activities such audits and nonconformance investigations—and act upon it to improve processes and the safety, quality, and efficacy of their medicinal products.[158]

If a device firm can prove that any changes in its manufacturing processes were done under a state of control, do not adversely impact the product, and were done proactively in response to monitoring information and trend analyses, the device firm need not submit a request to make such continuous improvements ahead of time. Indeed, the FDA actively encourages the continuous improvement of device production processes and device product quality, safety, and efficacy through its warning letter citations of device firms and their executives for failing to conduct continuous improvement activities. Under a quality by design rubric, biopharmaceutical firms can also rely on continuous improvement to provide a greater degree of regulatory flexibility.[159]

Process Analytical Technology

Notwithstanding the goals of continuous improvement and trying to apply it to a biopharmaceutical environment, the effects of process change on biological and pharmaceutical products can be difficult to predict. An essential part of quality by design is accepting that even if the complex interplay of process change and impact cannot be fully predicted, it can be monitored and controlled. Automating this monitoring and control is known as process analytical technology (PAT). PAT allows a firm to continuously monitor, test, analyze, trend, and adjust manufacturing processes to enhance control and improve efficiency.

Done well, PAT can help a firm shift quality control from an end of production activity to one that occurs at multiple points throughout production. This reduces the waste and cost of producing an entire batch or lot that may ultimately fail quality control. By embedding quality control checks throughout manufacturing processes, quality by design allows production optimization (without having to gain regulatory approval ahead of time for each change) and "real-time" quality control.[160]

Design Space

Product processes that do not impact product quality, safety or efficacy, or that always produce results that do not impact product quality, safety, or efficacy, are known collectively as "design space." Changes within design space do not require regulatory review or approval.[161]

The more information a firm has on the impact—or lack of impact— of a process on a product's quality, safety or efficacy, the more business flexibility a firm retains. This information originates during product development, and just as with the various critical process parameters, design space should also be confirmed and validated during changeovers and scale-ups from lab production to pilot plant production to full-scale manufacturing during clinical trials. Once a product is on the market, design space can be further refined and improved as production processes become more efficient and automated.

In essence, design space allows executives to carve out a virtual range of characteristics for any item in manufacturing such as a process range like temperature or speed, or an input characteristic such as a raw material or its purity, as long as the firm has demonstrated through product development and clinical trials that the medicinal product is not harmed by changes within those process ranges or inputs. Thus, with design space, a firm has a section of its manufacturing environ in which the company need not monitor or control for regulatory purposes. This further reduces compliance overhead and costs while improving operational flexibility. In 2008, the FDA and ICH published helpful examples of how to determine design space in their guidance documents on pharmaceutical development, the FDA's *Q8(R1) Pharmaceutical Development Revision 1* and the ICH's *Pharmaceutical Development Q8(R2)*. Readers can download copies of these documents from the book's website.

Design space also plays a key role in demonstrating a firm's ability to increase its product knowledge and continuously improve. In turn, using design space lowers production cost over time, reduces risk, and helps fend off eventual competitors.

MORE NEW MEDICINE DEVELOPMENT SPEED TACTICS

Quality by design, incorporating the voice of the customer, and open innovation collaborations are but three tactics in the growing arsenal of faster, less expensive, yet still compliant, new medicinal product development strategies that I have so far suggested. Consider adopting two other techniques that have proven their worth outside of the life sciences:

1. Bookshelving
2. Stage gates

Stage Gates

New product development plans with strongly defined go/no-go deci-sion points can take advantage of stage gates. In implementing stage gates, no product can move from one stage of development to the next without going through some form of structured review or gate.

Within an FDA compliance framework, stage gates can be designed in two ways:

1. Creating individual standard operating procedures for each stage gate review
2. Devising triggers for quality system activities

Executives familiar with medical device design control regulations and the requirement for a formal design review transfer standard oper-ating procedure (SOP) may want to explore creating an SOP that trans-fers a developing new product from each stage of design and develop-ment (*e.g.*, from preclinical to Phase I clinical trials, from Phase I clinical trials to Phase II clinical trials, and so on).

Triggers to initiate the transition review process can then be built into the SOP and the firm's overall product development organization. For instance, when approached by a development team to start planning clinical trials, compliance executives usually have two options: to start the work or to try to judge the priority and importance of the request, and thus possibly delay the work by making a poor choice. The "trigger" tactic adds a third alternative designed to force disciplined execution and informed, risk-based decisions.

The stage gate review generates documents that trigger appropri-ate quality systems and regulatory planning (I will discuss such plan-ning more in chapter eight); documents are the outputs of disciplined execution of processes—no documents, no need to spend monies and time on a particular quality and regulatory work task. And, as I will discuss further in chapters seven and nine, records are the proof that a particular SOP was followed, and thus that a firm is operating in a state of control.

By enforcing disciplined execution of an overall business process and its controls, stage gate trigger documents can clearly indicate to any regulatory inspector not only the firm's underlying logic, but also the point at which various quality system controls were applied. Each SOP can focus on the most critical pieces of information necessary to transition from one stage to the next. For instance, a preclinical stage gate checklist might include questions such as:

- Have upper limit boundaries been defined and tested for a specific process?
- Have lower limit boundaries been defined and tested for a specific process?
- Have samples (including photographs, etc.) of passing grade compounds, formulations, active pharmaceutical ingredients, etc., been shared? What about failure samples (or photographs thereof)?
- Do such samples (or photographs) note specific characteristics for easier identification?

BOOKSHELVING

Stage gate summary records can also be useful long-term indices of the growing knowledge and experience in the company. The ability to use prior knowledge—from previous products, from literature surveys, from personal experiences, and so on—is one way that quality by design improves product development. Incorporating prior knowledge and voice of the customer allows executives to identify, as early as possible, the specific characteristics a new product must meet for both regulatory approval and marketplace success.

This type of modular approach wherein a firm assembles pieces of information from various experiences, previous studies, and prior work is known as bookshelving to new product development professionals in the consumer products arena. Bookshelving cannot only speed product development and increase flexibility, but it can improve the success rate and return on investment of new products. Rather than relying solely on their own information and experiences, executives can draw upon other company projects, expanded literature surveys, and even prior collaborative partnership results. This allows executives to make medicinal product development planning decisions based on what has worked (or failed) for others as well as for themselves. Executives can avoid wasted R&D efforts, inadvertently repeating others' errors. Given that FDA-regulated medicines take such a long time to reach the marketplace, bookshelving is a perfect tactic to speed time to market and lower costs.

Firms should look to adopt bookshelving as early as possible, and certainly no later than at the preclinical development stage.

With bookshelving, the same data can be used multiple times to support several different new product regulatory applications. As a result, the cost of development is lowered by eliminating duplicate work. Modules of study results and data can be drawn upon by the firm to rapidly speed development of promising new products, or to quickly shut down avenues of research that have a high likelihood of ending in failure based on the historical information that has been bookshelved by the company.

Use of bookshelved information makes it imperative, however, that the data have integrity, which, given the electronic storage of such information, means compliance with FDA regulations intended to ensure electronic data integrity, 21 CFR Part 11 (in Europe, see Annex 11). While a firm can use literature surveys to help support its preclinical results and expected product characteristics, the company cannot rely solely upon such non-compliant information to allow a transition into clinical trials.[162]

One of the mistakes I made early on in my career was to assume that if some compliant bookshelved information translated directly to faster time to market and higher new product success rates, then even better results would occur if all preclinical laboratories were able to generate data compliant with 21 CFR Part 11. Unfortunately, because data has a long lifespan, nearly three-quarters of the cost of long-term compliance with 21 CFR Part 11 lies not in data acquisition or creation but in maintaining that compliance for as long as the data exists. The result is an ever-increasing escalation of costs. Readers can easily imagine a laboratory where every test, every result, every scrap of electronic datum was managed under rigid controls. While at first the cost was relatively minor, the scope of my mistake soon became apparent as more and more of my operational budget was consumed trying to maintain all these bookshelved data to 21 CFR Part 11 standards. To avoid repeating my mistake, judiciously apply 21 CFR Part 11 or any other regulatory control in the preclinical stage. One means to decide when to implement compliance controls is to follow the path I suggest when trying to ensure data from university collaborations is compliant with the FDA's Good Laboratory Practice regulations, below.

HOW TO ENSURE GLP COMPLIANCE

In chapter five I discussed open innovation collaborations, using the various ways in which a company can collaborate with universities as an example. I also noted in chapter two that universities often have questionable compliance with the Good Laboratory Practice (GLP) regulations, something that can cause compliance professionals to look upon university-generated studies with skepticism. To use data from university collaborations in any regulatory submission, and to use the data from any of the techniques discussed in this chapter—quality by design, bookshelving, and so on—the data must be compliant with GLP regulations.

This is the key distinction to keep in mind: the university or other lab need not be GLP compliant, only the actual data that a company plans to use in its regulatory submission must be compliant. This is how to take advantage of quality by design and open innovation collaborations in a compliant *and* flexible manner. Focus compliance efforts and controls more on the records produced and the intended usage of those records than on perfect compliance of the processes involved to generate those records.

Remember that the 20th century compliance and quality mindset was to ensure compliant results by ensuring compliant processes. As I have already noted throughout part one of this book, with the revolution in knowledge, technology, and sub-sub-specialties, trying to ensure every process is compliant is a Sisyphean task; no one has all the resources required. I do not mean that process controls are unimportant—far from it—rather, because there is an ever increasing number of processes due to an ever increasing amount of information, technologies, and combinations thereof, insisting that every process be compliant is simply no longer feasible. Instead, we have to focus on those aspects we are able to better understand, control, and manage: the actual process results and their intended usage. In other words, we have to do the same thing the FDA and other regulatory health agencies do when it comes to inspecting device and biopharmaceutical companies: examine the records produced for any indication that the processes involved were not done under a state of control.

In chapter five, I touched upon three ways to ensure university-generated study results can go into any regulatory submission:

1. Conduct confirmatory testing under GLP conditions in a company's own labs
2. Conduct upper and lower limit boundary testing under GLP conditions in company's own labs
3. Verify university results are within parameters expected from the literature survey

There are two additional steps to ensuring data integrity to GLP standards for data generated as a result of university collaborations:

4. Draw upon outside, independent verification of university results
5. Qualify the university as a supplier

Outside, Independent Verification of Results

Three tactics work well to demonstrate the GLP equivalency of university collaboration results by using outside, independent verification:

1. Other university labs can be contracted to perform similar work in parallel—if the results match (and the firm's internal confirmatory GLP studies corroborate the results), executives have a strong argument for complete GLP data compliance
2. Firms with a corporate partner can have the partner conduct its own confirmatory tests
3. Firms can hire a private contract research organization to conduct confirmatory studies under GLP conditions

Success with these third-party confirmations areas will still keep university collaboration costs significantly lower than trying to develop a new medicine alone and will add credence to university-derived results as scientifically valid, accurate and complete—the fundamental requirement for any claim that data are GLP-compliant.

Qualifying the University

The fifth and final step to ensuring GLP-equivalency of university generated data is to qualify the university as a supplier. The usual approach of supplier qualification to quality systems standards and regulations like the GLPs will not work with universities. Instead, consider an approach that blends the traditional with the innovative in six ways:

1. Selection
2. Onsite observational audit
3. Risk assessment
4. Contract and quality amendment
5. Overview of the new medicine
6. On-going review

First, selection of the university need not proceed down the normal path of putting together a supplier selection committee. Any accredited university or college—so long as it has at least a business school and a biochemistry department—will suffice. If you plan to undertake all the university collaboration tactics I suggested in chapter five, look for a school that has a strong pharmacology department (for my Virginia-based clients, I typically suggest Virginia Commonwealth University's department under Dr. Peter Byron) and a school with either a bioinformatics program or a collaborative arrangement with an informatics providers, such as Incogen. A review of peer-reviewed articles by various academics within such departments can help narrow down the choices.

Second, replace the typical on-site audit with an on-site visit focused on observation and targeted questions. Testing for adherence to specific standard operating procedures is often far too much to expect of a university setting. Rather, look to see if students in the labs use appropriate safety equipment. Ask how they handle review of test results—does the professor conduct the review personally, or hand it off to a colleague of the student? How does the lab segregate data from one project or research grant from another? Can firms get a full copy of the all the results—including any test methods—after the collaboration is complete? Is there some degree of control over lab space areas or is anyone free to use whatever they find? How is equipment maintained? Does the lab have service contracts with calibration providers? Does the lab conduct any supportive experiments for litigation cases (and if so, are there any special controls involved)? For university labs in the US, does the lab have a license from either the state pharmacy board or the US Drug Enforcement Agency?

While these are not typical laboratory GLP inspection questions, they do assess the university lab's level of control. Executives should assume that when it comes to asking a university lab to take on additional controls, especially those required for a rigorous interpretation of GLP requirements, unless a company is willing to pay for, constantly audit, and enforce contractual financial penalties for noncompliance, university labs will not even consider such additional controls. Qualifying universities is about putting controls around what is in place—not trying to morph academic environments into compliant corporate spaces.

After ascertaining the levels of control the university has over its environment (and thus, the levels of control it will have over lab protocols and test records), undertake a risk assessment to determine what additional controls, if any, may be required. Executives should expect the onus of most additional controls to be on themselves—not the lab director and the university. For example, if an executive wants to ensure that the lab notebooks used by the students in the lab working on the firm's project have quality control reviews that go beyond the professor's current review, the executive should be prepared to invest time and assign company personnel to audit these lab notebooks. As a result, consider very carefully any additional controls; costs can creep upward quickly to the point where any potential cost savings from the collaboration are consumed by 20th century compliance command and control efforts.

With the risk assessment and list of possible additional controls in hand, the contract with the university is ready to be executed. Major companies such as GlaxoSmithKline, AstraZeneca and Wyeth have learned several lessons from their contracts:

- Outline any publication rights up front
- Define patent rights and licensing, especially if you are starting without a defined compound
- Sign a contract that lasts between 3-5 years to encourage continuity and faculty strategic involvement
- Ensure that you receive a full copy of all data (including test methodologies, lists of equipment used, and so on)

A quality agreement with a university will, by necessity, need to be less onerous than an agreement one would sign with a contract research organization specialized in Good Laboratory Practices. As such, I recommend building the quality agreement into the contract rather than setting it up as a separate contract; from a perceptual basis, this will seem less onerous than a completely separate agreement and thus have a greater chance of meeting with approval by the university.

Additionally, write the quality agreement addendum with an eye to its eventual review by an FDA inspector. Clarify the controls the university already has in place, and then list any additional controls for which the company will be responsible (such as periodic on-site reviews). Requiring the university to go through any sort of formal change control or change notification is probably too much to ask. Instead, note that during the periodic on-site reviews, company representatives will be looking to see what has changed since the last visit and asking why those changes took place.

A further step in qualifying the university lab is to undertake a brief conversation with all the faculty and students involved in the collaboration. Cover your business basics, desired goals, and the regulatory lens under which their results may eventually be scrutinized. Lay out why you need to understand the logic behind certain things such as equipment changes or upgrades: your focus is on how it might impact the test results, not on how the lab runs its operations. Trust that professors and students alike will be fascinated by the major components of your business and the complex challenges posed by new medicinal development. The opportunity to meet executives trying to solve real-world dilemmas is a rewarding educational experience that extends far beyond academic case studies.

Lastly, some form of on-going review needs to be adopted to keep the university qualified during the collaboration. Consider using a three-pronged approach: periodic onsite visits (be cautious about calling them "supplier audits"), confirmatory testing, and periodic presentation of results. From a quality systems management review perspective, make sure to incorporate summaries of the presentations in any periodic review of your new product development programs.

SUMMARY

When I give workshops and presentations on tactics and strategies to speed the time to market of new medicines and lower costs, an attendee will often ask, "How does adopting quality by design in my lab improve the chances of our new product getting approved by the FDA?" This question is understandable. Trying to apply tactics like quality by design, voice of the customer, or open innovation collaborations to a specific, isolated context like an analytical lab or an active pharmaceutical ingredient (API) pilot plant will not lead to significantly faster time to market, easier FDA approval, higher success rates, or lower development costs.

When it comes to tactics such as quality by design and open innovation collaborations, the whole is greater than the individual parts. Adopting quality by design in one or two labs will not provide the benefits available from adopting an overall quality by design strategy from the preclinical benchtop to the postmarket study. This is the costly lesson that many pharmaceutical firms learned when they rushed to adopt process analytical technology in their manufacturing environments without incorporating any quality by design elements elsewhere.[163]

As Figure 9 makes clear, quality by design easily blends with bookshelving and stage gates in the 21st century new medicinal product development landscape.

The faster a new medicinal product is on the market, the greater the chance of a positive return on investment. Combined with voice of the customer information, the product and process knowledge gained under a quality by design rubric gives companies a long-lasting competitive edge. By using other techniques such as bookshelving to eliminate duplicative activities and using stage gate triggers to improve disciplined execution, executives help their organization cope with the demands of faster, smarter decision-making under the complex conditions of 21st century medicinal product development and personalization.

By ensuring that all of these techniques and strategies, from PAT and design space to open innovation collaborations universities, can result in data which can be used in submissions and to prove continuous improvement, compliance executives must provide their firms with a flexible, compliant new product development environment. The next step, then, is to determine how to expand this flexible, cost-effective approach to a firm's quality system, something I address in the next chapter.

EXECUTIVE'S CHECKLIST FOR CHAPTER SIX

Being able to bring the benefits of quality by design and other tactics for speeding time to market in a compliant manner is a crucial skill set for biopharmaceutical and device executives in the 21st century. Here's a step-by-step to-do list:

☐ Download and review the presentation slides from my

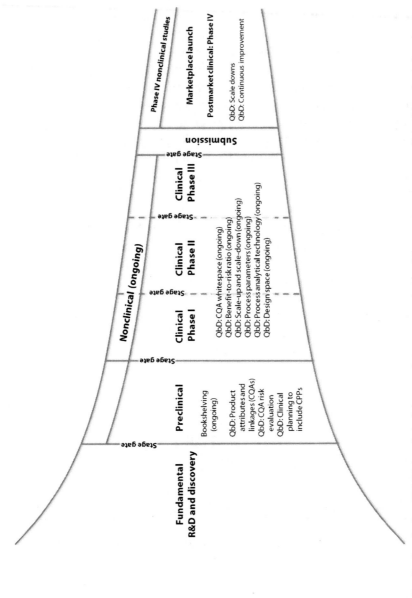

Figure 9: Quality by design (QbD), bookshelving, and stage gates in the 21st century new medicinal product development funnel

talk on quality by design client results (see the book's website http://www.Get2MarketNow.com)

☐ Download and review two FDA documents, *Q8(R1) Pharmaceutical Development Revision 1* and *Guidance for Industry: PAT—A Framework for Innovative Pharmaceutical Development, Manufacturing, and Quality Assurance* (both documents can be downloaded from the FDA website or from the book's website)

☐ Adopt a definition of quality by design that works in your company's environment, either the one I provided, the one the FDA uses in its guidance documents, or the one published by the ICH

☐ Create a matrix of product attributes and linkages (see Tables 1 and 2)

☐ Update your company's SOPs covering R&D activities to include some form of stage gate reviews and checklists to ensure a systematic, repeatable means of moving from each stage of development

☐ Discuss with your development and pilot plant teams (and your supplier management group if you use CMOs) the adoption of scale-up and scale-down techniques

☐ Work with your information technology (IT/ICT) department to implement databases for bookshelved data—this should include information generated in your firm and from outside your company (*e.g.*, literature surveys, etc.)

☐ Verify that your regulatory affairs submission SOPs appropriately include CQAs, CPPs, PAT, design space, and other elements of quality by design to expedite reviews

☐ Adapt the various techniques for qualifying universities and ensuring GLP-compliant data to your preclinical activities and any other open innovation collaborators

7 — Designing the Lean Quality System

With a 21st century medicinal product development structure in place—from collecting voice of the customer information through quality by design and bookshelving—it is now time to turn attention to a modern, 21st century quality system. Just as today's biopharmaceutical and device development rules are being rewritten to accommodate evolving scientific and engineering knowledge, the rules of the 20th century quality system are also being revised.

As I discussed in chapter three, traditional biopharmaceutical and device quality systems were built upon a post-World War II industrial era desire for uniformity and standardization. The very name of a quality system's basic component, the *standard* operating procedure, seeks to enshrine the uniform conduct of a process. And yet, how well does this quest for conformity and standardization fit in a landscape of rapid knowledge growth and daily scientific discoveries where technology capabilities double every two years, global competition and generics force mounting price pressure, and the Food and Drug Administration (FDA) increasingly turns toward guidance publications rather than new regulations to lay out its evolving expectations?

The 5th century B.C. Greek philosopher Heraclitus wrote, "You cannot step twice into the same river; by the second step the river's water has already changed." A similar message is true for quality system executives today: the rapid rate of knowledge growth, scientific discovery, technology advances, international regulatory harmonization, and global competition results in processes and controls that are out of date almost as soon as they are approved. To successfully compete and comply, firms must transform their 20th century-based quality system into a flexible, cost-effective quality system grounded in the regulatory, product development, and personalized medicine landscape of the 21st century. Such a structure calls for revisions in five core quality system components:

1. Standard operating procedures
2. Training
3. Risk-based decision-making
4. Cross-functional involvement
5. Continuous improvement

In this chapter, I walk through each of the changes necessary to build a lean quality system.[164] Each of these revisions combats the five weaknesses of traditional, 20th century-based quality systems I noted in chapter three:

1. Risk aversion
2. Two-valued system thinking
3. Operational silos
4. Cost inefficiencies
5. Customer exclusions

I conclude this chapter with a case study showing how all five of these changes play out in one of the most challenging aspects of 21st century medicinal product development and commercialization: supplier management.

STANDARD OPERATING PROCEDURES

A modernized, 21st century approach to standard operating procedures (SOPs) that balance flexibility, cost-efficiency, and compliance requires a company to:

- Link quality systems to business strategy
- Define a visual quality system framework
- Process-map and rapid prototype SOPs
- Write for flexibility
- Spell out the proof generated
- Strive for self-enforcement

Link Quality Systems to Business Strategy

Quality departments do not exist for the sake of quality. Rather, quality departments—quality assurance, quality management, quality control, etc.—exist to execute a component of overall corporate strategy. As an example, recall the slogan of the Ford Motor Co. in the 1980s, "Quality is Job 1." Ford's primary business objective was to sell more automobiles. However, in the 1980s, automotive sales were being driven by consumer perceptions of quality. To improve sales, Ford had to improve the public's perception of Ford quality. So, Ford strengthened the reliability of its automobiles, used Total Quality Management techniques to drive down costs, and embarked upon an advertising campaign to make the public aware of its renewed commitment to quality.[165] Quality was thus built into Ford cars not for quality's own sake, but to support Ford's business objective of selling more cars.

In a biopharmaceutical and device context, quality departments exist to implement and maintain the quality system required by regulatory health agencies and regulations. Additional quality system goals—achieving compliance with International Standards Organization (ISO) guidelines, implementing Six Sigma or Total Quality Management, etc.—should only be undertaken to support greater corporate strategies. Thus, biopharmaceutical and device corporate quality systems exist primarily to ensure compliance with FDA regulations and expectations, including appropriate rules from the International Conference on Harmonization (ICH) and the Global Harmonization Task Force (GHTF), so that the firm may develop and commercialize medicinal products.

Many quality management executives confuse this goal with a belief that their department's role is to ensure quality in medicinal products and quality in the company's processes and controls, assuming that by ensuring product and process quality, regulatory compliance is met. Unfortunately, quality is subjective; there can never be enough, especially when it comes to processes. As a result, quality executives strive for further and further control over processes, suppliers, product quality, etc., only to end up further and further away from meeting the business need of a balance between regulatory compliance and operational flexibility.

Just as Ford executives laid out that quality was only one tactic among many to achieve its overall business strategy, so too must biopharmaceutical and device executives make clear the role of quality in light of their business strategy (*e.g.*, the quality department's goal is to build operational procedures that comply with written regulatory expectations and rules so that the business may develop and sell its medicinal product).

I made this same distinction when it came to taking advantage of quality by design and open innovation collaborations with universities in a compliant and flexible manner in chapter six. Compliance and controls should focus more on the end goal—the records produced—rather than the compliance of university processes.

Throughout part one of this book, I described the rapid, continuously expanding amount of knowledge, technology, and sub-sub-specializations. Focusing on ensuring every process is controlled to a high degree of quality is a Sisyphean task. Instead, by focusing on the primary goal of a quality system—to ensure the company complies with written regulations and expectations in order to develop and sell medicinal products—ensuring process quality becomes only one tactic among many. Focusing on this end goal offers the company far more flexibility and opportunity for cost-effectiveness.

DEFINE A VISUAL QUALITY SYSTEM FRAMEWORK

When executives can work with the end business goal in mind, they can step away from the tactical to put together an overall quality system plan or framework that starts to balance compliance and control with cost-efficiencies and flexibility. Rather than tackle such a quality plan as a project, I encourage my clients to use a visual framework based on a tool they already have: the organizational chart. There are five steps to structure this framework:

1. Replace the typical job titles in each organizational chart box with potential SOP titles
2. Group these into functional areas; consider adopting something akin to the FDA's breakdown of a quality management system into seven groupings: management, laboratory or design controls, production and processes, records management and change control, facilities and equipment, and continual improvement and corrective and preventative actions[166]
3. Tie everything together, leading up to an overarching

quality policy

4. Connect the quality policy to a set of guiding ethical principles or a code of conduct

5. Over time, distinguish the boxes that represent each SOP as each SOP is implemented

The result should look something like Figure 10.

Many of the SOPs and policies created will be dependent upon each specific company and its operational environment (*e.g.*, the emphasis on privacy is greater in the European Union than in the US). The key is to keep the plan simple, structured, straightforward, and focused on complying with the regulatory expectations of a quality system.

Process Map and Rapid Prototype SOPs

The next step is to tackle the transience of processes and controls. If processes and controls risk becoming out of date faster, does that mean that SOPs are no longer feasible? No; documenting processes will always be necessary. It is the degree of documentation detail that is central to handling the transience of processes and controls.

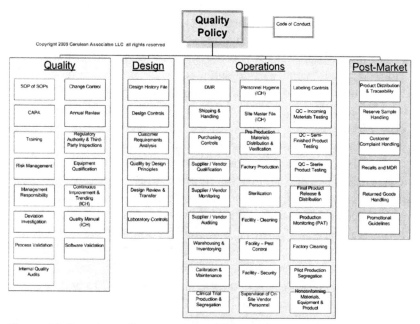

Figure 10: Sample quality system visual framework

To find a path forward, step back and consider the purpose of standard operating procedures. SOPs simply document processes in such a manner that by following the documented workflow, consistent results are produced within acceptable ranges and records are produced that prove this.

George Smith of the Office of Compliance in the FDA's Center for Drug Evaluation and Research has pointed out that as long as a company has a documented process and the records to prove that the process is followed, it does not matter if that process is "documented as a flowchart on a cocktail napkin or as a detailed 30-page SOP."[167] When it comes to SOPs, then, the only fixed compliance requirement is that the process and its decision-flow be documented; whether that documentation is in the form of a process diagram or a full-blown multi-page SOP is a business decision, not a regulatory requirement.

During my career as an executive in research and development (R&D) and new product commercialization organizations, I gained a deep appreciation for a development principle called "rapid prototyping." Rapid prototyping is the use of models or tools to quickly develop prototype products that can be assessed, often through formal testing or consumer focus groups. Rapid prototyping can also be used in determining and embedding the minimum controls as early as possible in any process, procedure, or system design.

One approach to capitalizing on rapid prototyping with quality systems is to draft a flowchart before writing a specific SOP and highlight critical decision points and potential controls. Then use a mock walkthrough or even a pilot plant test-run to assess the controls and the work flow. Refine and test again, this time in a different manner (*e.g.*, if a mock walk-through was used beforehand, use a pilot plant test-run the second time). Finally, write and wordsmith the detail behind the flowchart.

A second approach, often more amenable to the 21st century knowledge factory of offices and meeting rooms, is to combine rapid prototyping with process mapping. Process mapping plots the course of a business workflow from start to finish. Toyota pioneered process mapping in the 1950s when it assessed how information and materials flowed through its factories. Toyota then focused on which steps added value and which steps detracted from efficiency and raised costs. By eliminating the wasteful steps and keeping the value-added steps Toyota cut costs, increased efficiency, and improved operational flexibility.

I teach clients this same approach for SOPs. An SOP process map shows how information and materials (such as forms and checklists) flow through an organization's process and how decisions are made, resulting in a map that identifies:

- What initiates a process
- When decisions are made in a process
- Who makes those decisions
- Who communicates, shares, and documents those decisions
- What is used to communicate, share, and document decisions
- What information is used in evaluating potential decisions
- Where that information originates
- What process steps are required by regulation
- What process steps are business requirements

Because processes often cross departmental boundaries, the use of process maps increases the chance for cross-functional coordination and involvement. Additionally, process maps:

1. Leave little room for arguments around phrasing and terminology; this, in turn, allows a more holistic view to dominate, providing greater opportunity for flexibility to be retained
2. Demonstrate the consistent, repeatability of a process, thus achieving a regulatory requirement
3. Quickly allow participants to identify steps in the overall process sequence that can be eliminated, combined, or improved, balancing compliance with cost-efficiencies
4. Clarify who is responsible for each step of a process, improving accountability
5. Allow easier identification of records produced as a result of following a particular process
6. Are ideal training vehicles, providing a quick visual overview of a process
7. Help ensure that potential continuous improvement elements add value to the process

To combine process mapping and rapid prototyping, follow these four basic steps:

1. Draw the process map, identify decision-points, create any necessary forms, and clarify the records produced; this is the first SOP of any process
2. Use this process map, its forms, and its records for at least 3-4 months
3. During these 3-4 months, verify that the process works as mapped and that it produces the proper records which prove that the process was followed; ideally, identify opportunities for improvement—including consolidation or linkage to other SOPs
4. After 3-4 months, write out the actual SOP sections, making sure to include any process map revisions and other improvements identified over the previous 3-4 months

Executives can use the transition from process maps to fully written SOPs to show that continuous improvement has been achieved (see *Continuous Improvement* later this chapter).

WRITE FOR FLEXIBILITY

Just as quality by design, with its critical quality attribute and critical process parameter ranges, helps provide firms flexibility in medicinal product development, so too can SOPs be crafted to provide flexibility. There are two key components to keep in mind in drafting SOPs for flexibility:

1. Staying silent
2. Readability

Staying Silent

One of the most powerful lessons I learned in my career was from the general counsel of a *Fortune 50* subsidiary. We were in the process of crafting a service level agreement with an outside supplier and discussing how specific to make several requirements. As is typically the case with discussions on how best to spell out requirements and specifications to minimize supplier misinterpretations while providing the company the greatest flexibility, arguments soon emerged over phrasing and which specific words to use in the contract. After listening for a long while, the general counsel, highly respected because of his history of successfully defending client actions and contracts in court, stated simply: "If we don't need to say it, it's best to simply stay silent on the matter."

Keep in mind the goal of the quality department: to provide the company with a quality system that meets regulatory requirements so that the firm may develop and sell its medicinal product. If the regulations or guidance documents do not list the specific details expected in an SOP, then executives should question whether such details need to be present to implement the quality system. What business objectives are achieved by specifying such details? Do these objectives have to be spelled out in the SOP or can they be left to another means such as training? Can the SOP just stay silent on the matter? When it comes to writing SOPs, policies, and any other guidelines, take that counsel's advice to heart: unless specifically required to clarify details, it is often best to simply stay silent and not write such details into the document.

Readability

In 2009, the FDA published a draft guidance *Presenting Risk Information in Prescription Drug and Medical Device Promotion* that encouraged executives to consider "readability" as a key factor when presenting side effects and other risks.[168] As the name implies, readability assesses the ease with which text can be read and understood. In the guidance, the FDA points executives toward two methods for assessing readability, Flesch Reading Ease and the Flesch-Kincaid Grade Level. Just as more readable risk information allows consumers to better understand and appreciate the risks and side effects of a medicine, so too do more readable SOPs allow company personnel to better understand and comply with procedures and policies. As a result, SOP writers will want to target their SOP to be within the ideal readability score of these two measures based on the audience for whom the SOP is intended.

In the US, SOPs should target the typical reading level of the population, 30-45 on the Flesch Reading Ease scale or the 11th – 14th grade on the Flesch-Kincaid Grade Level scale.[169] Multiple factors influence readability including word count, use of acronyms and multi-syllable words, specific terminology, and sophisticated grammar. As a simple example, use of the word "car" in place of "automobile" would generate a better readability score.

Most commercially available word processing programs have readability measures built-in to them, typically under grammar and spell check options. Because of the ubiquitous nature of readability testing in commercial word processing software, I suggest taking advantage of this in any SOP drafting process.

Be cautious, however, about incorporating readability testing in any SOP that describes the process to create and maintain SOPs (the so-called "SOP of SOPs"). While this might seem the obvious place to put such a task, by placing readability testing as a sub-component of SOP creation, a firm will have to replicate the sub-process when it comes to label readability, packaging insert readability, promotional material readability, and so on. Soon enough, such duplicate sub-processes will get out of synch with each other, leading to questions of consistency. I suggest creating a simple, short SOP or work instruction on testing for readability that is broadly applicable from labels to SOP writing.

As part of this SOP on readability, consider adopting a definition similar to the one used by several of my clients:

> *Readability:* a measure—often expressed as "reading grade level"—that reflects how difficult a text is to read and understand. Unless otherwise identified through market research and analysis, the average reading grade level scores for the US population serve as a surrogate for the average patient or consumer reading grading level. Risk and claim information for consumers should target the 8th – 10th reading grade level (or 52-70 using the Flesch Reading Ease scale).

Improved readability is one way that quality executives can serve their department's customer: the other personnel in the company. By writing SOPs that are better understood by the average person in the company, the quality department improves compliance. Ensuring SOPs are more easily read and quickly understood, necessarily improves business efficiencies.

As an example of both principles—readability and staying silent—consider a comparison of two versions of an SOP scope (the first is the original scope from a client's SOP; the second is the revised scope based on the principles in this chapter):

Traditional: "This SOP applies to all regulatory and technical staff responsible for authoring and compilation of annual reports, recognizing that IND Annual Reports are to be submitted within 60 days of the effective date of the IND as stipulated in 21 CFR 312.33, and covering the 12-month period preceding the information cut-off date."

Revised: "This SOP applies to all regulatory affairs personnel responsible for authoring, compiling, reviewing, and/or submitting annual reports to regulatory health agencies."

The revised scope not only retains the intent of the original, but adds flexibility and readability. No longer is the SOP confined to the FDA and 21 CFR 312.33, but it can now apply to any regulatory health agency. By eliminating references to a specific regulation and its requirements, the company does not risk losing the initiative of whether an SOP needs to be revised and turning it over to regulatory writers. Under the more traditionally written scope, if the regulation changes, the firm needs to change its SOP or risk being out of compliance.

The readability review of the two scopes shows the differences quantitatively. The Flesch-Kincaid Grade Level of the traditional scope is 27.5 whereas the grade level of the revised scope is 19.2; the traditional scope scores eight grade levels higher than the revised version.[170] Based on the two principles of readability and staying silent, the revised scope better achieves the quality department's goal of achieving regulatory compliance while providing the business with operational flexibility.

SPELL OUT THE PROOF GENERATED

One section missing from most SOP templates is a clarification of precisely which records are produced as a result of an SOP being followed. As I noted in chapter three, this is a tremendous oversight: FDA inspectors spend nearly 80% of their time reviewing a firm's records, not its SOPs.[171] To better protect a firm from regulatory enforcement, quality departments need to ensure that each SOP delineates the records generated as a result of following the SOP.

Consider adopting a section toward the end of any SOP that clarifies the records produced. In the SOP template I have posted on this book's website (part of which is reproduced in Figure 11), section six defines the records produced in an SOP.

Defensible Documents SOP Template	The SmarterCompliance™ Toolkit

[your company name]	SOP #:
	Supersedes:
[SOP title]	Attachments:
	Effective date:

Step 4: [step from process map]
[Insert details of the process step here].

[Insert secondary details or clarification here as necessary; for referenced SOPs or other documents, use "see Title of Other SOP with a link to that SOP; for definitions, simply link to the company glossary or wiki].

5.0 Deviations
[Insert what personnel should do in the event of a deviation – could be to initiate a CAPA, contact their supervisor, notify a member of the compliance team, etc.].

6.0 Records
The following records are official outputs of this SOP:
- [insert form, record, document, or log name]
- [insert form, record, document, or log name]

These records will be filed in … [insert where filed, stored, or otherwise archived for future review or retrieval]. All records are to be retained as per the approved Records Retention Schedule.

7.0 Changes from Previous SOP
[Insert specific changes in accountabilities, process steps, deviation actions, or records].

8.0 Approvals

Function	Name	Title	Date	Signature
Author				
Reviewed				
Approved				

     info@ceruleanllc.com
www.ceruleanllc.com

Figure 11: Page two of the SOP template

Within that records output section, there are three important sub-points to clarify:

1. What specific official company records are generated as outputs of the SOP
2. Where these records should be stored and retained
3. How long these records should be stored and retained

As I will discuss in chapter nine, the FDA, along with other government agencies, has multiple regulations that require varying levels of record retention. Generating the record is only the first step in ensuring long-term compliance; additional efforts will be needed to maintain that record over its multi-year retention period.

STRIVE FOR SELF-ENFORCEMENT

At some point, executives will need to enforce compliance with quality system rules. Unfortunately, this can be a never-ending task that pulls money and time from new product development progress. In the worst case, an operationally damaging tension can arise between quality department personnel and the scientists and engineers who must design, develop, and test medicinal products and their production processes. Therefore, the key is to look for ways to change incentives such that compliance is in everyone's clear self-interest, both in the short-term and in the long run.

The traditional 20th century approach is one of command and control, with nonconformance resulting in punishment. Even FDA officials have noted that ideally, every nonconformance will have a documented disciplinary action associated with it. Unfortunately, creating a coercive environment is not conducive to good compliance, cost-effectiveness, business flexibility, morale, or safe, efficacious, quality products. Instead, executives may want to consider finding or developing incentives that reinforce a self-interest in compliance.

Start with two assumptions:

1. People prefer outcomes as close as possible to the way they view issues
2. Everyone likes the satisfaction that comes from getting credit for a good outcome

These assumptions mean that people are willing to compromise. And it is in compromise that a self-interested solution to compliance can be found. The goal, then, is to design process controls that are compromises and not dependent on another department's enforced cooperation; the controls should be in any department's immediate self-interest.

While reaching such a process control compromise can be a significant effort, and something that will be unique to each organization, consider:

- Defining and getting agreement on high-level controls first. For example, Should there be some control over protocol design for lab work to ensure consistency across labs? High-level controls are easier to get agreement on because they impact people's day-to-day less
- Taking advantage of the budget. Money is in people's self-interest and is therefore a great tool for self-enforcement. For example, in a manufacturing environ, each dollar saved in improvements without cutting compliance corners can be split between the manufacturing and the quality groups' budgets. The same distribution also works if time is saved; both parties get a "free" day off that is not subtracted from either vacation or sick leave.
- Hiring a mock FDA auditor, and for every finding successfully resolved during the course of the project, each person gets a bonus — a financial reward, an extra day off, etc.

All of these compromise, self-enforcing solutions require some level of creativity and a willingness to trust in the self-interest of the personnel involved. Creating this type of self-enforcing compliance — where compliance is in a person's direct interest — is another means by which quality departments can use a modern quality system to increase cross-functional cooperation, speed business results, and lower overhead costs.

TRAINING

In a May 2003 US Department of Health and Human Services' Office of Inspector General (OIG) document entitled *Compliance Program Guidance for Pharmaceutical Manufacturers*, the OIG noted that a fundamental prerequisite of an effective compliance program was "conducting effective training and education."[172] There are a number of specific recommendations from the OIG on the elements of effective quality system and compliance training programs, including:

- Identifying training needs through input from managers and employees, as well as internal and external audits
- Tailoring specific training to subsets of employees
- Regularly reviewing and updating training
- Documenting formal compliance training[173]

When it comes to compliance training, especially in SOPs, regulations, and other aspects of a company's efforts to ensure regulatory compliance, training that only focuses on information sharing and information retention does not necessarily ensure that attendee behavior will change. When I give workshops on designing effective quality system and regulatory compliance training I point to numerous studies by Kansai Gaidai University, the Work-Learning Research company, the National Training & Learning Institute, and others that show how little information is retained from traditional training sessions:

- After 7 days, only 33% of information is retained
- After 63 days, only 14% of information is retained
- After 91 days, only 5% of information is retained[174]

Unless a firm wants to repeatedly train employees every seven days, traditional means of training are simply not going to improve compliance.

BEHAVIORAL CHANGES

To improve compliance through training, understand that the goal of training is to change behavior. In that context, is the goal of an SOP training session to get attendees to know all the actual content of the SOP? Or is the goal to get attendees to change their behavior to start following the process the SOP simply documents? Under the traditional, 20th century focus of a quality system—having quality processes that then enable compliance—the goal of training was to ensure everyone knew the SOP and all the various process details. After all, without knowing all the process details, people would be unable to comply with the process, and thus put the desired level of quality at risk. In the 21st century mode, the current goal should be to encourage compliant behavior.

Given the true goal of a quality system I discussed earlier in the chapter—to put in place compliant processes that allow a company to develop, commercialize, and sell its medicinal product—training can and should focus on changing behavior rather than information retention. In other words, quality system training has a far greater chance of being successful and effective when it focuses more on behavioral changes than on information retention.

One of the examples I use in my workshops on how to design effective training is a five-slide presentation of the FDA's Quality Systems Regulations (QSRs). Three years ago, when a client first asked me to design training on the QSRs that would be broadly applicable to all new personnel, from summer interns to a newly hired company vice president, I realized two things: First, the traditional review of the regulations was inappropriate; I was not going to be teaching these new personnel how to be QSR experts. Second, for this training to be effective, it did not need to teach the details of the regulations, but rather would need to focus on teaching the behavior required in companies that must comply with the QSRs. In other words, my goal was to motivate behavioral changes in line with QSR expectations. As a result, I needed only to address four items:

1. What the expected behavior is
2. Why the behavior needs to change
3. The benefits of the expected behavior
4. How to know if the behavior is successful

By focusing on desired behavior, the training was able to speak directly to each attendee's self-interest. The result was that even today, three years later, executives and other individuals in that training still remember almost 80% of what we discussed, and my client continues to use that training in its new employee orientation program.[175]

EFFECTIVENESS MEASURES

To ultimately assess whether or not quality system training has been successful, executives are better off not waiting for an FDA inspector to voice his or her opinion. Executives need to determine whether training participants are applying the training appropriately. This type of evaluation requires two tactics:

1. Formal evaluation methods
2. Continuous assessment and improvement methods

Fortunately, biopharmaceutical and device executives already have the second tactic built in to their organizations: internal quality audits, corrective and preventative actions (CAPAs), and quality system management reviews. As an example, training effectiveness can be measured through comparing a department's nonconformance rate (*e.g.*, CAPAs) before and after training; this can then be trended during a quality system management review to ascertain any further insights such as a larger systemic issue (*e.g.*, the training was effective, but over time, pressure from a supervisor to cut corners led to increased noncompliance).

Formal evaluation methods appropriate to corporate environments include training simulations or on-site observations, performance checklists, post-training surveys, and interviews of training attendee supervisors. These types of evaluations can also reveal if workplace environments are conducive to compliance or if SOPs are unclear, inadequate, or otherwise bear little relation to realities in the actual workplace.

RISK-BASED DECISION MAKING

Modern quality systems need some type of documented—and followed— risk assessment and mitigation process. As I discussed in chapter three, without a defined process to assess and control day-to-day risks, risk management quickly becomes risk avoidance or risk allowance. The inability of a firm's quality system to tolerate some level of reasonable risk retards a company's ability to develop new medicines and compete in the global marketplace of the 21st century.

DRIVE RISK CONTROL INTO DAY-TO-DAY DECISIONS

Risk assessment and management can be complicated. However, as Leonardo daVinci wrote in the late 15th century, "Simplicity is the ultimate sophistication." Complex risk methodology tools are no substitute for good judgment, and good judgment can be used just as easily in a simple risk management system as it can in complex modeling methods. The key is to foster a culture used to thinking in terms of calculated risk-taking.

To create a quality system that tolerates a reasonable level of risk, quality executives need to craft a risk management process that can be used by everyone in the organization to make decisions, from the summer intern to the chief executive officer. Executives have many risk management methodologies such as Failure Mode and Effects Analyses (FMEA) or Hazard Analysis to Critical Control Points (HACCP) from which to choose. To push risk-based decision making across an organization, quality executives will need to redefine the methodology chosen into a simple, concise process that encourages broad adoption. One place to look for help is the FDA. In 1997, the agency published a guidance document for the food industry on HACCP, *Hazard Analysis and Critical Control Point Principles and Application Guidelines*, that simplified HACCP concepts and provided multiple examples well worth any quality executive's time to review.[176] Ironically, it was this guidance that helped encourage FDA officials to consider suggesting risk-based decision-making in the biopharmaceutical sphere.

To encourage wide scale adoption of risk-based decision making, biopharmaceutical and device quality department executives need to document a risk management SOP broadly applicable to any of their organization's processes and its decision points (as identified earlier in the process maps).

INCORPORATION RISK-BASED DECISIONS IN SOPs

One means of SOP adoption is to create a formal risk management SOP focused on one risk methodology such as FMEA or HACCP. For those executives considering HACCP, I recommend looking at the 2001 FDA guidance for the food industry, *Fish and Fisheries Products Hazards and Controls Guidance*, which provides fisheries a sample SOP with forms, a process flow, and a risk evaluation decision tree.[177] Along with the FDA's 1997 HACCP application guideline, the fisheries guideline provides an excellent model for the formal risk management methodology SOP.

However, such a defined and systematic risk evaluation process will be too much of a burden for day-to-day decision-making. As a result, some form of a simplified, preliminary risk assessment and evaluation process needs to be designed. One option is to create this as a separate SOP. Another option is the approach I recommend for my clients. Rather than having two SOPs to manage and maintain, create a two-part risk management SOP: the first part is a five step simplified preliminary risk evaluation and mitigation sequence usable by anyone in the company; the second part is the more in-depth, formalized methodology based on HACCP, FMEA, or whichever risk management tool company personnel know best.

In brief, the five steps of a preliminary risk assessment and control process are:

1. Describe the issue (for any equipment or materials, make sure to clarify intended use as appropriate)
2. Define what could reasonably go wrong, the likely causes of such failures, and the expected consequences
3. Define the severity and impact extent of the consequences using a simple three-tier scale such as low, medium, or critical
4. Identify risk control measures already in place
5. Identify further risk control measures that might be appropriate to either reduce or eliminate any risk, or to control the risk to a reasonable level

Note that I use the qualifier "reasonable" when it comes to identifying a possible risk and identifying potential risk control measures. To avoid arguments over just what "reasonable" is, draw upon the FDA's definition of reasonable as approximately equivalent to a 2% or greater chance of occurrence.[178] Also, make sure to clarify how and when an issue should be escalated beyond a preliminary risk evaluation to the second part of the SOP, the formal risk methodology. For example you might clarify that "All medium and critical risks that cannot be eliminated shall be escalated to the formal HACCP methodology and risk team."

While this type of preliminary process may not, dependent upon the risks involved, even need to be formally documented, consider at least encouraging personnel to adopt some level of documentation—even if it is in a memo to the file or in private notes. This will allow future review of the context of decisions and will determine if the risk control measures adopted are still relevant.

Because this preliminary part of the SOP does not specifically generate official company records, consider leaving the need to document preliminary risk evaluations out of the SOP—remember, stay silent if possible—but state it in any training on the SOP.

When it comes to training on two-part SOPs such as these, keep in mind the principle of teaching behavioral changes, not teaching process details. Everyone in the company needs to be trained on the five steps of the preliminary risk evaluation process. Everyone in the company needs to know how and when to escalate the preliminary process to the formal risk management methodology. However, beyond those core elements, any formal methodology training (*e.g.*, the second part of the SOP) should be reserved only for those individuals who will be conducting the formal methodology.

By taking this simplified, preliminary risk evaluation tact, and encouraging its widespread adoption, quality executives encourage smart risk taking, a better competitive posture, operational flexibility, and cross-functional coordination and cooperation. To use FDA terminology, such a risk management approach "has links to development, design, regulatory affairs, quality, purchasing, and so on."[179]

CROSS-FUNCTIONAL INVOLVEMENT

In August 2009, at the FDA Supplier Quality Management Congress I hosted, I spoke with two FDA officials—Dr. Barry Rothman and Mrs. Kim Trautman—on the agency's ongoing concerns about the drug and device industries' struggles with quality system compliance. Both Dr. Rothman and Mrs. Trautman repeatedly emphasized a single point: compliance failures continue to occur because companies inadvertently rely upon only their quality department when it comes to ensuring an effective quality system.

Dr. Rothman noted that regulation preambles and guidance documents repeatedly cite the phrase "integrated mix" when it comes to compliance as the only way to ensure product safety, efficacy, and quality. Mrs. Trautman was even more candid: "You must have an integrated compliance system—you *cannot* just rely on quality departments.

Everyone must be involved."[180]

For instance, when an FDA inspector scrutinizes a firm's supplier management records, the inspector follows threads from complaints, adverse events, submitted reports, and a firm's own internal corrective and preventative actions (CAPAs). When it comes to design and development work, FDA inspectors look for supplier controls around design work, formulations, clinical trials, non-clinical tests (especially toxicology and genomics testing), and other aspects of the overall new product development program to determine the reliability of submitted safety, efficacy, and quality information. Clearly such information is not all in the purview of a quality department.

RELATIONSHIP MAPPING

Another tactic compliance executives may want to consider, in addition to process mapping, striving for self-enforcing controls, and incorporating risk-based decision-making, is to enhance cross-functional coordination through relationship mapping. It's too late to figure out the structure of a cross-functional network while in the midst of an FDA inspection or product recall; better to map cross-functional relationships ahead of time to know whom—in an instant—to call for help. Relationship mapping, made popular by Madeleine Homan, is a system executives can use to understand how well each functional department and its personnel are serving the quality system objectives.[181]

There are four basic steps to creating a simple relationship map:

1. For each contact in another functional department, draw a box with the contact's name in it if they may be impacted by current quality system goals
2. For each box with a name in it, list that individual's own goals underneath the box
3. Given these goals, consider at least one worry which that individual may have about achieving his or her own goals given quality system constraints
4. Assess any similar goals and worries across the relationship map. Are there two or more individuals working on the same goal that can be put in touch with each other? Are there two people with similar quality system-based worries that can be assuaged at the same

time?

Executives who wish to learn more about the advantages of relationship mapping should read Madeleine Homan's article, "Have You Mapped Your Key Relationships?" in the August 2005 *Harvard Management Update*.[182]

CONTINUOUS IMPROVEMENT

As I noted earlier, the FDA is increasingly concerned that firms demonstrate continuous improvement, not only of medicinal products, but of compliance programs. The OIG's *Compliance Program Guidance for Pharmaceutical Manufacturers*, which I referenced earlier when discussing training, notes that executives should be regularly revising their compliance program.[183] Firms can achieve this continuous improvement in two ways:

1. Corrective action
2. Quality system management reviews

Look back at the definition of quality by design I provided in chapter six: "everything we do to directly promote and prove the safety, efficacy, quality, and personalization of our product." In the product development context, continuous improvement is a critical part of promoting and proving medicinal product safety, efficacy, quality, and personalization. But biopharmaceutical and device development is not conducted in a vacuum. Development proceeds under various regulatory requirements, including the need for a quality system. Continuously improving the quality system is therefore part of "everything we do to directly promote and prove the safety, efficacy, quality, and personalization of our product." In addition, by recognizing the importance of continuous improvement, a firm can move beyond the risk presented in traditional 20th century compliance polarized thinking, where something is either compliant or not. Continuous improvement recognizes that there are varying degrees of compliance, and this gives companies even greater flexibility.

Corrective Action

In general, corrective actions occur after a nonconformance has already occurred. For the purposes of using corrective action to demonstrate continuous improvement, quality executives will need to go beyond the traditional actions of a corrective and preventative action (CAPA) program (investigate, resolve, and verify) to specifically identify and resolve four items:

1. How the action will prevent or mitigate similar issues in the future
2. Why was the particular resolution(s) was chosen over others that might have also resolved future problems
3. What monitoring is in place to verify the positive long-term impact
4. What records will be generated as a result

Because FDA inspectors will examine the intended preventative controls and compare such intentions to the actual controls undertaken by reviewing the records produced, this latter step, identifying the records produced, is crucial to being able to demonstrate continual improvement.

Quality System Management Reviews

The ICH Q10 guidance, *Pharmaceutical Quality System*, espouses a regular quality system management review as a means to verify that a quality system is functioning effectively.[184] Take advantage of this review to also demonstrate continuous improvement.

I have spoken on numerous occasions about how to design and conduct an effective quality system management review, and will not repeat such details in this book (my focus here is on how to use a quality system management review to demonstrate continual improvement). For readers interested in setting up a quality system management review that meets FDA and ICH expectations, including example summary documents and checklists, look for the recorded seminar *Quality System Management Review (QSMR) Best Practices*, which may be accessed through the book's website.

There are three steps to use a quality system management review to prove continuous improvement and compliance:

1. Summarize the results
2. Communicate the results
3. Retain the records

Summarize Results

Following completion of the review session, draft a summary report highlighting trends, major improvements to be undertaken, and any specific projects or budget changes. I strongly encourage the delineation of the latter (projects and budget changes) because regulatory health agencies are well aware that corporations use budgeting and projects to actually implement tactics and strategies. By drawing attention in the summary to the project and budget changes that will occur as a result of the review session, executives are demonstrating that an effective, continually improving quality system is not only important, but has clear operational impact throughout the organization.

Keep the summary to less than five pages, focusing on the most critical 3-5 activities that will be undertaken. In the next review session, make sure to check on these activities. In the summary, state facts, conclusions, and deadlines (*e.g.,* "CAPAs for each department and each project were reviewed. As a result of this review, three improvements were deemed necessary to complete by September 26th..."). In addition, consider reiterating the relationship of any improvements or other changes to the company's overall quality policy and public safety.

Communicate Results

While the summary report may be written by the quality department's management team, corporate management needs to sign off and communicate the summary to organizational personnel. Keep in mind that FDA enforcement actions—warning letters, consent decrees, and the like—are addressed to the highest executive (the company president or chief executive officer) and tend to only identify individuals at a company who are vice-president level and above. As Annamarie Kempic, Associate Deputy Counsel for Litigation at the FDA, has stated, "If your name is in a press release, expect your name on any enforcement action or court document."[185]

Retain Records

Create a quality system management review "package" for each review undertaken. Putting all the records utilized in the actual review in one location allows an investigator to recreate the review as necessary. Note that at the time of writing, firms do not have to give these records to FDA inspectors; for inspectors from other regions such as Europe, firms must turn over such records upon request. Here are the records that typically comprise a quality system management review package:

- Trend graphs
- Presentations
- Lists of SOPs, contracts, and other documents reviewed
- Agenda of the review session
- Attendee lists
- Written communications of results to the organization
- Summary reports and any certification letters

Executives may also want to consider including any checklists used to gather and analyze the information, completed status reports, and even a copy of the SOP under which the review was conducted. If changes were made to supplier agreements, consider listing the suppliers and the agreements involved.

CASE STUDY: SUPPLIER MANAGEMENT

In August 2008, Midbern Pharmaceuticals[186] suffered through a six week FDA inspection of its supplier management controls. The inspection reviewed Midbern's selection, management, and oversight of its suppliers of:

- Pharmaceutical product raw materials
- Production line and quality control equipment
- Contract manufacturing and finished product distribution
- Other purchases services such as consultants

Inspectors also reviewed the processes used to evaluate, select, qualify, and manage suppliers, as well as the training Midbern personnel received on quality system controls dealing with supplier management.

In the inspection closeout meeting, inspectors identified a number of issues the firm needed to resolve to avoid a warning letter or stricter enforcement action. During informal follow-up discussions with the inspectors, my name arose as someone to help Midbern's management discern the underlying issues and revise their quality system. After reviewing the inspection documentation—both the formal FDA Form 483 observations and Midbern's internal inspection notes—and conducting my own overall gap analysis, we embarked upon an improvement and issue-resolution program tackling the five subjects covered in this chapter: modernizing the SOPs structure; implementing behavioral training; increasing risk-based decision making; strengthening cross-functional involvement; and using documented continuous improvement to demonstrate compliance and the company's commitment to safe, efficacious, quality medicines.

SOP IMPROVEMENTS

The first step was to fix the gaps in Midbern's existing SOPs on supplier controls, followed by tackling the larger gaps where Midbern was either missing an SOP or could consolidate SOPs to improve efficiencies without lowering the degree of control expected by the FDA. A process mapping workshop was conducted with the quality department, regulatory affairs, and other managers throughout Midbern's organization. As part of the workshop, we process mapped existing supplier control SOPs, identifying not only the gaps found by the FDA inspector, but those steps in the sequence that either did not add value or that did not fulfill their intention. For example, the Midbern computer department's review of data transfer controls between Midbern and its contract manufacturer had turned into an assessment of whether the contract manufacturer's virus control software was up to date and whether the manufacturer was using appropriate password controls—such controls added little value to supplier qualification and did not fulfill the intention of ensuring that the supplier could appropriately provide the services required. The outcome of the workshop was then a series of fixes to each of the existing SOPs that went beyond what the FDA expected and aimed to improve business efficiencies.

Additional SOPs were crafted, dividing the supplier evaluation and management process into four discrete processes:

1. Determination of supplier-type criticality
2. Supplier selection
3. Supplier qualification
4. Supplier monitoring

Supplier-Type Criticality Determination

In my experiences, most quality systems tend to rate suppliers for criticality on an individual basis. Given that the average company has hundreds of suppliers,[187] this is not an efficient approach. Rather, I suggested that Midbern break down its suppliers into categories based on criticality of risk to the end consumer of its products. As an example of a high criticality supplier-type, a finished product contract sterilizer would be in the "critical" category because if the sterilizer did not do its job, the patient would be directly harmed. A carton packaging materials supplier would be important, but not necessarily critical (while a poor quality carton might allow damage in certain situations to be done to the product, a poor quality carton itself will not directly result in injury or harm to the patient). Suppliers who did not impact the potential safety of the finished product, from equipment makers to process consultants, would be in the lowest risk category. The key risk driver was whether failure by the supplier would directly result in patient injury; there had to be a one-one relationship. As a result of the later quality system management review, we improved the risk criteria to also include whether the failure by the supplier directly caused product usage failure or critical product failure (*e.g.*, use of the product caused harm).

To ensure that an on-going evaluation of supplier criticality occurred, we also revised the complaint handling procedure such that trending of complaints was undertaken and thresholds were identified that would alert the quality department of an emerging supplier-related problem impacting the product or the patient. Using the newly implemented risk management core team (see below), the quality department could initiate a review of a supplier and the controls involved through a cross-functional risk evaluation and mitigation process.

Supplier Selection

The supplier selection process was dependent on three considerations:

1. Basic requirements
2. Advanced criteria

3. International criteria

Basic supplier requirements were just that—basic; if a potential supplier failed one or more of these criteria, that supplier was no longer considered. Suppliers had to have business liability insurance, not be on an FDA or other regulatory agency debarment list, not be in some sort of trouble (financial, legal, or publicity-wise), and have experience with what Midbern wanted to purchase or contract for. These basic requirements necessitated the involvement of multiple functional areas beyond the quality department: the purchasing department had to research financial stability and insurance coverage, the regulatory affairs department had to verify regulatory debarment status, and so on.

Advanced criteria were related specifically to how well the supplier could fulfill Midbern's requirements for that specific item or service. And criteria for international suppliers included indicating if the supplier was registered with the FDA, if the supplier had worked with customers in the US before, whether the supplier was in a country with export restrictions, etc.. Dependent upon the level of criticality of the supplier-type, Midbern would accept varying answers from its potential suppliers (*e.g.*, the more critical the supplier, the more criteria had to be met).

Supplier Qualification

After a supplier was selected, Midbern then had to qualify the supplier. Together, we designed a three-part program which included:

1. Remote due diligence
2. Onsite due diligence
3. Legal agreements

Remote due diligence was conducted for all suppliers and employed a single-page questionnaire, much of which could be completed by Midbern's purchasing department using information gathered from a supplier's website. This questionnaire was mailed to each selected supplier while the purchasing and quality departments worked with the computer department to design the questionnaire to be web-based so future suppliers could simply enter the information over the Internet. To ensure that Midbern received responses, I worked with their finance and purchasing departments to modify Midbern's accounts payable system with a simple trigger—suppliers who returned the questionnaire could have their invoices paid; suppliers who did not return the questionnaire would be reminded that until the questionnaire was completed (which could even be done over the phone with a Midbern purchasing agent), no invoices could be processed.

Results from this questionnaire were then used to help the quality department prepare for any onsite due diligence required. Because of the costs and time commitments involved in onsite due diligence (a minimum of $5,000 - $14,000 per supplier and 80-120 hours of work-time), we decided to tackle the critical suppliers first, then other suppliers in descending order of risk. In addition, non-critical suppliers with whom Midbern did not spend at least $20,000 annually would not ever receive an onsite audit unless a significant nonconformance, product failure, or patient injury was traced to that supplier.

Legal agreements with each supplier ran the gamut from basic purchase order terms and conditions to dedicated contracts with supplier quality agreement addendums. In general, the more common the item or service to be purchased, the lower the level of risk and the more inclination to rely initially on basic purchase order terms and conditions. Suppliers who provided off-the-shelf critical materials or services would receive a contract based on a standard Midbern template or Midbern would use that supplier's standard contract template. Customized supplies and services received individually customized and tailored contracts.

Supplier Monitoring

Midbern implemented a series of quarterly conference calls with its critical suppliers that included a review of trends associated with delivery of services, and any nonconformances. While Midbern had an approved supplier's list (*i.e.*, a list of suppliers who had been qualified and approved for use), the company was unable to answer a simple question from the FDA inspector: "How does a supplier come off the approved supplier's list?"

As a result, we implemented a series of thresholds which initiated a process by which a supplier was temporarily taken off the approved supplier's list and put on a defined supplier improvement plan. If the supplier was unable to achieve the agreed-upon measures of success in the plan, the supplier was no longer approved for use at Midbern. We also took an additional step of creating a disqualified supplier list—a listing of suppliers with whom Midbern would never do business again. Typically, suppliers would need to be deemed unethical or irresponsible to be placed on this list, and the only way a supplier could come off the disqualified supplier list was through a management and ownership change.

TRAINING IMPROVEMENT

Three tiers of training were created for Midbern: one for management, one for the general employees, and one for the personnel specifically responsible for carrying out the various supplier selection, evaluation, qualification, and monitoring tasks.

Management training was centered on encouraging behavioral changes for executives and other managers with budgetary and purchasing authority; those individuals who made decisions to seek outside suppliers. Training for the average Midbern employee also focused on behavioral expectations, but also dealt with why Midbern had to utilize a structured system, who was accountable for each of the major processes involved, and how to take advantage of the processes.

RISK-BASED DECISION MAKING

Midbern adopted a two-part risk assessment and management SOP similar to the one I discussed above. A formal risk management team was formed, comprised of representatives from quality, regulatory affairs, purchasing, legal, finance, and information technology (IT/ICT). Although not traditionally part of risk management teams, IT/ICT was asked to be a core member because so much of Midbern's activities involved electronic information, whether in the form of data capture in manufacturing and the laboratories, or data transfer between contract manufacturers and clinical sites. Additional representatives or subject matter experts from production, engineering, clinical, sales and marketing, records management, and so on, were brought in depending on the issues to be tackled by the risk management team.

The formal risk management team received detailed training on the risk management methodology selected (in Midbern's case, FMEA). An intermediate level of training was also designed to be given to any functional department representative or subject matter expert brought it to help the team. This training focused on shaping behavior by showing the individual what the risk management team needed in order to make effective decisions, along with an explanation of how criteria were typically weighted (*e.g.,* safety considerations were weighted more heavily than financial considerations).

To help ensure consistency and inclusiveness, we also created two guidelines. The first focused on typical triggers that would indicate a need to add another member to the team and how to determine from which functional department(s) to draw the representative or subject matter expert. The second listed potential risk control measures that could be adopted, or were already in existence, at Midbern. This second guidance document also made suggestions for the types of risks each control was ideally suited for controlling, mitigating, or otherwise eliminating.

When it came to supplier selection, qualification, and oversight, examples of how subject matter experts were to be chosen followed three guidelines:

1. Issues involving document, drawing, or other record transfers needed to involve a representative from records management and a representative from the functional area dealing directly with the supplier; for example, for a contracted clinical site, a representative from Midbern's clinical affairs department was to be brought in
2. For issues involving on-site contract staff, the human resources department was to contribute a representative
3. When risks arose revolving around potential recall handling by a contract manufacturer or distributor, a representative from Midbern's shipping and receiving department was brought in to serve as a subject matter expert

Some of the many supplier risk control measures available for adoption included:

- Independent verification testing of supplier-provided Certificates of Analyses or Conformity
- Onsite supplier audits (either by Midbern or a qualified independent auditor)
- Financial background reviews
- Public records reviews to ascertain if the supplier was

involved or had been involved in lawsuits or regulatory enforcements

- Quality agreement addendums to supplier contracts
- Supplier improvement plans
- Communication matrices and regular check-ins (both formal and informal) to provide multiple paths of communication and insight into supplier activities

CROSS-FUNCTIONAL INVOLVEMENT

As is clearly evident from the above tactics, supplier management became a cross-functional activity, no longer confined to the quality department. Indeed, one of the first changes we made was to identify the purchasing department as the "owner" of supplier selection, evaluation, and management. The quality department played a role more akin to an independent check on all supplier management oversight activities, acting, in coordination with regulatory affairs, as Midbern's senior executive watchdog as it related to FDA and ICH regulatory requirements and expectations.

CONTINUOUS IMPROVEMENT

Using both tactics highlighted above—the CAPA program and the regularly scheduled quality system management review –Midbern's quality department was able to demonstrate proactive continuous improvement. Corrective actions were used to document all the changes we implemented to resolve the FDA concerns, plus all the additional changes implemented as a result of my gap analyses and review of the inspection notes.

A quality system management review was scheduled a month after Midbern sent its formal response to the FDA Form 483 observations, so when the agency requested additional information from Midbern, the company was able to provide the requested information and the summary report from its quality system management review to demonstrate further proof of its commitment to effective oversight of suppliers.

The result of all these efforts saved Midbern from receiving an FDA warning letter, or worse. In addition, the revisions and improvements cut compliance overhead requirements by at least 120 working days, saving Midbern money and giving the firm more flexibility while ensuring FDA and ICH compliance.

SUMMARY

As the Midbern case study makes clear, the five major tactical revisions outlined in this chapter—from SOPs to continuous improvement—are designed to overcome the five weaknesses of 20th century-based quality systems that the FDA and other regulatory health agency inspectors are increasingly highlighting as hindrances to regulatory compliance and the development of safe, efficacious, quality medicinal products.

Revising the SOP process to rely on process mapping and records outputs helps to balance regulatory requirements with business necessities. Designing training to focus on behavioral modification rather than SOP document details strengthens the impact and effectiveness of training while raising a company's compliance competence. Risk-based decision making provides a company with options that reflect improved agility, preventing polarized thinking. All three of these—balanced SOPs, behavioral training, and risk-based decision-making—require a firm to move beyond its quality department to rely on cross-functional involvement and cooperation to comply with regulatory expectations around quality systems. In turn, the operational flexibility and cross-functional dependencies force a company to continually review and revise its quality system, demonstrating continual improvement.

EXECUTIVE'S CHECKLIST FOR CHAPTER SEVEN

Implementing a cost-effective, flexible quality system is a crucial part of getting a new personalized medicine to market faster, easier, and for less money and risk. Here's a step-by-step to-do list:

- ☐ Clarify the business goal of the quality department in an internal memorandum or other document describing each functional area's primary purpose
- ☐ Draw a visual framework of your current quality system based upon your organizational chart and Figure 10
- ☐ Process-map your SOPs, including the completed process map as an attachment within each SOP (see page three of the SOP template on the book's website at http://www.Get2MarketNow.com)
- ☐ Draft a readability SOP, including the definition of

readability (*e.g.*, Flesch Reading Ease or Flesch-Kincaid Grade Level) I provided

☐ As part of your next quality system management review, initiate a project to assess the readability level of your current SOPs; monitor trends in these readability levels

☐ Create a "records output" section in your SOPs that clarifies the records produced, where the records are stored, and for how long the records are to be retained (see page two of the SOP template on the book's website)

☐ Work with your human resources and finance departments to identify possible self-enforcing measures that could complement formal disciplinary actions

☐ Download and review the OIG's *Compliance Program Guidance for Pharmaceutical Manufacturers* (links to this are in appendix two and on the book's website)

☐ Download and review a copy of my five-slide overview of the Quality Systems Regulations from the book's website at http://www.Get2MarketNow.com

☐ As part of your next quality system management review, revise training presentations to be more behavioral focused

☐ Download and review the FDA's *Hazard Analysis and Critical Control Point Principles and Application Guidelines* (from the FDA website or the book's website)

☐ Develop a simple, preliminary risk evaluation and mitigation process everyone in the company can follow

☐ Use the FDA's expectation of "2% or greater" as a measure of what is "reasonable" in your risk evaluation and mitigation process

☐ Consider mapping each of your internal organization cross-functional relationships so you know whom to contact for help in compliance-crises

☐ Update any CAPA procedures to clarify the need to document how actions will prevent or mitigate future problems, the logic behind the resolutions chosen, the monitoring put in place, and the records produced

☐ Download and read the ICH Q10 guidance, *Pharmaceutical Quality System* (from the ICH website or the book's website)

☐ If you do not already undertake regular quality system management reviews, or wish to improve your reviews to meet FDA and ICH compliance best practices, obtain a copy of the recorded seminar, *Quality System Management Review (QSMR) Best Practices*, through the book's website at http://www.Get2MarketNow.com

☐ Following your next quality system management review, communicate the results of the review with all personnel using a summary report that clearly indicates projects and changes to be initiated

☐ After your next quality system management review, assemble the QSMR records package, including a summary report and any additional notes on what to make sure to cover in the next review session

8 — Ensuring Lean Regulatory Affairs

U nder the traditional 20th century new medicinal product development and commercialization model, regulatory affairs seemed like an afterthought, stuck somewhere between the quality, legal, and clinical departments. In the 21st century model, regulatory affairs plays a leading role far beyond submissions, annual reports, and promotional claim reviews. Companies lacking strong regulatory affairs leadership will lose the race to market. And regulatory affairs executives unwilling to step outside the boundaries set in the previous century will cripple their companies and hurt the very patients they profess to protect.

In the 21st century drive to bring a new medicine to market, regulatory affairs executives play two critical roles:

1. Share the compliance burden with the quality department
2. Blaze the path for product commercialization and launch

The tactics outlined in this chapter allow any regulatory affairs executive to succeed in these two strategic roles.

REGULATORY AFFAIRS ROADMAPPING

When developing new personalized medicines, companies cannot take advantage of the tools I discussed in chapters five and six—the voice of the customer, quality by design, bookshelving, open innovations, and stage gates—without a sound regulatory affairs department. Regulatory affairs executives are the ones who must make sure each of the new medicinal product development tools is accounted for in development plans so the results can be put into submissions and future postmarket reports.

A high-level roadmap is required to achieve a level of coordination that ensures each available product development tool is incorporated at appropriate stages throughout development so that its results can be assessed for inclusion in regulatory submissions. Regulatory affairs executives are best suited to develop such a roadmap. This roadmap can help improve their company's strategic decision making and serve to guide the firm's new product development efforts. This is a similar concept to the technology roadmaps first promoted by Motorola in the late 1970s.[188]

According to former Motorola CEO, Bob Galvin, "The fundamental purpose of ... roadmaps is to assure that we put in motion today what is necessary in order to have the right technology, processes, components, and experiences in place to meet the future needs...."[189] Roadmapping is a strategic-level, organizational planning and coordination process designed to help a company achieve its strategic goals. A roadmap outlines the requirements necessary over a specific timeline across an organization to achieve the strategic goals. At its essence, the new medicinal product development funnel I have used in this book is one type of roadmap.

Roadmapping for regulatory affairs, just as for any organization, enables strategic alignment across company-wide projects (such as developing a new medicine), enhances collaboration and communication, improves product quality, and decreases development time.[190] The end result is a product that gets to market faster, with greater quality and less cost to the company. In terms of new medicinal product development, roadmapping is a means to assemble all the various components such as voice of the customer, quality by design, and bookshelving, with all of the various requirements such as establishment of a quality system, timing for clinical trials, comparative effectiveness studies, and triggers for pre-submission meetings with regulatory health agencies such as the Food and Drug Administration (FDA). The first step in roadmapping is for regulatory affairs to create a clinical regulatory integrated strategic plan.

CLINICAL REGULATORY INTEGRATED STRATEGIC PLANS

The clinical regulatory integrated strategic plan (CRISP) is comprised of many elements such as:

- Confirmation of the regulatory health agency division overseeing the new medicinal product
- Known development guidelines
- Anticipated clinical trials and requirements
- Probable pharmacokinetics
- Key test and monitoring criteria
- Potential manufacturing sites (for a multi-site company or if the firm uses contract manufacturers)
- Global submission timing
- Target product profile

As a strategic plan, the CRISP can be constantly updated by the regulatory affairs department with input from other functional areas. The CRISP serves as the guiding document tying each functional area's projects (*e.g.*, the clinical department's project plan for Phase I clinical trials, the project plan for Phase II clinical trials, etc.). By developing and using a CRISP, regulatory affairs executives help streamline new medicinal product development and minimize the risk of redundant activities and gaps.

In general, a CRISP should have the following main strategy summary headings:

- Regulatory
- Clinical
- Nonclinical
- Safety / efficacy
- Postmarket surveillance
- Quality by design coordination
- Voice of the customer
- Open innovation collaboration

Under each heading, the major elements of a project and any dependencies are then identified. As part of its regulatory strategy section in the CRISP, the regulatory affairs team may want to answer questions such as:

- What actions has the FDA taken in this treatment area over the past few years?
- What are the specific concerns the FDA has raised in competitor products?
- What concerns have government agencies such as the Centers for Medicare and Medicaid Services (CMS) or the National Institute for Clinical Excellence (NICE) raised about this treatment area or any competitor products?
- Is there any recent recall history in this treatment area?
- Are there any current product liability lawsuits related to this treatment area?

These questions go beyond 20th century regulatory affairs basics and speak to the increasingly strategic role required of regulatory affairs executives in 21st century medicinal product development.

One practice to consider is graphing the CRISP so it shows the evolution of major project tasks over time. This will help other functional departments provide input and allow the organization to better identify gaps and duplications. An example of part of a CRISP graph is shown in Figure 12.

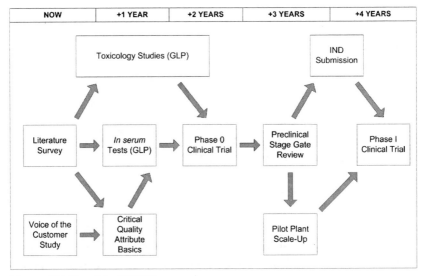

Figure 12: Graphical CRISP example

Given the large number of activities in any new medicinal product development effort, regulatory affairs executives will need to work with their cross-functional counterparts in other departments to draft the overall CRISP and its various components. This will help a firm further minimize internal operational silos. In addition, this cross-functional coordination will benefit the company by helping overcome customer exclusions and polarized compliance mentalities (these were described in greater detail in chapter three).

In order to balance multiple demanding departmental needs, regulatory affairs professionals inclined to polarized compliance thinking will need to acknowledge the impossibility of maintaining compliance of every item in the laboratories before preclinical testing starts, compliance of all items in the pilot plant before clinical trials start, and so on. Degrees of compliance will need to suffice in order for the company to achieve its strategic goals and meet reasonable timelines. Finally, by delineating the voice of the customer components in the CRISP, the customer's concerns become an important consideration of bringing a new personalized medicine to market.

Regulatory Strategy Triggers

Companies often reinvent existing elements when it comes to planning their regulatory strategy for a new medicine, even backtracking to conduct an additional study or two. Admittedly, parts of a new medicinal product's regulatory strategy will always be unique, but any plan should aim to reuse regulatory affairs and quality systems activities as new product development triggers. Executives who work in small companies and have to handle the roles of quality and regulatory affairs concurrently already take advantage of some of this reuse intuitively. A manager serving as both the regulatory affairs and the quality department for a company knows what each aspect of his or her role is currently working on and is planning to do next, and then intuitively coordinates such work. Executives who do not serve as both regulatory affairs and quality departments need to replicate that intuitive knowledge so that each department is not caught unaware, which can put a new product development project at risk of delay and/or additional cost.

Consider crafting a table of the standard strategy for any new medicinal product. What are the regulatory affairs activities associated with different product development stages? For instance, using Table 3

Table 3: Sample regulatory affairs activities by development stage

Stage	Activities
Fundamental research and discovery	Candidate selection • Identify appropriate regulatory health agency directorate(s)
Preclinical	Preclinical design • Describe *in vitro* studies • Describe animal studies • Meet with local regulatory health agency office
Clinical	Clinical plans • Select clinical sites • Identify adaptive trial thresholds Pilot design • Select API production location • Select finished product CMO

as an example, the drug candidate is selected in the fundamental research and discovery stage. During this time, regulatory affairs needs to identify the appropriate regulatory agency directorate under which the medicine will fall.

Then, add a third column for the new product development activities that trigger regulatory affairs activities (see Table 4). In this example, regulatory affairs needs to describe the *in vitro* studies as part of preclinical design. What action occurs that notifies the regulatory affairs department that it is time to describe the *in vitro* studies? Perhaps the lab director sends a draft report to the regulatory affairs director. Or perhaps, as a result of participation in a fundamental research stage gate review, the regulatory affairs director is now aware of the need to start preclinical planning.

Eventually each trigger will flow into a distinct project plan with activity linkages, resource leveling, and so on. For now, though, this type of table allows executives to identify repetitive activities (such as a literature surveys) and to create templates for the end product of the survey in order to streamline the actual work involved.

Years ago, I worked with a regulatory affairs director who maintained this type of table on a laminated poster on the wall in her office. She would circle the big-picture activities (in the middle column) that her team was currently working on, and draw arrows to different activities in the development space to which they related. On several occasions, this table allowed us to either identify gaps in a specific product's project plan or to identify activities (in one case, a toxicology test) that

Table 4: New medicinal product development triggers matrix

Stage	Activities	NPD Triggers
Fundamental research	Candidate selection • Identify appropriate regulatory health agency directorate(s)	
Preclinical	Preclinical design • Describe *in vitro* studies • Describe animal studies • Meet with local regulatory health agency office	
Clinical	Clinical plans • Select clinical sites • Identify adaptive trial thresholds Pilot design • Select API production location • Select finished product CMO	

could be eliminated because it had already been conducted for a related product.

This type of table can also translate directly into a CRISP, and from there, into the organization's overall new medicinal product development roadmap. One consideration is to tie the start of a CRISP in with Phase 0 clinical trials.

PHASE 0 CLINICAL TRIALS

Phase 0 clinical trials are very small (10-12 patients or less), very brief (7 days or less) clinical studies designed simply to validate the viability of a technology or new molecular therapy as worthy of further development for humans.

The device and diagnostic field originally pioneered the concept of Phase 0 clinicals as "feasibility tests." The goal for devices is simply to ensure that the technology can work on humans. Efficacy and safety parameters are typically not part of such device feasibility testing, although, as I suggested in chapter six, firms should consider collecting such parameters if possible. In a 2006 guidance document, *Exploratory IND Studies*, the FDA recommended biopharmaceutical firms collect such data in any Phase 0 clinical trials for new drugs and biologics.[191]

In the context of new personalized medicinal development—especially when taking advantage of quality by design—Phase 0 clinical trials can help companies clarify product critical quality attributes, verify specific biomarkers, and verify that a new medicine is able to influence specific molecular targets.

There are eight key considerations when planning for Phase 0 trials:

1. Phase 0 trials are an essential part of quality by design, moving from the preclinical stage to the clinical trial stage
2. Use Phase 0 trials to further refine potential molecular therapies, already identified during quality by design activities in the preclinical stage
3. Consider implementing a Phase 0 clinical trial as part of a stage gate review to move from preclinical into clinical trials
4. Phase 0 clinical trials must be conducted in compliance with Good Laboratory Practice (GLP) regulations and, as much as possible, Good Clinical Practice (GCP) regulations
5. Phase 0 clinical trials are limited in scope, require less extensive documentation, and pose very low risks to clinical patients; as such, they are a low cost means of identifying those molecular entities that have a strong chance to make it through the normal clinical trials process
6. Phase 0 clinical trial results can help executives design more detailed comparative efficacy studies, thus providing a better opportunity for premium pricing and reimbursement
7. Phase 0 clinical trials require a good understanding of pharmacogenomics to design, analyze, and draw conclusions
8. Phase 0 clinical trials require early involvement of statisticians in their design to ensure data results can be appropriately extrapolated to larger patient populations

A final benefit of Phase 0 clinical trials applies specifically to small startup companies: such trials can dramatically substantiate any claims when trying to license a potential new therapy. This substantiation then reduces the barrier to revenue.

Although Phase 0 trials have been around for several years, few biopharmaceutical companies have taken advantage of them.[192] As personalized medicines are increasingly developed, expect Phase 0 clinical trials to become the standard practice prior to the initiation of an application to proceed with the more traditional clinical testing. As a result, regulatory affairs executives need to plan for and incorporate Phase 0 clinical trials into any CRISP, just as they will need to plan for another increasingly common type of clinical trial, the adaptive clinical trial.

ADAPTIVE CLINICAL TRIALS

An adaptive clinical trial is one that allows accumulating data to be used to modify aspects of the clinical trial after its initiation, without undermining its validity or the integrity of its results. Modifications can result from dwindling patient numbers, new genetic profile information, changes in dosing levels due to purity variability, shorter duration of treatment, and so on.

Because adaptive clinical trials may be modified as they proceed, they require significant amounts of forethought and planning to ensure results are valid and not viewed with skepticism by regulatory reviewers. As a result, regulatory affairs executives need to consider questions such as:

- How will comparative effectiveness be proven if the competitor medicine has an entirely different dose regimen?
- Should separate sub-trials (arms) be established for patients who have been on prior treatments and those who have not?
- Will the adaptive design put randomization in jeopardy?
- Are the clinical trial endpoints and midpoints acceptable to the FDA (or other regulatory health agencies)?
- What statistical methodology will be used?
- Is enrollment going to be so complex that it puts trial completion at risk?

By segmenting more traditional clinical trials into different arms, adaptive clinical trials give clinical investigators and the clinical trial sponsor more information across many different treatment conditions, such as dosing, route of administration, frequency, male versus female response levels, etc.. As I noted in chapter five, a natural fit exists between quality by design and the validation of various product critical quality attributes.

Sophisticated predictive models, using Bayesian statistics, are typically required to design and monitor an adaptive clinical trial to ensure meaningful data and conclusions. As a result, firms without adequate biostatistician personnel are at a disadvantage and may need to outsource design of adaptive clinical trials (see one such method in chapter five when collaborating with universities).

Despite the complexities of adaptive clinical trial planning, such trials have a powerful potential to redefine regulatory new medicinal product development strategies and costs. In September 2009, Merck announced that an adaptive clinical trial for one of its new medicines saved the company $70.8 million compared with what a traditionally designed clinical trial might have cost.[193] This is precisely the type of cost-savings that will help companies compete in the 21st century.

The types and purposes of adaptive arms vary by type of new medicinal product, but consider conducting at least some Phase I adaptive arm clinical trials to finalize a new medicine's critical quality attributes. This will provide three immediate benefits:

1. A demonstration to the FDA of the firm's intent to follow the agency's quality by design initiative
2. Validation of critical quality attributes as early as possible, allowing a greater focus in remaining clinical trials on refinements of the new medicine
3. Initial verification of various critical process parameters, especially when it comes to product changeovers in pilot manufacturing

Executives will want to schedule a meeting with the appropriate FDA division, including its biostatisticians, prior to any pre-Investigative New Drug or pre-Investigative Device Exemption submission to discuss adaptive clinical trial design. Use this meeting to get insights from FDA officials on what they will expect to see in order to assess the validity of adaptive clinical trial goals. Make sure and clarify any additional information that might help speed a review of the new medicine for market launch. Having at least a tentative adaptive trial design plan is critical to the success of this meeting.

With the maturation of statistical methods and the increasing availability of more powerful statistical analysis technology and computer hardware, adaptive clinical trials are part of the regulatory affairs executive's toolkit in the 21st century. However, in adopting clinical trials, regulatory affairs executives need to be cognizant of a growing concern among biostatisticians: the impact of clinical patient psychology on trial results.

Clinical Patient Psychology

A patient's emotional state affects certain biomarkers such as heart rate and blood pressure (e..g., the "white coat" syndrome results in some patient's blood pressures being measured higher in the presence of physicians and nurses), rendering these two biomarkers less useful in assessing cardiovascular health. The more scientists learn how the mind influences the body's response mechanisms, the greater the risk to valid clinical trial results due to a patient's psychological state. While some controls can be put in place—for instance, the patient can be asked to take his or her blood pressure at home—the psychological impact on all biomarkers is not so easily addressed. Thus, when patient response to a new treatment is assessed, it is not certain how much of his/her response exists because the patient believes he or she is undergoing testing for a new "solution" as opposed to a new *possible* solution which may end up not being effective.

When I discussed this dilemma with an FDA biostatistician, he provided me with two suggestions that the FDA is increasingly urging firms to adopt as a condition of any approval for clinical trials to begin:

1. Clinical investigators must clarify in the informed consent form, and then re-emphasize in discussions with prospective clinical patients, that the treatment is investigatory only and may either not work, work only as well as one currently available, or work as hoped
2. Regulatory affairs executives need to ensure that clinical trial designs specifically rely upon at least one measure of efficacy that is independent of patient psychological state at the time of treatment whenever

possible (*e.g.*, long-term observational measurements); this independent measure can be used to verify that any acute observations are relevant

Efficacy-Threshold Graph

The efficacy-threshold graph is a third tactic to combat clinical trial patient psychology, and can pay dividends in reimbursement benefits. To product an efficacy-threshold graph, plot the efficacy of other comparative treatments on the market today and connect each treatment's plotted points with a line (see Figure 13).

During clinical trials, any efficacy measurements of the new medicine that exceed the highest threshold line of comparative medicines can visually demonstrate the superior efficacy of the new treatment. If the result is a dramatic difference, then this type of efficacy-threshold graph can be used as part of any submission to reimbursement agencies to justify premium pricing and premium reimbursement.

END-OF-PHASE II MEETINGS

Regulatory affairs professionals agree that end-of-Phase II meetings with the agency are crucial to refining final clinical trial and regulatory submission strategies. In January 2006, the FDA released a report, *Independent Evaluation of FDA's First Cycle Review Performance—Retrospective Analysis Final Report*, showing a direct correlation be-

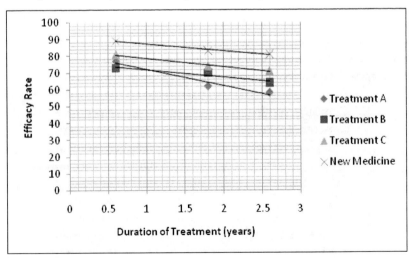

Figure 13: Example efficacy-threshold graph

tween a strong end-of-Phase II meeting and the likelihood of first-cycle approval.[194] Regulatory affairs executives must include end-of-Phase II meetings in the CRISP, as well as a buffer to accommodate changes that might need to be made as a result of the meeting. Executives who are unfamiliar with the details on planning an end-of-Phase II meeting should review the 2009 FDA guidance, *End-of-Phase 2A Meetings*.[195]

REMS AND RISK COMMUNICATION

As I noted in chapter one, the FDA and other regulatory health agencies are increasingly emphasizing post-approval monitoring and surveillance as a means to ensure medicines incorporate relevant new scientific findings related to the medicinal product's safety and efficacy. In September 2009, FDA published two documents with which regulatory affairs executives need to be well versed: a guidance entitled *Format and Content of Proposed Risk Evaluation and Mitigation Strategies (REMS), REMS Assessments, and Proposed REMS Modifications*, and the agency's own strategic plan for communicating risk to the public, *FDA's Strategic Plan for Risk Communication*.[196] The latter document is important because, by defining the agency's underlying philosophy of risk communication in its own strategic plan, the FDA has specifically stated the importance of risk communication to consumers and thus expressly laid out its expectations of industry.

Three key aspects in the *FDA's Strategic Plan for Risk Communication* need to be acknowledged:

1. Throughout the document, the FDA calls for risk communication to be "clear and easily understood information" (*e.g.*, within a target readability score range)[197]
2. The agency's emphasis on risk communication as a two-way dialogue means that regulatory affairs executives need to be prepared to engage customers directly and not just rely upon press releases, website postings, and field alerts
3. By elevating risk communication to a strategic level, the FDA is suggesting that risk communication represents a core competency for regulatory affairs executives

Along with the FDA's risk communication plan, the REMS guidance adds a number of additional burdens to companies, and therefore, it is incumbent upon regulatory affairs executives to begin planning to accommodate this as soon as possible. REMS require a significant amount of supporting documentation. While I will address some of the record retention issues in the next chapter, within the context of regulatory affairs roadmapping, executives need to assess these documentation requirements and determine how best to achieve them with the least amount of work. The sooner regulatory affairs is able to identify various documents and records that may be needed in a REMS, the sooner such documents and records can be identified and flagged as medicinal product development proceeds. Companies can then minimize their need to go back and recreate or assemble new documents to meet any REMS requirements.

Executives whose firms do not yet have a standard operating procedure (SOP) on how to create and maintain a REMS need to create one; assume that if a recall or other such significant health event occurs, a documented risk plan and set of monitoring controls (*e.g.*, a REMS) will need to be part of any return to the market.

Finally, when it comes to managing and communicating risk, executives may want to consider drafting a preliminary REMS as part of each new medicinal product's development process. While this preliminary REMS need not be included in the final submission, having it will allow the company to better answer any FDA questions that indicate the agency is considering requiring a REMS as part of marketplace approval. A preliminary REMS will also provide the company three additional benefits:

1. When dealing with pre-informed patients, nonprofits and consumer advocacy groups, a preliminary REMS can help drive discussions into meaningful dialogues to better incorporate the voice of the customer
2. A preliminary REMS can help a company drive the design of any anticipated Phase IV clinical trials or studies suggested by the agency
3. A preliminary REMS can help a company define any additional controls necessary to ensure it avoids civil monetary penalties for violating a REMS requirement; Because civil monetary penalties start at $250,000 for

the first 30-day period, the time and effort put into proactively determining if any additional internal controls need to be put in place can be well spent[198]

SHARING THE COMPLIANCE BURDEN

Evolution in the statutory and regulatory landscape—from the 2007 Food and Drug Administration Amendments Act that provided civil monetary penalties for REMS violations to global harmonization efforts and the rise of reimbursement considerations—combined with the rapid rate of scientific, engineering, and technological knowledge explain why a company can no longer rely solely upon its quality system to ensure compliance with the FDA, even in its manufacturing environment. Regulatory affairs executives need to step forward as equal partners under a 21st century compliance framework.

This compliance partnership role requires regulatory affairs executives to initiate, coordinate, and manage four strategic compliance responsibilities:

1. Regulatory requirements assessments
2. Compliance forecasts
3. Compliance budgets and coordination
4. Enforcement protection

Some of the components of each of these responsibilities are already embedded in basic, 20th century regulatory affairs activities. It is the growing scope and amount of activities required to deal with all the trends and evolutions in the 21st century that require such separate aspects to be crystallized under these four tactics.

DEVISING A REGULATORY REQUIREMENTS MATRIX

Most regulatory affairs executives are familiar with the basic regulatory matrix that cross-references various FDA statutes and regulations with necessary activities as a new medicine moves through product development and onto the marketplace. Because of regulatory harmonization, the increasing role of reimbursement agencies, and the need to accommodate regional and global considerations, a regulatory matrix confined to FDA considerations will quickly cause a company to inadvertently forget some of its regulatory obligations.

When dealing with just US requirements, regulatory affairs professionals must account for multiple regulatory agencies with an interest in medicinal product development, or aspects thereof, beyond the FDA's safety, efficacy, and quality concerns. As a result, regulatory affairs professionals may want to expand the regulatory matrix to account for each of these agencies, the relevant regulations or statutes, and the activities or records necessary in the company to prove compliance. Such a matrix might look like the example in Table 5.

Other regulatory considerations in the US include the Department of Transportation and the Department of Homeland Security. State rules also need to be monitored. In 2008, the District of Columbia passed a new law requiring pharmaceutical sales representatives to be licensed as pharmaceutical detailers.[199] As result, records of pharmaceutical promotional items, sales logs, and communications with Washington, D.C.-based healthcare providers need to be retained by a pharmaceutical company for at least five years, and be available for review by the

Table 5: Excerpt from Regulatory Requirements Matrix

US Agency	Regulation or Statute	Corresponding Corporate Compliance Activity
Centers for Medicare and Medicaid (CMS)	National Coverage Determination (NCD) – Reimbursement Health Insurance Portability and Accountability Act (HIPAA) Clinical Laboratory Improvement Amendments (CLIA)	
Occupational Safety and Health Administration (OSHA)	Federal Occupation Safety and Health Act Needlestick Safety and Prevention Act	
Environmental Protection Agency (EPA)	Federal Water Pollution Control Act Amendments Pollution Prevention Act	
Bureau of Industry and Security (BIS)	Export Administration Regulations	
Drug Enforcement Agency (DEA)	Chemical Diversion and Trafficking Act	

District's Board of Pharmacy within 10 days of request.[200] This is the type of information that needs to be captured in a regulatory requirements matrix. To prepare such a matrix, regulatory affairs executives need to work cross-functionally, especially with counterparts in the legal department to identify the specific regulations and statutes and then with colleagues in various functional departments to identify the corresponding compliance activities.

The individual statutes and regulations need not go into a CRISP, but as part of the overall regulatory affairs roadmapping process, some of the corresponding company activities will need to be identified. For instance, if a firm plans to ship complex magnetic resonance imaging equipment as part of a clinical trial to an international site, regulatory affairs executives will need to verify the equipment is not on the prohibited list of the Export Administration Regulations. If export of such equipment is prohibited, the company will either need to try to obtain a waiver (which may very well delay the trial by many months), or make alternative plans. Executives unversed in the basics of compliance with the US Export Administration Regulations and their application to medicinal product development may want to read my 2008 article, "Export Compliance for Life Sciences," from the *Journal of Commercial Biotechnology*[201] (a copy is available for download on the book's website).

DEVELOPING A COMPLIANCE RADAR

As should be clear from the new law regarding pharmaceutical sales representatives operating in Washington, D.C., the evolution of laws and regulations makes it imperative that regulatory affairs executives take the lead in developing a company's compliance radar. Such a compliance radar provides advance knowledge of possible situations the company will face in the months and years ahead. For firms regulated by the FDA, a well-structured compliance radar allows executives insight into:

- Emerging regulatory compliance expectations
- New quality systems requirements
- Additional regulatory rules
- New medicinal product development best practices
- Regulatory enforcement trends

These components comprise advanced knowledge of likely challenges a company may face as it proceeds with new medicinal product development. Executives who do not know the compliance situations they may face will inevitably put themselves and their companies into great difficulty.

Gathering basic compliance intelligence is not unduly difficult. There are hundreds of articles, blog postings, warning letters, guidance documents, special presentations, and other material all widely available on the Internet. It is the beyond-the-basics analyses, forecasts and recommendations that denote good regulatory and quality systems intelligence. Basic who-said-or-did-what information is a commodity, so any compliance intelligence program that simply regurgitates this information is not as helpful as one that goes into more detail.

Five Components

Compliance intelligence programs need to focus on analyzing trends and providing practical recommendations geared to the challenges a firm already faces or soon will. Such perspectives and forecasts should be well-thought out, logical, and relevant. There are five components of an effective compliance radar:

1.   Local intelligence
2.   Internal intelligence
3.   Competitive intelligence
4.   Market intelligence
5.   Independent intelligence

Local intelligence is gathered from those people who are aligned directly with either a company's business or an executive's profession: business colleagues, other quality, regulatory or compliance professionals, industry or profession-specific articles, industry conferences, professional associations, and medicinal product development business partners are all sources of local intelligence.

Internal compliance intelligence is learned from people who hold government positions—FDA officials, employees of Health Canada, and even representatives from regulatory harmonization groups such as the ICH (International Committee on Harmonization) or the GHTF (Global Harmonization Task Force).

Competitive intelligence is information gathered on competitors, their products, and their customers. It may come from sources inside an executive's own organization (for instance, marketing and business development personnel assigned to gather competitive intelligence), or from gleaning insights from published documents such as a 510(k) submitted to the FDA.

Market intelligence comes from people who operate in a firm's overall marketplace but are not direct competitors or partners. This includes suppliers, professional services (lawyers, accountants, consultants, etc.), venture capitalists, financial analysts, healthcare providers, patients and their advocacy groups, not-for-profit trade groups, and even public-private collaborative ventures.

Independent intelligence is gained from people who provide reports, insight, and advice independent of all of the above. Such intelligence typically sees the relationships between specializations and niches, and thus can be the most powerful—and subtle—of all the types of intelligence that go into an effective compliance radar. Determining what is "independent" and what is not can be difficult, but is of utmost importance to provide the regulatory affairs executive objective insights and advice. Therefore, I will provide examples of each type of intelligence using various public sources.

Component Examples

Two examples of local intelligence are *Focus*,[202] the journal of the Regulatory Affairs Professionals Society, and Elsevier's *The Silver Sheet*.[203] The latter's target audience is medical device executives; the former targets regulatory affairs practitioners.

Examples of internal intelligence include the FDA website and agency presentations at industry conferences (many of which are then made available on the FDA's website).

Competitive intelligence comes from many sources –websites and press releases of competitors, complaints from competitor customers, published meeting minutes between a competitor and the FDA, etc..

Marketplace intelligence can come from the publications of law firms, patient advocacy groups, and nonprofits. When I speak with executives about developing an idea of the emerging challenges they may face, I often suggest subscribing to a free version of a venture-capitalist publication such as the *Burrill Report*[204] or *FierceBiotech*.[205] This will help executives keep an eye on trends and innovations in the marketplace that concern venture capitalists and investors, something that, in turn, offers a window into what lobbyists expect (which, in turn, influences governmental and regulatory actions).

In this context, there are few independent sources of information and intelligence available. In the investment sector, many people hold up *The Kiplinger Letter*[206] as an example of independent intelligence; the newsletter is not tied to a specific sub-sector such as biotech or venture capital, but rather reports on a broad spectrum of trends (anything from international shipping rates to impending health legislation) that will impact the overall marketplace and thus influence investment decisions. When it comes to regulatory compliance and quality systems, intelligence that is independent is more difficult to find. For this reason, executives who are able to identify and benefit from such independent intelligence will invariably achieve great success.

One approach to developing a compliance radar with independent strength is to hire an independent firm or consultant to help develop such a program. Structure the project so that it is based largely on knowledge sharing, so the consultant engagement is only temporary: perhaps have the consultant conduct research and submit reports for six to twelve months, and then, as the biopharmaceutical or device firm's personnel have become more comfortable determining how to obtain the intelligence most relevant to the company and its products, they can take over from the consultant. This tactic requires executives to conduct four activities (in addition to selecting and qualifying the consultant and signing a confidentiality agreement):

1. Make a list of the short-term items the firm needs monitored; in this context, define short-term as anything the company is actively working on (*e.g.*, a Phase II clinical trial) or will work on (*e.g.*, an end-of-Phase II meeting) within the next 6 months

2. Compile a second list of longer-term items the firm needs to be kept abreast of, but only as the items relate to the company and its products; for instance, a device company might want to know about FDA and GHTF activities that deal with devices or combination products, but only be aware of isolated ICH publications

3. Create a third list of regulatory enforcement subjects to be alerted about; these should be relevant to the company and its products (*e.g.*, executives within a

company without overseas suppliers and which is not expecting to have such suppliers within the next two years need not waste time learning about enforcement actions on firms with overseas suppliers)

4. Assemble examples of each category to go along with the three lists, and then provide these to potential consultants to create potential summary reports; this will allow executives to judge comparative samples from each provider

Executives considering an outside firm to help them develop an effective compliance radar will want to make sure that all intelligence provides analyses and specific recommendations from warning letters, breaking news, newly published guidance, etc. The key is for the analyses to be predictive, with recommendations for proactive steps to consider.

As a simple example of what separates commodity intelligence from the useful compliance radar, consider this information:

- At an August 2009 conference, FDA officials from the Center for Drug Evaluation and Research (CDER) announced they were in the latter stages of qualifying portable tools to allow inspectors to conduct onsite, real-time sampling

This is an internal intelligence component (*e.g.*, it comes from FDA officials) but by itself the information is just a commodity. What should a biopharmaceutical or device executive do with this information? An effective compliance radar provides analyses and specific recommendations:

- At an August 2009 conference, FDA officials from the Center for Drug Evaluation and Research (CDER) announced they were in the latter stages of qualifying portable tools to allow inspectors to conduct onsite, real-time sampling. *As a result, executives will want to consider two points: first, if FDA inspectors can conduct real-time sampling of chemicals, formulations, and other items at a facility, quality departments will have a difficult time justifying why regularly sampling of in-process*

*chemicals, formulations, etc. is not a standard procedure;
and second, consider contacting officials at CDER to find
out what these tools are—if the FDA has already qualified
the tools, there is no need to redo such qualification, and
firms can simply adopt such tools now under the rubric
of process analytical technology (e.g., in-process sampling
and real-time quality control).*

While multiple recommendations are built within this additional
information, executives may want those specifics further delineated, in
which case the recommendation list might be:

1. Be prepared for the FDA to conduct real-time sampling
    at the firm's facilities (or the contract manufacturer's
    facilities)
2. If the firm is not already conducting similar sampling,
    the time to start is now so that the firm has records that
    prove it has been conducting such sampling by the time
    inspectors arrive
3. Make sure other quality system processes support real-
    time sampling, including being able to act on findings in
    a timely manner
4. If a firm can get the make and model of these tools—and
    assuming the tools are commercially available—then
    significant monies and time can be saved by purchasing
    the same tools and verifying their use in the firm's
    facilities
5. Portable sampling techniques should strongly be
    considered as part of a firm's adoption of process
    analytical technology

As I noted earlier, compliance intelligence that simply regurgitates
public information will not provide the advanced knowledge and advice
that comprise an effective compliance radar. An effective compliance
radar gives regulatory affairs executives a singular opportunity to demonstrate long-term strategic value and enhance their company's competitive edge.

Budgeting and Compliance Coordination

Part of honing a competitive edge is making the best use of company resources and tools to strengthen compliance while ensuring cross-functional coordination and operational flexibilities. Regulatory affairs executives may want to consider adapting a program called "Person to Person" from Australia's Department of Human Services. Person to Person is a welfare-service program wherein a group of families choose a program coordinator who allocates the resources and services based on criteria jointly arrived at by all the families. This allows families to prioritize the services they receive based on their anticipated needs for the upcoming year with additional flexibility administered in a non-partisan, previously agreed upon manner.[207]

Executives are well acquainted with elements of such allocation schemes in terms of making budget for the upcoming year or quarter. Resources are allocated for various projects to support different activities in the organization (*e.g.*, training for new hires will be made, a mock FDA audit for laboratories planning to start preclinical studies next year, etc.). But it is in taking this allocation a step further and creating a cross-functional consensus set of criteria that enhanced funding flexibility emerges, especially when it comes to regulatory compliance.

Under this approach, regulatory affairs executives work with their counterparts in other departments such as quality, medical affairs, clinical, formulations, information technology, and so on, to create a series of criteria for funding allocations. For instance, a project team whose intellectual property is destined to be licensed could have its regulatory affairs and quality systems-related priorities placed on laboratory data quality and record integrity, rather than on new regulation overview training or revised SOP writing. A project team focused on shifting Phase I clinical trial active pharmaceutical ingredient (API) production from the labs to the pilot plant could have its quality and compliance resources prioritized to implementing process analytical technology and conducting scale-up validations.

Regulatory affairs executives—because of their unique position between regulatory compliance, a quality system, and operational execution—are perfectly poised to initiate the creation of, and take an objective role in the administration of, this type of funding system. Not only does the adoption of this funding system based on mutually agreed upon criteria then encourage other functional areas to see regulatory affairs executives as strategic partners, it also helps encourage cross-functional coordination, business planning, and assignment of priorities in line with business strategy. As a result, a company's operational efficiency, speed, and flexibility are increased.

PROTECTING AGAINST REGULATORY ENFORCEMENT

Ultimately, however, success with regulatory affairs roadmapping, funding criteria coordination, compliance radar completion, and so forth, will mean little if a company stumbles into compliance enforcement actions such as warning letters, consent decrees, civil money penalties, and corporate integrity agreements. Regulatory affairs departments stand as one of the bulwarks against such disasters. While there are many aspects involved in protecting a company against regulatory enforcement, one vital aspect is preparing for, conducting, and responding to the inevitable regulatory inspection. Again, regulatory affairs executives, with their access to regulatory officials and their understanding of regulatory nuances, can best help a company successfully undergo an inspection with the least worries and risk.

When I speak to organizations and offer advice on passing inspections and audits, I relate an experience I had several years ago:

I was sitting in on a meeting with a C-level executive whose organization had not successfully passed a single inspection or even an internal audit in at least a decade. My role was to offer my advice to help them succeed in their next inspection or audit. As the meeting closed, the executive gave a very good motivational talk to his various department heads, and then began going around the room to each vice-president and each director, pointing at an individual and asking, "How many audit findings are we going to have?" And the person would shout "Zero!" And then the next person would be asked, "How many inspection findings are we going to have?" He or she would shout "Zero!" And finally it was my turn, "John, how many findings are we going to have?" And I said, "One…maybe two, although I'd suggest three might be good too." The room went quiet. But before anyone could say anything, I continued, "Look, if the inspector doesn't find anything, his boss is going to think he did a lousy job. And all that's going to happen is we'll get inspected again, this time with a different team or larger group who will look harder. We need to figure out, what is the one, maybe even two or three, things we want that inspector to find."

Regulatory affairs executives are perfectly poised to play this type of strategic role when it comes to compliance and regulatory enforcement. If maintaining a universal, perfect level of compliance is not realistic, then what one (or two or three) thing(s) are reasonable to expect the inspector will find? Regulatory affairs can then work with the functional groups involved in those less than perfect compliance areas to determine how to strengthen and improve compliance. Lessons can also be drawn from strengthening those areas that might be applicable elsewhere, thus allowing a firm to show that not only will it correct the deficiencies uncovered in the audit or inspection, but it is going to go beyond the specific findings to improve compliance at an overall systemic, strategic level. By critically examining its compliance infrastructure and accepting that compliance is not an all-or-nothing proposition, a firm can better position itself to respond to an audit or regulatory inspection.

SUMMARY

As this chapter has shown, there are powerful opportunities available to regulatory affairs executives to lead their companies to success in developing and bringing to market 21st century personalized new medicines. From sharing the compliance burden with quality departments to coordinating a cross-functional roadmap of development and all the components necessary, regulatory affairs executives stand poised to play the strategic role demanded as a firm adapts its new medicinal product development processes to personalized medicine, regulatory harmonization, and other 21st century trends.

The tactics in this chapter are designed to elevate regulatory affairs to a position of critical strategic accountability. Regulatory affairs departments are strategic assets, and are not to be defined by exclusion between clinical, quality, and legal. As I noted in chapter three, because regulatory harmonization is increasingly commoditizing regulatory affairs tasks such as submission assembly and annual reporting, regulatory affairs executives have a unique opportunity to shift to a more strategic role. And as part two of this book has made clear, bringing a new personalized medicine to market in the 21st century requires such a strategic, holistic perspective. A strategic compliance perspective, and the know-how to act upon it, is one of the few differentiators between 21st century marketplace success and failure.

Firms that adopt all of the suggestions I have made so far—incorporating the voice of the customer; relying on open innovations; tackling quality by design, building in bookshelving; setting up stage gates; process mapping and rapid prototyping SOPs; structuring behavioral training; preventing nascent intellectual property loss; improving cross-functional coordination; using risk-based decision making; laying out a clinical regulatory integrated roadmap; devising a compliance radar; and protecting against regulatory enforcement—will still lose the marketplace race without a holistic framework that allows a company to take the best advantage of the tactics and techniques in this book. And it is this framework that I tackle in the next chapter.

EXECUTIVE'S CHECKLIST FOR CHAPTER EIGHT

Just as quality executives need to take a more strategic, cross-functional role in the 21st century, so too do their regulatory affairs counterparts. Here's a step-by-step to-do list:

- ☐ Process-map and draft an SOP to create and maintain a clinical regulatory integrated strategic plan (CRISP)
- ☐ Create a table of new medicinal development triggers of regulatory affairs (and, ideally, quality system) activities by stage of development (see Tables 3 and 4)
- ☐ Find out how many of your colleagues and staff members are familiar with Phase 0 clinical trials
- ☐ Download and read the FDA guidance, *Exploratory IND Studies*, on Phase 0 clinical trials (a copy can be found on the FDA website or downloaded from the book's website at http://www.Get2MarketNow.com)
- ☐ Review any internal processes and SOPs to ensure that you can accommodate Phase 0 clinical trials; for example, do any of your SOPs need to be rephrased or have new definitions added to them?
- ☐ Conduct a literature survey on best practices for adaptive clinical trials as they relate to your specific new medicinal product
- ☐ Use the results of this survey to assemble a tentative adaptive clinical trial plan, especially for Phase I and Phase II clinical trials (if you have not already conducted them); make sure to incorporate advice from any

biostatisticians you have on staff; otherwise, see if a nearby university can help

☐ With the tentative adaptive clinical trial plan, contact the local regulatory agency district or regional office to schedule a meeting to get agency feedback (even if it is at an informal level)

☐ Review your clinical protocol and investigator qualification SOPs to ensure you discuss with investigators the importance of tackling clinical patient psychology

☐ Make sure your clinical trial design plans always identify at least one measure of efficacy that is independent of patient psychological state at time of treatment

☐ Consider creating an efficacy-threshold graph as part of your analysis of clinical data

☐ Download and read the FDA guidance, *End-of-Phase 2A Meetings*, on end of Phase II clinical trial meetings (a copy can be found on the FDA website or the book's website); incorporate its suggestions into your timelines

☐ Download and read the FDA guidance, *Format and Content of Proposed Risk Evaluation and Mitigation Strategies (REMS), REMS Assessments, and Proposed REMS Modifications*, and the agency's current *Strategic Plan for Risk Communication* (copies can be found on the FDA website or downloaded from the book's website)

☐ Verify that readability measures are used in any risk communications to the public such as labels, promotional materials, recall notices, field alerts, web site postings, etc.

☐ If you do not already have one, process map and draft an SOP on creating and maintaining a REMS; make sure any REMS incorporate those monitoring controls your firm or its distributors may already have in place

☐ As medicinal product development proceeds into Phase III clinical trials, consider drafting a preliminary REMS

☐ Create a regulatory requirements matrix that goes beyond FDA, ICH and/or GHTF requirements to capture other rules impacting your medicinal product development (see Table 5)

- ☐ Download and read the article "Export Compliance for Life Sciences" from the book's website at http://www. Get2MarketNow.com
- ☐ Draft a high-level guideline or policy statement on the components of a compliance intelligence program (*e.g.,* a compliance radar); if you are going to hire a third-party to help develop your program, this guideline or statement might be one deliverable to consider as part of a contract
- ☐ Consider creating a preliminary set of criteria, to be used to allocate budgetary line items and personnel, based on compliance requirements necessary to achieve business objectives for the upcoming financial year or quarter; share these criteria cross-functionally for review and ask for commitment on using them to fund compliance-related activities
- ☐ Make sure you have an SOP on preparing for, managing, and responding to inspections and other audits; this SOP should have various checklists to help ensure tasks and records have been appropriately identified or conducted (for sample checklists see the recorded seminar, *Bulletproof Yourself against FDA Enforcement*, which you can access through the book's website at http://www. Get2MarketNow)
- ☐ If you are actively preparing for an upcoming inspection or audit, make sure your audit preparation team has identified those 1-3 things you want the inspector to find

9 — Driving a Holistic Regulatory Compliance Framework

T o show investigators, shareholders, and patients that a new medicine is safe, efficacious, and personalized, the tactics I have reviewed so far are not enough. These tactics will produce records—the study results, statistical analyses, clinical regulatory plans, process maps, training presentations, quality system review summaries, etc.—all of which need to be carefully captured and controlled.

Regulatory compliance and quality system rules require records. A new medicinal product needs a plan blending compliance and innovation. And these records and blending of compliance and innovation call for a framework tailored to each company. Such an overall new medicinal product compliance framework is comprised of four components:

1. Modern quality system
2. Modern regulatory affairs
3. Records retention and controls
4. Compliance organization

I have already discussed the first two components—a modern quality system in chapter seven and 21st century regulatory affairs in chapter eight. This chapter tackles the remaining two components: records retention and the reporting structure of compliance. I end this chapter with a discussion of a simple yet sophisticated tactic to internalize this compliance framework, the application of Foucault's panopticon, so that company energies can better focus on developing and bringing a new medicine to market now.

COMPLIANCE AND RECORDS RETENTION

Records prove compliance. So why, at the time of writing, had 271 companies over the previous 14 months received Food and Drug Administration (FDA) enforcement notices citing records-related problems such as "failure to maintain accurate, complete, and current records..." or "failure to retain all required records...?"[208] Did the executives in these companies equate having standard operating procedures with FDA compliance? Standard operating procedures (SOPs) are just written intents, nothing more. Without the records and documents to prove an SOP was actually followed, an intent to comply is just that—an intent—and not a result.

Crucial to bringing a new personalized medicine to market is a systematic approach that takes advantage of all the tactics I have discussed—process mapping, compliance radars, quality by design, voice of the customer, and so on—and adds the controls and boundaries necessary to capture and maintain the records generated. In other words, compliance and product development require a records retention strategy.

STRATEGY SUMMARY

To implement such a strategy, start with a focus on the basics that tie in directly with regulatory health agency (*i.e.*, the FDA) compliance. Over time, as the strategy is implemented and controls mature, look to add other business records more typical of a corporate-wide records management program—material safety data sheets, legal contracts, purchase orders, approved budgets, and so on. At first, though, the immediate goal is to be able to identify and maintain the records proving FDA compliance and the new medicinal product's safety, efficacy, quality, and personalization.

To establish an FDA-compliant records retention and control program, executives should follow these twelve steps:

1. Establish baseline knowledge
2. Research retention requirements
3. Craft a records retention matrix
4. Assess the environment and plan controls
5. Inventory information locations
6. Complete the records matrix

7. Draft records management policies and SOPs
8. Implement and train
9. Revise current SOPs to reference records controls
10. Conduct an annual review
11. Include records control checks in quality audits
12. Assess and revise in a quality system management review

Step 1: Establish Baseline Knowledge

When I conduct workshops for companies on implementing a practical, FDA-compliant records retention and control program, the first thing I do is to ensure that everyone is working from the same starting point. I begin with a very brief quiz designed solely to elicit attendee assumptions about records. The sooner these assumptions are revealed, the faster they can be dealt with, and the quicker we can drive to a common knowledge base. Take a look at the question in Figure 14.

Which of the following are records? (circle all that apply)

a. An unapproved SOP draft
b. Meeting minutes
c. Someone's scribbled comments on a printout of the new drug development project plan
d. Email
e. Voicemail
f. A wet lab sample leftover from a completed study
g. All of the above
h. None of the above

Figure 14: Records compliance quiz excerpt

Few people answer "g. All of the above"—and yet, that is the correct answer. Each of these items is a record, which is why any argument attempting to delineate between information, data, records, and documents is not productive. Records contain information or data. Information can be in documents, images, sounds, or countless other formats (including materials like blood samples or marketing displays). In the eyes of regulators and the courts, they are all records, and they are all proof.

Inevitably, this realization begets the number one pitfall in retaining records: the assumption that "If records prove compliance, then let's just keep everything." Look again at the list above and imagine how quickly a business would grind to a halt if it had to retain every voicemail, every SOP draft, every email, and every piece of paper with an employee or onsite contractor's scribbled comment. And trying to find anything useful in an ever growing mountain of records would be a Herculean task. Ultimately, the philosophy of "keep it all and let the lawyers sort it out" does not make for good business sense or compliance smarts.

What does make sense is a plan for what to retain, why to retain it, and for how long to retain it. Establishing a uniform knowledge base allows executives to move forward with informed, risk-based decisions.

STEP 2: RESEARCH RETENTION REQUIREMENTS

Once an understanding is reached on what constitutes a record, it's time to research the specific regulatory requirements that apply to the organization. To keep from getting overwhelmed, limit research to the FDA regulations—Good Laboratory Practices (GLPs), Good Clinical Practices (GCPs), and Good Manufacturing Practices (GMPs). Consider using the regulatory requirements matrix I discussed in chapter eight to document the research results.

Unfortunately, identifying required records is not as simple as looking at a sub-section in the applicable regulations. At minimum, statutes such as the Health Insurance Portability and Accountability Act (HIPAA) and the Food and Drug Administration Amendments Act (FDAAA) will need to be reviewed. Guidance documents, such as the FDA's 2008 *Guidance for Sponsors, Clinical Investigators, and IRBs: Data Retention When Subjects Withdraw from FDA-Regulated Clinical Trials*, will need to be culled for their requirements. And guidelines from the International Conference on Harmonization (ICH) and the Global Harmonization Task Force (GHTF) will need to be examined.

FDA records retention requirements are not static. In addition to changes driven by the agency, a firm's business activities also drive retention variability. A record from a nonclinical GLP-study conducted today only needs to be kept for two years after the study is complete (as per 21 CFR 58.195(b)) unless that record is needed to support a planned submission in the future, in which case the firm needs to retain the record for at least two years after the agency has approved the submission.

For example, given current FDA review times, a record generated today that will support a submission planned for 2019 might need to be kept until 2024.

Thus, the clinical regulatory integrated strategic plan (CRISP) I discussed in chapter eight can be extremely helpful. The sooner executives can define when submissions are planned along with the tasks necessary to support the new medicinal product development, the faster they can clarify the records needed to prove compliance, safety, efficacy, and personalization, and the easier it will be to identify and implement the records controls required. One control to establish as early on as possible is the functional or departmental group that "owns" a record.

STEP 3: CRAFT A RECORDS RETENTION MATRIX

Record ownership can be a complicated subject and is something to be covered when establishing baseline knowledge. For the purposes of this chapter, assume the owner of a record is the department or function that generates or approves it; purchasing orders are owned by the procurement department, lab notebooks by the laboratories, budgets by the finance department, etc. This ownership structure holds whether the record is on paper or in some other format. Establishing who owns each set of records required under the regulations is crucial to achieving accountability.

Take the information already gathered from the previous records control steps—the types of records the FDA expects and the regulatory retention required—and then add the list of record owners. I find it easiest to put this in a matrix with multiple columns such as record types, retention period, and owner (see Table 6).

Do not quibble over who owns specific documents such as calibration records for an HPLC versus an electron microscope—use record categories like "laboratory equipment calibration records"—and the departmental group that is responsible for these records (e.g., under whose watch these records are generated). Executives used to clarifying department heads (i.e., "Director, Research & Development") may do so,

Table 6: Base records retention matrix

Record Type	Retention Period	Functional Owner

but recognize that for the initial matrix, simply stating the functional area is good enough.

Step 4: Assess the Environment and Plan Controls

Compliance missteps speak to an organization's culture and the imprints it leaves in its wake—the documents and records of everyday activities and decisions. To define the controls necessary, an assessment of the company's culture is needed.

Culture and behavior are intertwined. Without a supportive culture, behavior falters; without compliance-mindful behavior, culture regresses. Firms can have the best quality system and documentation rules, but without abiding behavior, executives in the firm will be better off just preparing for the inevitable FDA Form 483 observations and warning letters.

When I conduct records management and control audits, I always ask at least a handful of questions to try to discern the underlying culture and individual attitudes:

- When was the last time the firm's record inventory was updated? How was the inventory verified?
- When someone in the company is unsure if they should keep a record or throw it away, what is the usual decision?
- Who is the person in charge of electronic records?
- When a fellow scientist needs information from a study recently conducted, how does he/she get it?

There are more questions to ask but, for now, notice the pattern— there are zero "Yes/No" questions and there are no questions that risk a defensive reaction (*i.e.*, none of them ask "why"). The questions themselves are innocuous and fact-gathering; it is the responses which speak to the culture.

When asking these four questions, if I receive answers similar in tone to the ones below (lifted from actual experiences), I know cultural barriers exist:

- "Let's see—a record inventory...you mean what chemicals we have?"

- "When we're not sure what to do with something, we just keep it"
- "Well, it's supposed to be the computer department, but you know them…" or "Oh, all that stuff is right here in this drawer on these CDs"
- "Let's see…a scientist down the hall. Is it analytical chemistry that wants the information or (*pause*) you know…QC?"

The more that cultural factors inhibit good compliance practices, the more controls are needed to ensure information integrity, whether in paper or electronic form. Base such controls on a risk assessment of the environment, considering risks ranging from missed signatures to computer viruses. Make certain to address three common problems that lead to FDA Form 483 observations:

1. Uncontrolled changes in materials, protocols, etc.
2. Equipment problems, including untrained or inexperienced personnel
3. Absence of contemporaneous results records

Executives will also want to make sure, as part of this assessment, to identify controls already in place that can be leveraged such as:

- Inventory management systems
- Calibration and maintenance programs
- Protocol and deviation approval SOPs
- Computer security controls
- Internal quality audits

Note where each control aligns with a quality system control. This will minimize redundancy and cost while further reinforcing the quality system.

STEP 5: INVENTORY INFORMATION LOCATIONS

The next step is to conduct an inventory of where the records actually exist in the organization. There are four ways to go about this:

1. Send out a questionnaire
2. Conduct one-on-one interviews
3. Undertake detailed audits of the computer network, offices, labs, and any other storage areas
4. Hire an outside records compliance expert

A combination of all four is the best way to obtain the information necessary while balancing risk and cost. The most expensive alternative is to simply choose method four and completely outsource the inventory. As such, I rarely recommend this. Executives in a small start-up company should consider steps 1-3 and only bring in an outside expert on an as-needed basis for advice, rather than for actual onsite work. For all other firms, I suggest a breakdown as follows:

- Hire the outside records compliance expert to conduct baseline knowledge sessions (see step one above), preferably with one session oriented toward senior management, one session designed for middle management and line supervisors, and one session for line workers and general staff
- Use the outside expert on an as-needed basis to either conduct the records requirements research (see step two above) or to serve as an impartial reviewer to ensure nothing significant was missed
- Then, conduct as much of the actual inventory using internal staff as possible, with the outside expert only used on an as-needed basis for reviewing plans, results, etc.

For more details on tactics for conducting this inventory and hiring an outside firm to get the results desired, read my articles "How to Meet Compliance and Records Requirements of the US Food and Drug Administration"[209] and "Getting the Results You Expect from Consultants."[210]

The key is ensuring that this inventory is current—the inventory period is not the time to start moving records from one location to another. At minimum, identify what records exist, what records do not (or cannot be found), where the records are (or ought to be), and in what format they exist.

Step 6: Complete the Records Matrix

This information can then be placed into a base records retention matrix (see Table 2). Populate the columns with the data gathered in the inventory. Chances are, some records required under the regulations (for instance, clinical records) may not be held within the company. This is especially true for firms that outsource some aspects of their business functions such as clinical trials, payroll, or personnel departments. For now, simply note what records are located elsewhere (see Table 7 for examples).

Handling records between outsourced suppliers and collaborative partners is complicated and the complexities involved should not be underestimated. The more a company's compliance records network stretches across outside entities, the greater the risks and liabilities involved. Executives may want to work with an outside expert and with legal counsel to define specific controls and expectations when it comes to outside suppliers and a company's required regulatory records. Because of the potential for regulatory enforcement and business-to-business litigation, executives who insist on going it alone put themselves and their companies in grave risk.[211]

Step 7: Draft Records Management Policies and SOPs

Executives need to process-map, write, and implement a set of records management and control policies and SOPs that tie into the quality system. Remember: records prove compliance. As a minimum, consider one high-level, overarching "Records and Information Management

Table 7: Records retention matrix

Record Type	Retention Period	Functional Owner	Location	Format
Lab equipment calibration logs		R&D labs	R&D record storage room	paper
Clinical consent forms		Clinical project team – Product Alpha	ABC clinic	paper
Adverse event report raw data		Clinical project team – Product Alpha	ClinDATA company	electronic

Policy" and six SOPs that respectively cover:

1. Retention requirements
2. Records disposal
3. Annual review
4. Confidentiality, security and privacy
5. Long-term archival
6. Litigation disposal-suspense

When tied with the firm's quality system, such a structure might look like Figure 15.

The retention requirements SOP specifies records retention rules, answering common questions such as:

- Does retention start after the record is created or after the business activity under which the record was generated is complete?
- Does the approved SOP, the draft SOP, or do both need to be retained?
- Who is allowed to make modifications to the records retention matrix?
- Who reviews and approves such changes?

Records disposal is the records management profession's terminology for approved destruction of previously required records. For example, after keeping a nonclinical GLP-study record for 2 years, a firm decides not to pursue a submission and can now dispose of the record. The records disposal SOP needs to cover who is allowed to make these decisions, what authorization is required, and so on.

The annual review SOP describes the process personnel need to periodically follow to review their records—in their offices, network storage locations, computers, etc.—to ensure they are retaining appropriate records still in use while sending "closed" records off to long-term storage. The SOP on confidentiality, security, and privacy can cover basic rules for the confidentiality of company records, the privacy of individual information (such as medical records), and the minimum security criteria expected—locked storage rooms or file cabinets, password-protected network storage, and so on.

The long-term archival SOP should describe how records—whether

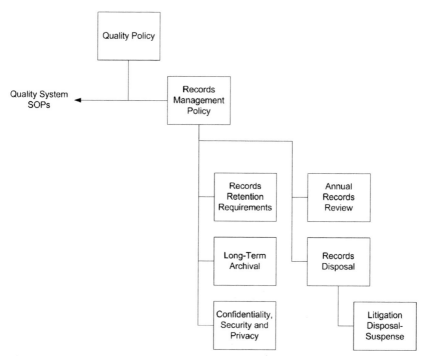

Figure 15: Sample records management policy & SOP structure

in paper or other formats—are stored for the long-term. Remember that some records may move from a two-year retention period to a ten or twelve year period, and vice versa, depending on business activities and decisions. This is the SOP used to clarify the process involved so a record is not accidently kept too long or mistakenly destroyed. Be aware that accidental loss of records has resulted in multi-million dollar court fines. The SOP on litigation disposal-suspension needs to define when to stop routinely destroying records, the authorizations required, and how such notification works. Recognize that in the event of a lawsuit, records control SOPs will be some of the first documents scrutinized by the court.

STEP 8: IMPLEMENT AND TRAIN

Draw upon the suggestions I provided in chapter seven on training for behavioral changes. Training should provide employees examples of how FDA inspectors discover records issues along with examples of such problems in the context of common documents and emails.

Consider scheduling an annual review (see step ten below) as soon as possible after training. The annual review is where a company reinforces records program rules and requires personnel to demonstrate they understand their accountabilities, their tasks, and appropriate behavior.

STEP 9: REVISE SOPs TO REFERENCE RECORD CONTROLS

As the records retention and control program is implemented, firms may need to revise the quality systems SOPs to better integrate with the various retention rules. As I noted in chapter seven, make sure each SOP identifies the records generated as a result of someone following the SOP. For instance, an incoming materials inspection SOP may generate a signed or "quality checked" stamped bill of materials or packing slip; the training creation SOP might generate an attendance sheet, a training outline or agenda, the training presentation slides, and the trainer's specific notes. Having a process map of each quality system procedure will greatly simplify any revisions necessary to clarify the records produced.

STEP 10: CONDUCT AN ANNUAL REVIEW

After the records retention and control program has been implemented, and preferably immediately following training, conduct an organization-wide records review. This is a supervised review of records conducted by all employees to determine what records they have in their possession. In over a decade of conducting audits and inventories, no matter how thorough I thought an inventory was, something was inevitably missed that appeared during this first review.

Some type of documentation will need to be created for this review. Consider three forms:

1. An employee's self-certification that he or she reviewed his or her own records
2. A list of records sent off to archive by the employee
3. A summary of each department or functional group's activities

The first time this review is conducted, expect employees to take at least 2-5 days to review all of their various records (typically, the longer the person has been with the organization, the longer the review will take). Consider this first review as a "review week," while from that point forward just a day or so a year will suffice.

Some practitioners suggest holding these reviews quarterly or bi-annually. While the choice of frequency is not a critical factor; my experience is that getting management and staff to agree to pause normal business once a year, for at least a day or two, is hard enough; trying to schedule a review every quarter calls for a level of authority and commitment that records retention does not generally command.

STEP 11: INCORPORATE CONTROL CHECKS IN QUALITY AUDITS

Just as in chapter five where I suggested incorporating corporate espionage protection questions into standard quality audits, so too should records control questions be built into quality and due diligence audits. Flag problems for further scrutiny. Examples might include missing signatures on an approval form or out of order approvals (on a series of progressively timed activities); these are discrepancies FDA inspectors are trained to look for. Part of any internal company quality audit should also be to find such records problems.

Building such records control checks into quality and due diligence audits not only avoids duplicate internal efforts, it has the added benefit of helping to prepare for a regulatory inspection. At a minimum, ask questions such as:

- Are all records that should be marked "confidential" so marked?
- Are people actually deleting files and disposing of records no longer required for retention by company policy? How is this verified?
- How often is the compliance of record retention schedules with current laws and regulations verified?

In addition, consider sampling the records of ten to fifteen random personnel such as a scientist, an analyst, and a director to identify any categories of personnel who are not following the records program. And make sure to coordinate any audit with the firm's information technology (IT/ICT) group to ensure electronic files are considered. Readers may download a list of 27 sample questions to include in internal quality and supplier due diligence audits from the book's website.

STEP 12: ASSESS IN THE QUALITY SYSTEM MANAGEMENT REVIEW

Part of the quality system management review (see chapter seven) needs to be an assessment of records controls and retention. Remember: records are proof of compliance. Questions to consider for the review include:

- Have all records been indexed before being sent to long-term storage?
- Do you know the rates of corruption or breakdown for your electronic data storage (*e.g.*, DVDs, computer tape, etc.)? Is it is time to migrate electronic data from one format to another?
- Was a random audit of archived records conducted? What were the results?
- Have any new record retention expectations from the FDA come out since the last review?

Firms that cannot control their records cannot hope to convince regulators of the safety, efficacy, and quality of their new medicines.

OTHER RECORDS COMPLIANCE CONSIDERATIONS

Seemingly small details can play significant roles in determining the line between success and failure. Five of the most common challenges I have come across over the past 16 years are:

1. Using email as a substitute for written notification
2. Drafting a communications policy
3. Tracing data ownership
4. Handling inspector requests
5. Relying too much on supplier documents

EMAIL AS WRITTEN NOTIFICATION

To use email as a substitute for written notification of compliance-related activities, such as the approval of a new SOP or the resolution of a problem, emails must comply with the 2006 Amendments to the Federal Rules of Civil Procedure. These amendments require email notifications to clearly identify the individuals addressed or involved, they must be retained appropriately (*e.g.*, as a record under the firm's quality system), and they must specify the issues, nonconformance, or other information without using phrasing that might be construed as disingenuous by an objective third-party.

Firms need to be careful not to retain written notifications or other regulation-required records within their email system. Trying to make an email system compliant with 21 CFR Part 11 or Annex 11 is a waste of time and money. A potential compromise, enabling the use of emails for written notification, is to save email messages individually as electronic documents or printed out and retained as hard copy documents.

DRAFTING A COMMUNICATIONS POLICY

Firms without a communications policy that discusses email usage and retention rules, particularly around compliance with the Federal Rules of Civil Procedure, need to draft one. Email tends to bring out a less formal, less structured type of writing, and as a result, inappropriate comments or opinions can easily slip into these corporate records.

To minimize the risk of inappropriate statements in email, create a communications policy that discusses email usage in the context of a quality system or retention of FDA-required records. Keep in mind that in the event of a product liability lawsuit, an email holds just as much validity as a formally approved clinical trial protocol in the eyes of the court. Nancy Singer, a former FDA prosecutor, has noted that emails written by busy executives frequently include phrases that can easily be taken out of context by inspectors and investigators to imply inappropriate conduct:

> *An excellent example is the company president who asked of his regulatory group "Let me know the types of claims outside our approved indications that we can get away with." Or the marketing official who wrote an email stating, "I know this goes against the regs, but I*

*think we should make the claim and wait for the gov-
ernment to take regulatory action."*[212]

A good communications policy will describe the reasons why email is a company record, detail any expectations of privacy, and provide specific rules to follow when composing and/or replying to email.

Tracing Data Ownership

Data accountability transparency can be crucial to organizations trying to demonstrate FDA compliance and information integrity. Address accountability transparency by combining the concepts of flowcharts and organizational charts. For accountability trace the documented proof of patient safety and product efficacy through various levels of management, and for data trace the same documented proof through computer systems. Then, correlate the two charts to identify relationships. The goal is to be able to determine, at any time in the information's lifecycle, who in an organization is accountable for its integrity and where the supportive records are located.

Handling Inspector Requests

One question I am frequently asked in corporate workshops is "What happens if I'm there with the FDA inspector, he asks for something, and we cannot find it?" How a firm handles this situation can be the difference between a formal FDA Form 483 observation and a more informal remark by the inspector. Companies who have a records retention and control program in place are going to handle this successfully, if not avoid this situation completely.

Assuming the worst case, however, there are four steps to keep in mind:

1. First, call a meeting of everyone who might be involved in handling the record; this is where identifying the "owner" of a category of records is crucial
2. Second, assess whether the record might be stored under a different name or incorporated in a different document; ask the computer department to run an inventory search on the network or pull a backup tape from previous months to look either for the file itself or

copies thereof
3. If the record still cannot be found, start a corrective and preventative action (CAPA) investigation, and explain to the inspector the situation and what has been done so far
4. Commit to finding the record within ten days or sooner, depending on how long the inspection is expected to last; as part of any delivery of that record, make sure to include not only the closed CAPA investigation, but also the various new controls put in place to prevent this from happening in the future

RELYING TOO MUCH ON SUPPLIER RECORDS

Relying too heavily on supplier provided Certificates of Analysis or Conformance can jeopardize compliance as well as product efficacy, safety, and quality.

In August 2009, the FDA's Dr. Barry Rothman asked attendees of the Supplier Management Congress, "If you have no idea of the quality of the actual materials maker, and you have no idea of the conditions under which the materials were transported and stored, how can you rely upon the accompanying Certificate of Analysis?"[213] Such certificates may be copies the distributor or broker had from a previous batch, or the default certificate the distributor provides for all batches of that chemical, or it could be a genuine analysis but made from composite samples taken from a large shipment.

Over-reliance on supplier documents can be avoided by implementing a risk-based supplier qualification program (see the case study in chapter seven). In addition to supplier evaluation and on-going monitoring, supplier controls can include thorough testing of the first shipment from any new supplier, and then more thorough sampling and testing if the supplier's manufacturing site has made any recent, significant changes. Proof of this testing can be as simple as a hand-written note on the Certificate of Conformance or Certificate of Sterility.[214]

THE MODERN COMPLIANCE ORGANIZATION

Records, however critical they may be to proof of regulatory compliance and new medicinal product safety, efficacy, and personalization, are ultimately the result of human judgments. And the best scientific evaluations and risk-based decisions will come to naught without the compliance advice, help, and expertise necessary to bring the medicine to market. For shareholders expecting financial returns and for patients wanting personalized medicines, the compliance organization is the fulcrum upon which success and failure hinge.

ROLE OF THE COMPLIANCE OFFICER

When it comes to a company's compliance program, the compliance officer is the ultimate authority and has three main responsibilities:

1. Planning
2. Implementation
3. Oversight

Guiding the compliance officer's actions should be his or her direct reports: regulatory affairs, quality, and records management. Firms with a separate auditing function should also consider having that group report to the compliance officer.

The US Department of Health and Human Services' Office of Inspector General (OIG) document entitled *Compliance Program Guidance for Pharmaceutical Manufacturers* which I referenced in chapter seven suggests that the compliance officer report directly to the head of the company or to its board of directors.[215] In practice, however, the latter is unlikely—an informal reporting relationship between the compliance officer and the board of directors is probably more pragmatic. In such a case, I also suggest having the company's legal counsel serve as an informal advisor to the compliance officer (and vice versa). This structure is depicted in Figure 16.

Internal Compliance Agreements

As part of the implementation of an integrated compliance program, the compliance officer may want to work with his or her human resources departmental counterpart to craft an internal compliance agreement which all employees and contracted staff would need to review and sign. Such an agreement should be based upon the corporate integrity agreements espoused by the OIG, and cover: codes of conduct, policy rules, audit and training expectations, as well as complaint reporting and handling, risk management principles, and the corporate protections

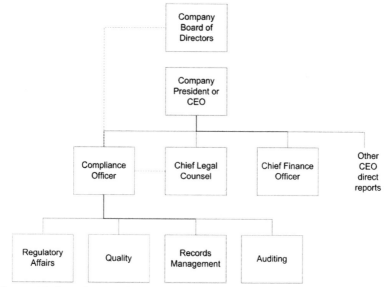

Figure 16: Sample compliance organization reporting structure afforded to internal whistleblowers.[216]

Organizational Conflict Resolution

Adopting many of the tactics in this book will extend an executive's influence outside the mold of traditional 20th century FDA quality and regulatory compliance bailiwicks. As such, these tactics may cause organizational resistance and resentment. A myriad of books, self-improvement classes, articles, personal coaches, etc., exist to help leaders deal with organizational resistance to change. That such a variety and multitude of resources exist indicates that no one "right" approach exists. There are, however, three fundamental rules that do seem to cut across the various methodologies:

1. Overcoming organizational resistance takes time; years if handled poorly, months if handled well

2. Clarity of conduct and associated measures of success are crucial. To encourage colleagues and staff to adopt the suggestions in this book, identify and communicate clear targets (*e.g.*, "Let's schedule a meeting so we can get a firm 'go/no-go' decision before starting clinical planning" rather than "Let's setup a preclinical stage

gate"). This shifts the focus from the psychologically-loaded concept of "something new to worry about" to something more limited and tangible. Assuming the meeting goes well, then a more formalized, repeatable structure (*e.g.*, stage gate) can be suggested

3. Avoid implementing all the changes at once. Break the newness into parts, preferably to be adopted singly to allow teams and departments to tailor each change to their specific environment; just make sure to keep the end goal in mind so these departmental adjustments do not end up reflecting the 20th century model

In addition, when executives allocate resources to these new initiatives—or draw them from older, less competitive projects—expect stubborn opposition from those who support the traditional strategies.

Thus, if possible, approach any necessary conflict by keeping in mind long-term demographics and minor quick-wins. When China first began to embrace modernization and shift toward an information economy, its president at the time, Jiang Zelin, pushed for a "city-first" approach. He recognized that the strongest opposition he faced regarding modernization was from Communist party members based in rural districts. Once the cities began to modernize, job openings rapidly skyrocketed. This, in turn, led millions of younger, rural Chinese to move to the cities to take advantage of the opportunities. Thus, the strength of the eventual opposition was minimized.[217]

Just as the modernization strategies of part two in this book are designed for the long term as part of an adaptation to the trends and changes identified in part one, recognize that demographics will support adoption of many of these tactics over time. Large firms may want to consider choosing a single division, facility, or subsidiary, in which to first implement the suggestions in this book. Younger knowledge workers will embrace these changes, for they quickly grasp the inherent flexibilities and opportunities available, and will be much less worried about any potential risks and conflict with the status quo.

Many years ago, when I worked for a large, multi-product *Fortune 50* company, we set up two new factories—one was a traditional plant with all the rules, SOPs, and policies of other manufacturing sites; the second factory was designed as an experiment in modernization wherein only the highest level policies (anti-discrimination, etc.) of other manufacturing sites were duplicated, and all the SOPs were to be created anew by the new factory's personnel. Given the choice of working under the old-style or the new-style factory, both blue- and white-collar workers under the age of 40 consistently chose the latter. So powerful was the incentive to move to an environment where SOPs and rules were flexible and open to innovation, the company had to increase worker salaries by 15% at the traditional factory in order to ensure enough experienced workers were transferred there.

Punishment and Compliance Enforcement

When coaching clients on ways to minimize organizational conflict, some form of the following question always arises: "I have identified someone who is intentionally not following the new rules. Why shouldn't that person be punished?"

This is a reasonable question. After all in his book *The Prince*, Niccolo Machiavelli noted that the fear of punishment is always an effective means of enforcement.[218] However (and this part is typically forgotten), Machiavelli was unequivocal: fear-based enforcement is only effective when the punishment occurs suddenly, dramatically, and publicly, leaving all "...at once satisfied and stupefied."[219] Chances are, unless the firm's chief executive officer has an unfettered board mandate and the active backing of regulatory agency officials, this type of discipline cannot be carried out effectively. As I have noted repeatedly in this book, the command-and-control style of compliance cannot achieve the objectives of cost-effective compliance balanced with innovation and improved productivity. Tactics for the 21st century include the use of self-interested enforcement (see chapter eight) and the adaptation of Foucault's panopticon, which I will discuss later in this chapter.

COMPLIANCE IMPACT AWARENESS

Any holistic compliance framework that seeks to ensure consistent compliance balanced with cost-efficiency and R&D productivity will need to share gained compliance intelligence. This can be as simple as sending out departmental-relevant briefs synopsizing the information from an effective compliance radar (see chapter eight) to holding "Compliance 101" awareness and training sessions for employees and onsite contracted staff.

Compliance 101

This is a basic awareness training session or overview given to all company personnel. The session should cover:

- Core groups that make up the company's compliance department (regulatory affairs, quality, etc.)
- The primary purpose of each group within the department
- The normal points in business processes when members from the compliance department become involved, such as clinical trial planning, review of promotional activities, and so on
- The major regulations governing the company's business activities (recall the five slide Quality Systems Regulations presentation I discussed in chapter seven)
- Who in the department to contact for typical questions
- What to expect over the next six months (*e.g.*, the major compliance projects and activities); this session should also cover what to do with any compliance intelligence synopses training attendees might receive in the future

Dependent upon the audience, this awareness session might also include a sample SOP as well as examples of how SOPs are to be used. At a minimum, this type of session should be included as part of all new hire orientations, and the compliance officer will need to work with his or her human resources counterpart to ensure this happens. Holding regular compliance awareness sessions is just one way to ensure that compliance is part of basic day-to-day behavior. It is through application of Foucault's panopticon that compliance becomes embedded in daily activities.

APPLYING FOUCAULT'S PANOPTICON

In 1975, French philosopher Michel Foucault published a landmark study of the panopticon—a building, such as a prison or hospital, with all parts of its interior visible from a single point—and of the panopticon's impact on human behavior.[220]

RULES, JAILORS, AND MONEY

The panopticon was originally proposed in 1785 by Jeremy Bentham as a circular prison with cells placed around a central observation guard station. The panopticon was designed to be cost-efficient. With only one central observation post for all the prisoners, the panopticon would require less jailors and thus less cost.

Bentham supplemented this with a brilliant, but at the time, risky innovation: one could create the observation post such that the prisoners outside of it could not see into it. This meant that the jailor need not be on duty all the time. Bentham argued that one man could watch an entire prison.[221] It was sufficient for prisoners to believe there was an observing jailor on duty; whether there actually was a jailor on duty was beside the point.

FOUCAULT'S ANALYSIS

Almost 200 years later, Michel Foucault put forth the argument that modern hierarchical structures (*e.g.*, a company) resemble a virtual panopticon. By constantly observing employees and colleagues, behavior is normalized through multiple means of feedback and discipline.

Feedback can be formal, such as an employee's annual review, or informal, such as discussions or whispered conversations in the hallway. Discipline can be delivered during a one-on-one meeting with a supervisor, as a required training session, as suspension with or without pay, or as a company-wide memo admonishing poor performance or bad behavior, etc.

For Foucault, discipline allows individuality and innovation but only within formats approved by the company and its management. Underlying this discipline is the understanding that employees are being observed—in meetings, in email, walking through the hallway, in the break room, and so on (even, as some would argue, during family fun days and company barbecues that employees are invited to voluntarily attend).

Foucault noted that modern society creates disciplinary careers that are backed by the authority of science and criminal punishment. These include police officers and prosecutors, forensic scientists, regulatory agency inspectors and reviewers. Indeed, Foucault pointed out that any hierarchical society like a corporation, functioning as it does as a virtual panopticon, eventually produces a specialized class of people who act as proxies for the government in surveillance—to wit, corporate compliance officers, regulatory affairs managers, quality assurance directors, quality management directors, environmental health and safety officers, and so on.

INTERNALIZING COMPLIANCE TO BOOST INNOVATION

Foucault saw that each of us follows, without thinking about it, a particular set of rules and behaviors based on the displayed expectations of the hierarchy around us and the presence of observation. For example, we often stop at red lights not because we anticipate that a police car is nearby ready to enforce the law, but because stopping at red lights is expected by all the drivers around us. Once such rules become habits, we do not actively recall the rule (I know I certainly have not read the actual legal statute requiring me to stop at a red light or put on my seatbelt when I drive) nor do we actively reflect on our behavior (*e.g.,* "Should I wear the seatbelt today?"), but act automatically within the rules.

Foucault argued in support of Bentham's original proposal—that given our tendency to "internalize" rules and just follow them automatically because we *might* be observed and because we are expected to follow the rules—that active observation and enforcement can be removed. Turning rules into habits minimizes the costs associated with compliance and allows each of us to go about our daily business without risk to the community in which we live or its members. Executives can take advantage of Foucault's panopticon to make compliance with regulations, policies, and SOPs more effective, more cost-efficient, and more internalized such that employees and contracted staff spend their energies on new medicinal product innovation and productivity while subconsciously following the compliance rules out of habit.

BRUTAL SIMPLICITY

When I served as the head of records management and information technology (IT) for an FDA-regulated firm, we accidentally discovered that a scientist was sending proprietary, confidential information (including intellectual property) out of the company to unknown locations on the Internet.

After a thorough investigation, the scientist was dismissed and noticeably escorted from the building. From that day forward, and for the next three years, not a single individual in the company (including new hires) broke any IT policy. The rumor mill had spread the perception that the scientist had been let go because he broke some IT rule, whereas he was really fired for breaking intellectual property security and records management rules. It was because IT personnel were heavily involved in the investigation that company employees and onsite contractors naturally assumed that when the scientist was dismissed, it was due to something that IT had discovered while it observed people's actions over the Internet and on their computers.

From the standpoint of Foucault's panopticon, the lesson was clear: the panopticon works. As I noted in chapter seven when I discussed SOPs and training, when it comes to compliance, the goal is not adherence to specific terms and phrases within today's written policy or SOP, but for automatic adoption of the underlying principles and framework (*e.g.*, behavioral changes).

SUMMARY

Building a holistic compliance framework that is internalized by company personnel is a significant undertaking. And yet, as I discussed throughout part one of this book, and re-emphasized in chapters seven and eight, compliance cannot rest upon regulatory affairs and quality department personnel alone. Cross-functional cooperation and coordination is critical. Proof of compliance and of product safety, efficacy, and quality must be identified, captured, and retained over the long term. And an appropriate organizational structure must be present to minimize conflicts-of-interest and temptations to falsify records.

As a new drug or device goes through the 21st century new medical product development funnel (see Figure 17), from gathering voice of the customer and quality by design inputs to clinical regulatory integrated strategic plans and records management, compliance plays an increasingly important role. A medicinal product development funnel without compliance cannot bring a new medicine to market or keep it there.

The next chapter concludes this book by reviewing how each of the tactics I have discussed can overcome the major challenges of medicinal product development in the 21st century era of personalized medicines. It is through adoption of these tactics that executives can bring their new personalized medicine to market now.

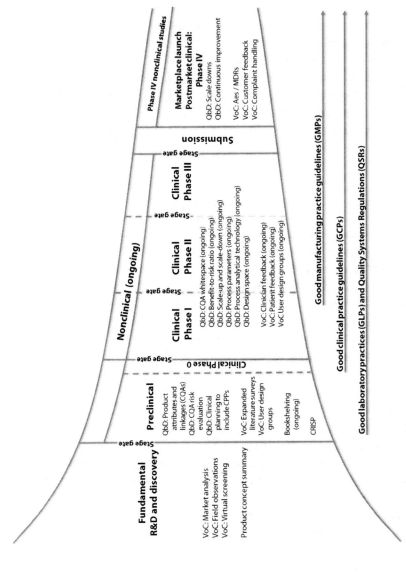

Figure 17: The 21st century new medicinal product development funnel

EXECUTIVE'S CHECKLIST FOR CHAPTER NINE

Matching organizational structure with a records retention and control program that maintains the proof of compliance and product safety, efficacy, and personalization is required to ensure the success of a modern compliance program. Here's a step-by-step to-do list:

- ☐ Hold an awareness session on FDA records requirements with your staff; consider using my recorded seminar, *FDA Quality Systems Records Requirements and Retention for Pharmaceutical, Biotech, and Devices— GLPs, GCPs, GMPs, QSRs,* as a guide (obtain a copy through the book's website at http://www. Get2MarketNow.com)
- ☐ Research your company's records requirements from the FDA, ICH and/or the GHTF, plus any other regulatory health agency; you can use the nine-page matrix in my recorded seminar noted above as a starting point
- ☐ Compile a records retention matrix identifying the record type, retention period required, and the functional owner in your company (see Table 6).
- ☐ Download and use my 27-question records management and control checklist from the book's website to conduct an assessment of your company's culture of control
- ☐ Conduct an inventory of your company's records, hiring an outside expert as necessary, and inputting the information into the records retention matrix
- ☐ Download and read "How to Meet Compliance and Records Requirements of the US Food and Drug Administration" and "Getting the Results You Expect from Consultants" from the book's website before you select any outside expert
- ☐ Process map and draft the appropriate records management SOPs and policies
- ☐ Revise any quality system and other SOPs to reference the appropriate controls and SOPs of the records retention and control program
- ☐ Set aside at least three days to conduct your first company-wide records review; schedule a one-day

review for the following year

- [ ] Ensure each employee's record review is documented, a list of records sent off to archive is created, and a summary of each department's activities is documented
- [ ] Adapt some of the 27 questions from my records management checklist (available at http://www. Get2MarketNow.com) into your quality system audits and due diligence audits
- [ ] Review and assess your progress in implementing a records retention and control program in your next quality system management review
- [ ] Draft a communications policy that covers email usage and retention rules
- [ ] Consider having your records management team work with your computer department to assemble a data traceability flowchart
- [ ] Verify that your supplier management controls do not have an over-reliance upon supplier documents such as Certificates of Analysis or Conformance
- [ ] Consider working with your executive team to realign regulatory affairs, quality, records management, and internal audit to report to a compliance officer; if you cannot afford to hire a full-time compliance officer this individual can simply be the senior-most executive of one of these four teams
- [ ] Consider crafting a simple, one-page internal compliance agreement which all personnel sign as part of new hire orientation (perhaps following a compliance awareness session)
- [ ] Work with your human resources department, as necessary, to establish a tiered disciplinary approach to noncompliance. Be cautious about punishment; motivate enforcement based on self-interest and Foucault's panopticon
- [ ] Learn more about applying Foucault's panopticon to your organization by reading about the panopticon (consider the suggestions listed in appendix two)

Summary of Part Two

Over the last five chapters I have laid out the specific components of the 21st century medicinal product development funnel and the compliance infrastructure required to answer five critical questions:

1. Within the confines of the GLPs, GCPs, and design control, how can innovation and R&D productivity be improved?
2. How can quality and compliance become more involved earlier in product development without inhibiting the flexibility and innovation necessary to create new medicines?
3. How can flexibility and adaptability in FDA quality systems and other compliance programs be strengthened?
4. How do FDA quality systems and other compliance programs achieve cost-efficiency?
5. How do all of these strategies and tactics integrate to bring new medicines to market faster, easier, and for less?

Here is a summary of the recommendations:

☐ To improve innovation and R&D productivity, adopt the voice of the customer, open innovation, and bookshelving

☐ To drive quality and compliance into product development without risking innovation and creativity, adopt quality by design, process analytical technology, design space, and stage gates

☐ To build flexible, adaptable compliance programs and quality systems, adopt process mapping and rapid SOP prototyping, behavioral training, risk-based decision making, cross-functional involvement, and continuous improvement processes such as a quality system management review

☐ To encourage cost-efficiencies in regulatory affairs and quality systems, adopt regulatory affairs roadmapping tactics such as a CRISP, link quality systems to business strategy, and strive for self-enforcement

☐ Tie all of this together with records retention and control, an overall compliance organization reminiscent of the Office of Inspector General's suggestions, and take advantage of Foucault's panopticon to internalize compliance

As a result, we have moved from the traditional 20th century new medicinal product development model (Figure 18) to the new model that incorporates each of the above recommendations, thus addressing the regulatory revisions and personalized medicine expectations of the 21st century (Figure 19).

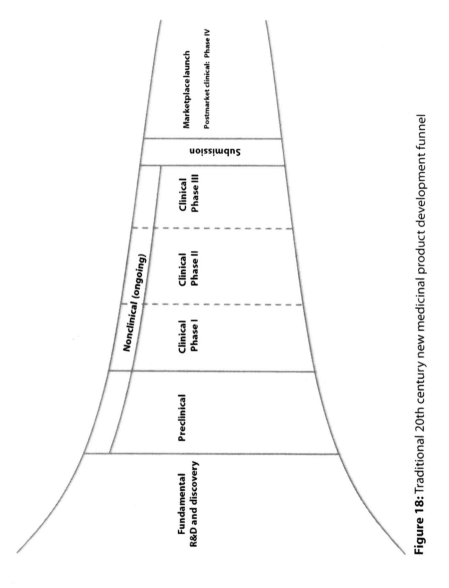

Figure 18: Traditional 20th century new medicinal product development funnel

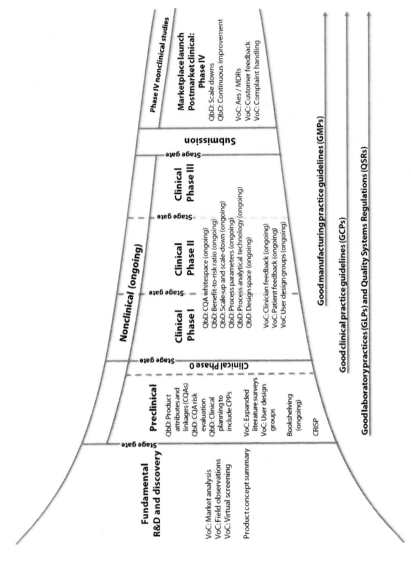

Figure 19: The 21st century new medicinal product development funnel

10 — Conclusion: Bringing It All Together

Throughout this book, I have tried to show that for all its newness, elements of the 21st century new medicinal product development funnel and its matching modern compliance infrastructure are already at work today.

Regulatory agencies such as the US Food and Drug Administration (FDA) have revised 20th century regulations, leaving companies relying on old paradigms to adapt, or see approvals for their new medicines delayed or denied. Virtual companies and independent contractors are driving traditional biopharmaceutical and device firms to transform their supplier qualification and oversight programs or face regulatory enforcement actions and cost overruns. And the exponential expansion of scientific knowledge, technological capability, and engineering expertise has caught many medicinal product development programs and compliance systems off-guard, leaving them to struggle with new requirements, costs, and risks.

These trends suggest that rapid and constant change in new medicinal product development and regulatory compliance is already occurring, and it is growing at a faster and faster pace. Executives will have to make important decisions, not in a matter of decades, but in the months ahead. These changes will continue to take place whether we are ready for them or not.

NOSTALGIA IN THE MIX

New methodologies and tactics inevitably invite criticism from those who have benefited from and attained great success with traditional methodologies. 21st century tactics and strategies are as-yet ill-formed and incomplete in comparison to those of the 20th century. Yet, new knowledge, changing regulatory rules, emerging expectations, and globalization are bringing surprises, challenges, and opportunities that escape last century's either-or dichotomy of compliant versus non-compliant. Compliance is not an absolute.

Retaining last century's regulatory understanding weakens the ability of firms to develop personalized medicines. The FDA, the European Medicines Agency, and other members of the International Conference on Harmonization (ICH) and the Global Harmonization Task Force (GHTF) are shifting the landscape to accommodate the new dynamics of the 21st century.

PERSONALIZED PATHWAY

Executives have to adapt to regulatory changes that include harmonization, records control, and reimbursement considerations. My attempts to integrate discussions of these regulatory changes and their impact on new medicinal product development in a single book have undoubtedly raised many questions about personalized medicine manufacturing, postmarket approval monitoring, and finished product improvements.

It is clear that the traditional pathway to develop a new medicine contains many potential pitfalls for a personalized medicine. Tactics such as quality by design and process analytical technology will need to become mainstays within the next few decades for firms to have any hope of improving time-to-market and avoiding a never-ending cycle of adding more and more nonclinical studies and clinical trial arms to accommodate the constant increase of relevant scientific knowledge. Pre-marketplace approval submission meetings are not the time to learn that the FDA wants more clinical trials conducted using biomarkers which were validated only a few months beforehand. Executives need a means to incorporate such new knowledge during product development, not as a result of end-of-Phase III clinical trial meetings with the FDA. Adopting voice of the customer, clinical regulatory integrated strategic plans, bookshelving, risk-based decision making, compliance intelligence programs, and all the other tactics I have suggested is how executives can stay ahead of the marketplace and the regulators.

A SOLID FOUNDATION

Before setting out to take action on the strategies and tactics covered in this book, let us briefly look back at the essence of each section.

First, I laid the foundation for the ideas in this book by discussing fundamental changes in the regulatory and new medicinal product development landscapes: reimbursement and efficacy considerations, international harmonization, records integrity, and scientific and engineering convergence. Medicinal efficacy is increasingly being tied to reimbursement; the greater the efficacy, the greater the reimbursement. Medical science is subordinate to monetary value; we have reached a technological level wherein we can extend life indefinitely but only a few can afford to pay the cost associated with the convergence of today's technological and scientific innovation. Regulatory harmonization will continue to grow as governments are forced to evaluate medicines developed, manufactured, and distributed across the global marketplace. And the only common means to ensure compliance with regulations, guidelines, and safety, efficacy, and quality expectations is evaluating the integrity of a firm's records.

Second, I covered the five ways in which compliance infrastructures left over from the 20th century hinder the ability of firms to bring new medicines to market and to stay compliant: all-or-nothing compliance mentalities, risk aversion, operational silos, cost inefficiencies, and customer exclusions. Cost inefficiencies occur as standard operating procedures (SOPs) are written and revised with more and more detail. Customers are inadvertently excluded by a pre-occupation with avoiding any hint of marketing an unapproved medicine and through an all-or-nothing mentality that sees product development through the lens of applicable regulations rather than as stages of product knowledge. Operational silos result from over-specialization and poor cross-functional coordination and communication amongst compliance groups. And when risk management is interpreted by an all-or-nothing mentality to become risk elimination, businesses are left to struggle with compliance infrastructures that value risk avoidance above innovation and creativity.

Third, I reviewed a number of the larger landscape trends with which companies must contend: the pre-informed patient, increasing executive liability, the drive for cost containment, and exponential scientific and engineering knowledge growth. In an industry that currently takes 7-13 years to bring a new medicine to market, there is a significant business risk for firms unable to rapidly adapt to the potentially disruptive impacts of nanotechnology, stem cells, diagnostic and drug convergence, and other innovations. Shareholders, investors, and patients increasingly see compliance a key strategic component, and hold executives liable for failing to disclose risks to new medicinal product approval due to noncompliance. Generics, low-cost overseas competitors, and cost-sharing as a condition of regulatory approval are driving cost-containment in the development of new medicines and regulatory compliance operations. And pre-informed patients can either help personalize a new medicine or reduce its chances for marketplace success.

Fourth, I laid out each of the new product development tactics that will help firms bring safe, efficacious, more personalized medicines to market in the 21st century: voice of the customer, quality by design, open innovation collaborations, and caring for nascent intellectual property. Executives can make smart use of pre-informed patients by soliciting and incorporating voice of the customer insights from the preclinical stage through post-market monitoring; this in turn will make new medicines more personalized. Quality by design can help lower costs and speed time to market, especially by incorporation of ideas such as bookshelving, process analytical technology, and design space. Open innovation collaborations can help companies rapidly adapt to new technologies and new scientific innovations without compromising compliance or new medicinal safety or efficacy. And compliance teams can incorporate intellectual property protection considerations into basic activities such as supplier due diligence and quality audits.

Fifth, I explained the many compliance tactics and overall strategies involved in supporting more personalized medicinal development by offering suggestions for some of the major players in a 21st century modern compliance infrastructure: the quality, regulatory affairs, and records management departments. Quality departments will need to adopt process mapping, behavioral training, risk-based decision-making, and continuous improvement components in order to ensure quality systems balance flexibility, cost-efficiency, and compliance. Regulatory affairs groups will need to increasingly coordinate with their compliance counterparts through roadmapping, compliance radar initiatives, post-market monitoring and reporting, and structuring a modern compliance organization that strives for self-enforcing rules and behaviors. And records management is crucial for establishing and maintaining long-term records integrity, from initial preclinical studies through regulatory submissions and post-market monitoring reviews.

FINDING THE RIGHT BALANCE

I have tried to identify an overall strategy for executives to not only meet the demands of 21st century compliance and personalized medicinal product development, but also to ultimately succeed. The 21st century new personalized medicine development funnel intimately relies upon compliance and quality systems that balance rules with room for creativity and innovation. Thus Foucault's panopticon and a cynical reliance upon self-interest may be the foundations upon which we will achieve the right balance.

I have looked at how quality by design, process analytical technology, and design space offer some of the answers but are, by themselves, lacking. Quality by design is incomplete because it does not incorporate voice of the customer aspects such as the pre-informed patient, the realities of reimbursement, or the concerns of primary caregivers; process analytical technology is incomplete because it is too easily mistaken for process improvement through automation and thus misses the mark on implementing real-time quality control to minimize costs and maximize product quality; and design space is incomplete because without pre-defined product characteristics and pre-defined process control ranges, it is only applicable to pilot plant production and thus cannot provide the regulatory flexibility firms need for personalized medicines.

To resolve this incompleteness I have added other successful new product development tactics—open innovation, bookshelving, stage gates, scale-up, and scale-downs—to enable companies to develop medicines more quickly, to adapt faster to global competition and technology evolution, and, perhaps more importantly, to make best use of their money, time, and personnel.

FRAGILITY OF COMPLIANCE

Even the shrewdest strategy can be blunted or made irrelevant if it fails to take into account the greater marketplace and regulatory landscape. Companies and regulatory agencies will continue to prioritize their own perceived self-interests. Because these self-interests change with time, any state of compliance is temporary. The policies and mindsets of last century's compliance infrastructures overemphasized process adherence, rather than process results. Process adherence is, of course, important. But a process without agility—without a focus on its end result—is reactive. Overemphasis on process adherence subordinates a person, an operational group, or a company to someone else's strategy and objectives, or simply to chance.

Processes, like the humans who devise them, are not perfect. Processes must therefore be flexible to avoid constant revision. Indeed, an ideal process will take into account not just potential future changes, but the possible rates of change. 21st century compliance requires a fragile balance of process adherence, flexibility, and forward-thinking strategies. Admittedly, this balance is easy to describe, but hard to carry out on a day-to-day basis. One solution I have suggested throughout this book is to focus compliance efforts on end results and desired behaviors.

COMPLIANCE AS A WAY OF CONDUCT

The modern quality system and 21st century regulatory affairs support a flexible, innovative, faster-paced business environment with process mapping, behavioral training, compliance radars, and a focus on end outputs (*e.g.*, records) rather than complete process compliance. My goal has been to remove any perception of compliance as an obstacle or strategic liability, and turn it into a strategic asset: a means by which a company achieves its objectives for new medicines brought to market that are safe, efficacious, and personalized.

Compliance executives can rely upon the tactics in this book to help them manage collaborations with independent contractors, universities, startups, and virtual suppliers around the world. Those executives able to adapt the tactics in this book will get safe, efficacious, quality, personalized medicines on the market faster, easier, and for less cost and with less developmental risk than their competitors.

FASTER, EASIER, FOR LESS

A company whose compliance infrastructure is flexible and internalized in day-to-day activities is one that is more innovative, adaptive, and efficient. It is a company whose executives will be able to take calculated risks faster and with more confidence than their counterparts, and bring new medicines to market sooner. And it is in this context that compliance executives can serve another crucial role in the 21st century: preventing their companies from pursuing poor opportunities.

COMPLIANCE AS STABILITY

Long-time observers of corporations and the role they play in society have noted that the more innovative, adaptive, efficient, and flexible an organization becomes, the more it risks becoming overconfident, leading to impetuous and poor decisions.[222] By insisting on tactics such as product concept summaries, stage gates, and clinical regulatory integrated strategic plans (CRISPs), compliance executives can give their companies stability and structured moments of pause to prevent the pursuit of poor options. By encouraging adoption of voice of the customer, bookshelving, and quality by design, compliance executives can help their company accept fast, early failures to identify clear candidates with the best chance of success in which to invest further development efforts.

PUTTING A PLAN INTO ACTION

Success in putting compliance to work as a competitive edge requires planning. In this book's introduction, I offered a challenge to map out your own timeline and plan to adapt as many of the strategies and suggestions as possible. Now, having read through this book, it is clear how much work it will take to transition from last century's compliance and product development model to 21st century frameworks. Whether firms undertake this work themselves, outsource it, or choose a path somewhere in between, executives will still be required to provide regulatory input and make decisions. Losing momentum trying to put into practice every tactic and strategy is a real risk. The key is to work out a plan that is right for you and your organization. Consider the following steps to start adapting compliance as a competitive edge in your organization:

1. Use the checklists at the end of each chapter, along with the links in appendix two and the book's website (http://www.Get2MarketNow.com) to systematically obtain the various resources I have suggested.
2. Review these resources. You may want to assign staff members or coordinate with colleagues to reduce the

burden for each person.

3. Highlight key points in these resources that you think are most applicable for your organization and/or the new medicines under development. Take notes on the specific tactics you like and those you do not. Remember that not everything I have discussed is going to be a perfect fit for your organization.

4. List two end goals: what you hope to accomplish for yourself, and what you hope to accomplish for your organization. Perhaps improving compliance agility is the most important objective for your organization, while you would like to personally be able to strengthen your comfort-level making risk-based decisions to get away from an all-or-nothing compliance mindset.

5. Select the tactics that will best achieve these two goals. For organization agility, process mapping and staying silent in SOPs might be appropriate tactics. To improve your comfort level making risk-based decisions, consider adding a preliminary risk evaluation to half a dozen SOPs such as complaint handling or corrective and preventative actions. Concentrate on processes with forms easily adapted to add a line or two for documenting the results of preliminary risk analysis.

6. Set up a project calendar. Identify when you would like to have each tactic selected above actually implemented. Make sure each target date has some buffer to build flexibility into your plan. Work backward from the selected dates to identify the necessary lead time so you can prepare and coordinate necessary tasks such as drafting SOPs, updating forms, holding review sessions, and so on.

7. Implement the items at the times designated on your project calendar. Try to plan ahead to stagger revisions, new meetings, and other changes that demand attention so they do not delay your deadlines.

8. Measure performance. Monitor how well each tactic is serving to accomplish the goals you have chosen. If you have adopted process mapping for SOPs, assess if process nonconformances have increased or decreased; assess if

product quality has been affected. On the basis of your review, you may decide successes merit selecting two new goals and implementing more of the tactics in this book.

LEARNING FROM MISTAKES

When adopting any plan, expect to make mistakes. Additionally, every tactic in this book may not fit your environment. Here are a few final tips:

- Talk to your colleagues. What tactics would they like to see adopted into your organization first? Which of the tactics in this book would increase your organization's agility or lower your costs?
- Get expert help. Although I have tried to explain these tactics and provide enough supporting resources that you should be able to accomplish everything yourself, organizations have their own sets of quirks, complexities, and day-to-day realities that will make adopting some of the ideas in this book difficult without independent help.
- Find like-minded executives. Implementation of the tactics and strategies in this book will require more than a month or two. Sustaining long-term implementation projects can be a struggle and building an informal support network to help keep you motivated can be crucial.
- Continue to research and adapt. Use the Internet to locate more resources and more ideas. The more examples and insights you can find and share, the greater your chances of swaying skeptics and cynics.

FINAL THOUGHTS

Transitioning from the traditional 20th century model is not going to be easy. Executives will need to make choices that are far more difficult in the context of daily realities and workplace emotions than the ones I have portrayed in these pages. Progress in the 21st century era of personalized medicines will bring with it a host of challenges for executives, shareholders, customers, and patients. How debilitating these challenges are will depend upon how we meet them.

Executives who work on any of the tactics and strategies in this book will see improvement in their firm's compliance and research and development programs. Those who work a little on all of these tactics and strategies will see even more improvements in compliance and R&D productivity. Executives who master all of these strategies and tactics will consistently bring new, safe, efficacious, more personalized medicines to market and generate steady, predictable profits.

My hope is that you will take the tactics, tips, and templates from this book and its website and use them to develop the potential of the 21st century into your success.

Are you ready?

Appendix One: List of Acronyms

Although each of these is defined at least once within the text, readers may find it helpful to have all the main acronyms used in the book in one location.

CBER – Center for Biologics Evaluation and Research (at FDA)
CDER – Center for Drug Evaluation and Research (at FDA)
CDRH – Center for Devices and Radiological Health (at FDA)
CFR – Code of Federal Regulations
CHMP - Committee for Medicinal Products for Human Use (at EMA)
CMS – Centers for Medicare and Medicaid Services
CPP – critical process parameter
CQA – critical quality attribute
EMA – European Medicines Agency
EPA – Environmental Protection Agency
EU – European Union
FDA – Food and Drug Administration
FDAAA – Food and Drug Administration Amendments Act (of 2007)
FMEA – failure modes and effects analysis
GHTF – Global Harmonization Task Force
HACCP – hazards analysis and critical control points
HIPAA – Health Insurance Portability and Accountability Act
ICH – International Conference on Harmonization
ISO – International Standards Organization
NICE – National Institute for Clinical Excellence
NIH – National Institutes of Health
NPD – new product development
OIG – Office of the Inspectors General
PAT – process analytical technology

QbD – quality by design
REMS – risk evaluation and mitigation strategy
SOP – standard operating procedure
UK – United Kingdom
US – United States
VoC – voice of the customer
WI – work instruction

Appendix Two: Further Resources

The resources I have listed are some of the ones that over the years I have found most helpful in providing tools, insights, and advice. For more resources, see the source notes and bibliography. Each resource below is listed in a grouping relevant to primary topic area. Website links are active as of the printing date, but check the book's website for more current information as necessary.

COMPLIANCE ORGANIZATIONS AND STRUCTURE

HHS Office of Inspector General Corporate Integrity Agreements http://oig.hhs.gov/fraud/cias.asp

HHS Office of Inspector General's *Compliance Program Guidance for Pharmaceutical Manufacturers* http://oig.hhs.gov/fraud/docs/compliance guidance/042803pharmacymfgnonfr.pdf

COMPLIANCE RADAR / REGULATORY INTELLIGENCE

GMP Newsletter, PO Box 10 21 68, 69011 Heidelberg, Germany; http://www.gmp-compliance.org/eca_newsletterabo.html

SmarterCompliance newsletter, PO Box 498, Williamsburg, VA 23187-0498 USA; http://www.ceruleanllc.com/Newsletter/

CORPORATE ESPIONAGE

Patent Baristas blog http://www.patentbaristas.com

Securing Innovation blog http://www.securinginnovation.com

Spies Among Us by Ira Winkler. Wiley Publishing (2005).

CROSS-FUNCTIONAL ORGANIZATIONAL IMPROVEMENT

The Fiefdom Syndrome by Robert Herbold. Currency Doubleday (2005).

Sun Tzu for Execution by Steven Michaelson. Adams Media (2007).

FOUCAULT'S PANOPTICON

13 Things: Internalized Authority and the Prison of the Mind: Bentham and Foucault's Panopticon http://proteus.brown.edu/13things/7121 (includes two photographs of panoptic prisons from the inside)

"Foucault and Panopticism Revisited" edited by David Wood, in *Surveillance & Society* journal (2003); http://www.surveillance-and-society.org/journalv1i3.htm

"Post-Panopticism" by R. Boyne in *Economy and Society* (2000).

Theorizing Surveillance: The Panopticon and Beyond edited by David Lyon. Willan Publishing (2006).

NANOMEDICINE

NIH nanomedicine website http://www.nihroadmap.nih.gov/nanomedicine/index.asp

NEW PRODUCT DEVELOPMENT

Design for Six Sigma by Greg Brue and Robert Launsby. McGraw-Hill (2003).

ISO 16982: Ergonomics of Human-System Interaction – Usability Methods Supporting Human-Centered Design http://www.iso.org/iso/iso_catalogue/catalogue_tc/catalogue_detail.htm?csnumber=31176

The Medical Device R&D Handbook by Theodore Kucklick. Taylor & Francis Group (2006).

Winning at New Products: Accelerating the Process from Idea to Launch, 3rd Edition, by Robert Cooper. Perseus Publishing (2001).

OPEN INNOVATION AND BOOKSHELVING

Collaborative Drug Discovery http://www.collaborativedrug.com

CoDev and Open Innovation Community blog http://openinnovation.ning.com

InnoCentive's Open Innovation Marketplace https://gw.innocentive.com/ar/challenge/marketPlace

NCI Developmental Therapeutics program http://dtp.nci.nih.gov/index.html

Open Source Drug Discovery http://www.osdd.net

PRE-INFORMED PATIENT

2009 Pew Internet & American Life Project report http://www.pewinternet.org/Reports/2009/Generations-Online-in-2009.aspx

Drug Recall http://www.adrugrecall.com

DrugWatch http://www.drugwatch.com

RateADrug http://www.rateadrug.com

WebMD http://www.webmd.com

PROFESSIONAL ORGANIZATIONS

ARMA International, 11880 College Boulevard, Suite 450, Overland Park, KS 66210 USA; http://www.arma.org

Drug Information Association (DIA), 800 Enterprise Road, Suite 200, Horsham, PA 19044-3595 USA; http://www.diahome.org

Ethics & Compliance Officer Association (ECOA), 411 Waverley Oaks Road, Suite 324, Waltham, MA 02452 USA; http://www.theecoa.org

Food and Drug Law Institute (FDLI), 1155 15th Street NW, Suite 800, Washington, D.C., 20005 USA; http://www.fdli.org

Health Care compliance Association (HCCA), 6500 Barrie Road, Suite 250, Minneapolis, MN 55435 USA; http://www.hcca-info.org

Institute of Internal Auditors (IIA), 247 Maitland Avenue, Altamonte Springs, FL 32701-4201 USA; http://www.theiia.org

International Association of Risk and Compliance Professionals (IARCP), 1220 N. Market Street, Suite 804, Wilmington, DE 19801 USA; http://www.risk-compliance-association.com

International Society for Pharmaceutical Engineering (ISPE), 3109 W. Dr. Martin Luther King, Jr. Boulevard, Suite 250, Tampa, FL 33607-6240 USA; http://www.ispe.org

Management Roundtable, 92 Crescent Street, Waltham, MA 02453 USA; http://www.roundtable.com

Parenteral Drug Association (PDA), 4350 East West Highway, Suite 150, Bethesda, MD 20814 USA; http://www.pda.org

Pharmaceutical Compliance Forum, 100 N. 20th Street, 4th Floor, Philadelphia, PA 19103 USA; http://www.pharmacomplianceforum.org

Pharmaceutical Quality Group, 12 Grosvenor Crescent, London SW1X 7EE, UK; http://www.pqg.org

Product Development and Management Association, 15000 Commerce Parkway, Suite C, Mount Laurel, NJ 08054 USA; http://www.pdma.org

Regulatory Affairs Professionals (RAPS), 5635 Fishers Lane, Suite 550, Rockville, MD 20852 USA; http://www.raps.org

Regulatory Compliance Association (RCA), 909 Third Avenue, New York, NY 10022 USA; http://www.rcaonline.org

Society for Clinical Data Management (SCDM), 555 E. Wells Street, Suite 1100, Milwaukee, WI 53202 USA; http://www.scdm.org

Society of Corporate Compliance and Ethics (SCCE), 6500 Barrie Road, Suite 250, Minneapolis, MN 55435 USA; http://www.corporatecompliance.org

Society of Quality Assurance (SQA), 154 Hansen Road, Suite 201, Charlottesville, VA 22911 USA; http://www.sqa.org

The Organization for Professionals in Regulatory Affairs (TOPRA), Bellerive House, 3 Muirfield Crescent, London E14 9SZ, UK; http://www.topra.org

QUALITY BY DESIGN

Pharmaceutical Development Q8(R2), ICH; http://www.ich.org/cache/compo/276-254-1.html

RECORDS MANAGEMENT

Records and Information Management: Fundamentals of Professional Practice by William Saffady. ARMA International (2004).
Winning Strategies for Successful Records Management Programs by Mark Langemo. Information Requirements Clearinghouse (2002).

REGULATORY ORGANIZATIONS

Centers for Medicare and Medicaid Services (CMS): http://www.cms.hhs.gov
European Medicines Agency: http://www.ema.europa.eu
Food and Drug Administration (FDA): http://www.fda.gov
Global Harmonization Task Force (GHTF) http://www.ghtf.org
Health Canada: http://www.hc-sc.gc.ca
International Conference on Harmonization (ICH) http://www.ich.org
Medicines and Healthcare products Regulatory Agency (MHRA): http://mhra.gov.uk
National Institute for Clinical Excellence (NICE): http://www.nice.org.uk
Pharmaceutical Inspection Co-operation Scheme (PIC/S): http://www.pic-scheme.org
World Health Organization: http://www.who.int/en/

RISK MANAGEMENT

Hazard Analysis and Critical Control Point Principles and Application Guidelines, FDA (August 1997); http://www.fda.gov/Food/FoodSafety/HazardAnalysisCriticalControlPointsHACCP/ucm114868.htm
ISO 14971: Medical Devices – Application of Risk Management to Medical Devices (2000).

SOPS AND POLICIES

Achieving 100% Compliance of Policies and Procedures by Stephen Page. Process Improvement Publishing (2000).
Seven Steps to Better Written Policies and Procedures by Stephen Page. Process Improvement Publishing (2004).
Writing to Learn by William Zinsser. Harper & Row, Publishers, Inc. (1988).

TRAINING

Training for Dummies by Elaine Beich. Wiley Publishing, Inc. (2005)

VOICE OF THE CUSTOMER

Acquiring, Processing, and Deploying Voice of the Customer by M. Larry Shillito. CRC Press (2001)

Voice of the Customer: Capture and Analysis by Kai Yang. McGraw-Hill (2008).

WEBSITES FOR COMPLIANCE EXECUTIVES

Biotech Blog: http://www.biotechblog.com

Cerulean Associates: http://www.Ceruleanllc.com

ComplianceHome: http://www.compliancehome.com/topics/FDA/

ComplianceOnline: http://www.complianceoneline.com

ComplianceZen: http://www.ComplianceZen.com

Data Quality Research Institute (DQRI): http://www.dqri.org

European Compliance Academy: http://www.gmp-compliance.org/eca_index.html

Eye on FDA blog: http://www.eyeonfda.com

Glossary of Common Clinical Trial Terms (at Weill Cornell Medical College): http://www.med.cornell.edu/icr/resources_and_services/glossary.html

Institute of Validation Technology: http://www.ivthome.com

Pharmacy and Pharmaceutical Information on the Internet: http://www.pharmweb.net

WEBSITES FOR NEW PRODUCT DEVELOPMENT EXECUTIVES

Bad Designs: http://www.baddesigns.com/examples.html

Innovation Tools: http://www.innovationtools.com

Institute for the Future: http://www.iftf.org

Personalized Health Care: http://www.hhs.gov/myhealthcare

World Future Society: http://wfs.org

Yet2.com: http://www.yet2.com

Source Notes

INTRODUCTION

1. DiMasi, Joseph, Ronald Hansen, Henry Grabowski (2003) "The Price of Innovation: New Estimates of Drug Development Costs," *Journal of Health Economics*, vol. 22, p. 151-185.
2. *FiercePharma* (2009), "J&J Researchers on the Future of Personalized Medicine," 11 June.
3. *Wall Street Journal* (2009), "FDA Approves a Novel Novartis Drug," 19 June.
4. *Wall Street Journal* (2009), "New Recruits: Enlisting Genes in the Campaign Against Cancer," 29 May.
5. *FiercePharma* (2009), "Sanofi CEO: Think Small in Big Pharma," 19 June.
6. *Journal of Life Sciences* (2009), "The Next Big Thing," 21 May.
7. Anders, Donald (2004) "Attention ABLS…Are You Undervaluing Your Borrower's Greatest Assests?" *ABF Journal*, July/August, vol. 2, no. 7.
8. Bielski, Michael and Christine Ford (2007) "Combination Products and Intellectual Property Strategy: What Drug Companies and Device Makers Should Know", *Regulatory Affairs Focus*, July, pp. 40-42.
9. Emanual, Ezekial (2002) "Session 2: Regulation 6: Institutional Review Boards (IRBs)," President's Council on Bioethics, 12 September 2002, http://bioethics.gov/transcripts/sep02/session2.html and Nancylynn-GA (2004) "Google Answers," 17 July, http://answers.google.com/answers/threadview/id/374774.html accessed on 17 November 2009.
10. Avellanet, John (2008) "Want a Good Partnership? Know How to Ruin One First," *BioProcess International*, November (Supplement), pp. 44-47.

CHAPTER 1

11. FDA (2002), *Concept Paper, Pharmaceutical cGMPs for the 21st Century: A Risk-Based Approach*, August.
12. FDA (2003), *Pharmaceutical cGMPs for the 21st Century – A Risk-*

Based Approach: Second Progress Report and Implementation Plan, August, http://www.fda.gov/Drugs/DevelopmentApprovalProcess/ Manufacturing/QuestionsandAnswersonCurrentGoodManufacturing PracticescGMPforDrugs/UCM071836, accessed 22 September 2009.

13. FDA (1995), *Medical Device Premarket Approval Inspection Process,* 7383.001, p. 3.

14. Author conversations with Helen Winkle in November 2007 and Thom Savage in July 2008.

15. FDA (2004), *Innovation or Stagnation: Challenge and Opportunity on the Critical Path to New Medical Products,* March,: http://www. fda.gov/ScienceResearch/SpecialTopics/CriticalPathInitiative/ CriticalPathOpportunitiesReports/ucm077262.htm, accessed 4 August 2009.

16. FDA (2004), *Pharmaceutical cGMPs for the 21ˢᵗ Century – A Risk-Based Approach,* September, http://www.fda.gov/Drugs/Development ApprovalProcess/Manufacturing/QuestionsandAnswersonCurrentGood ManufacturingPracticescGMPforDrugs/ucm137175.htm, accessed 4 August 2009.

17. Trautman, Kimberly (2007), *Regulatory Perspective on quality management Systems in the Medical Device Industry – Lessons Learned.* Speech to the Joint PDA/FDA Conference on Modern Quality Systems, 1 November.

18. Trautman, Kimberly (2007), *Regulatory Perspective on quality management Systems in the Medical Device Industry – Lessons Learned.* Speech to the Joint PDA/FDA Conference on Modern Quality Systems, 1 November.

19. Warning Letter 320-08-01 (2008), 21 April, http://www.fda.gov/ICECI/ EnforcementActions/WarningLetters/2008/ucm1048332.htm, accessed 4 August 2009.

20. Welch, Jan (2009) *Recent Developments in the International Compliance Landscape: From a US FDA Perspective.* 11 February.

21. This is an illustrative example only; NICE actually has a much more complicated scoring algorithm named "QALY" which calculates quality of life improvements, average price per day of improved quality of life due the new medicine, and so on.

22. Goldstein, Jacob (2009) "The Next Step in Cancer Drugs: Who Should NOT Get Them" *Wall Street Journal Health Blog,* 14 January, http://blogs. wsj.com/health/2009/01/14/the-next-step-in-cancer-drugs-who-should-not-get-them/, accessed 4 August 2009.

23. Bowers, Brent (2009) "Investors Pay Business Plans Little Heed, Study Finds." *New York Times,* 14 May.

24. Burns, Lawton Robert (2008) <u>The Business of Healthcare Innovation</u>. Cambridge, UK: Cambridge University Press, p. 130.

25. Pisano, Gary P. (2006) <u>Science Business</u>. Boston, Massachusetts: Harvard University Press, p. 155.
26. Kelland, Kate (2009) "Interview – UK Watchdog Offers Health Rationing Tips to World" Reuters, 9 October.
27. FDA (2008) *Integrated Summary of Effectiveness*, August, http://www. fda.gov/downloads/Drugs/GuidanceComplianceRegulatoryInformation/ Guidances/ucm079803.pdf, accessed 4 August 2009.
28. Rogers, Michael C. (2008) *Inspections/Investigations – the ORA Perspective*. Speech at the Joint FDA/FDLI Enforcement and Litigation Conference, 19 February.
29. Avellanet, John (2008), *Securing Intellectual Property from the Inside Out.*, in Friedman, Yali (ed.) <u>Best Practices in Biotechnology Business Practices</u>. Washington, D.C.: Logos Press, p. 37.
30. Piche, Greg (2008) *Pfizer's "Double Blind" Bextra Bind – The Value of Clinical Data*, 30 December, Healthcare Law Blog, http://www.holland-harthealthcare.com/healthcare/2008/12/pfizers-double-blind-bextra-bind-the-value-of-clinical-data.html, accessed 14 August 2009.
31. Autor, Deborah (2007) *How to Avoid Warning Letters and Other Troubles with the FDA*. Speech at the Joint FDA/FDLI Enforcement & Litigation Conference, 6 February.
32. Rivera-Martinez, Edwin (2008) *Inspections/Investigations, the CDER Perspective*. Speech at the Joint FDA/FDLI Enforcement and Litigation Conference, 19 February.
33. FDA (2009) Warning Letter to Lupin Limited, http://www.fda.gov/ ICECI/EnforcementActions/WarningLetters/ucm162745.htm, accessed on 22 September 2009.
34. FDA (2009) Warning Letter to Arkray Factory, http://www.fda.gov/ ICECI/EnforcementActions/WarningLetters/ucm172497.htm, accessed on 22 September 2009.
35. Reuters (2009) KV Pharma: FDA Accepts Plan to Resolve Manufacturing Issue, 2 September.
36. Richmond, Frances J and Nancy Singer (2007) *Hiring and Training Needs in the Medical Products Industry: Focus on Regulatory, Quality and Clinical Professions*, Los Angeles, California: School of Pharmacy, University of Southern California.
37. Ibid.
38. Silverman, Ed (2008) "Fleeing the FDA for Industry and Retirement," 3 June, *Pharmalot Blog*, http://www.pharmalot.com/2008/06/fleeing-the-fda-for-industry-and-retirement/, accessed on 14 August 2009.

CHAPTER 2

39. PhRMA, *Drug Discovery and Development*, Pharmaceutical Research and Manufacturers of America, Washington, D.C., March 2007.
40. Grabowski, H., J. Vernon and J. DiMasi, "Returns on research and Development for 1990s New Drug Introductions," *Pharmacoeconomics* 20 (December 2002): suppl. 3, pp. 11-29.
41. Pisano, Gary P. (2006) Science Business. Boston, Massachusetts: Harvard University Press, p. 25.
42. Ibid, pp. 29-30.
43. Author conversation with Dr. Cherney, May 2007.
44. Pisano, p. 46.
45. Pisano, p. 56.
46. Burns, Lawton Robert (2008) The Business of Healthcare Innovation. Cambridge, UK: Cambridge University Press, p. 56.
47. Burns, p. 17.
48. Sherma, Debra (2009) "Abbot, Pfizer in Pact for Lung Cancer Screening." Reuters, 27 August.
49. Friedman, Yali, editor (2008) Best Practices in Biotechnology Business Development. Washington, D.C.: Logos Press.
50. Pisano, p. 104.
51. Avellanet, John (2009), "Trend Watch: CRO Industry to Double." *SmarterCompliance*, volume 3, issue 4, April, p. 4.
52. Rydzewski, Robert M. (2008) Real World Drug Discovery. Oxford, United Kingdom: Elsevier Ltd, p. 148.
53. Pisano, p. 50.
54. Ibid, p. 99.
55. Winslow, Ron (2009) "Roche Drug Shrinks Tumors in Study," *Wall Street Journal*, 3 September.
56. Rydzewski, p.148.
57. Pisano, pp. 51.
58. Rydzewski, p. 148.
59. Government Accountability Office (2006) *New Drug Development: Science, Business, Regulatory, and Intellectual Property Issues Cited as Hampering Drug Development Efforts*, November, p. 25.
60. Emanual, Ezekial (2002) "Session 2: Regulation 6: Institutional Review Boards (IRBs)," President's Council on Bioethics, 12 September 2002, http://bioethics.gov/transcripts/sep02/session2.html and Nancylynn-GA (2004) "Google Answers," 17 July, http://answers.google.com/answers/threadview/id/374774.html accessed on 17 November 2009.
61. Steenhuysen, Julie (2009) "Risks to Personalized Medicine Seen In U.S. Reform," *Reuters India*, 27 October.
62. FDA (2009), *Guidance for Industry: Postmarketing Studies and Clinical*

Trials – *Implementation of Section 505(o) of the Federal Food, Drug, and Cosmetic Act*, July.

63. In 2009, Health Canada has also revised its GMPs to adhere more closely to those expectations laid down in the ICH for risk-based quality systems.

64. Cherney, Barry (2007) *Quality Product Attributes and Linkages*. Speech at the PDA Workshop Quality by Design for Biopharmaceuticals: Concepts and Implementation, 22 May.

65. FDA (2008), *Guidance for Industry: CGMP for Phase 1 Investigational Drugs*, July.

CHAPTER 3

66. Dr. Barry Rothman quoted in "FDA Officials on Supplier Control," (2009) *SmarterCompliance*™ newsletter, volume 3, issue 10, page 6.

67. FDA (2006) *Guidance for Clinical Trial Sponsors: Establishment and Operation of Clinical Trial Data Monitoring Committees*, March, page 17.

68. *FiercePharma* (2009) "FDA Experts Reject King's Imaging Drug," 29 July, http://www.fiercebiotech.com/story/fda-experts-reject-kings-imaging-drug/2009-07-29 accessed on 29 July.

69. Rivera-Martinez, Edwin (2008) *Inspections/Investigations, the CDER Perspective*. Speech at the Joint FDA/FDLI Enforcement and Litigation Conference, 19 February.

70. Welch, Jan (2009) *Recent Developments in the International Compliance Landscape: From a US FDA Perspective*. 11 February.

71. Rockoff, Jonathan and Julia Mengewein (2009) "J&J in Setback Over Antibiotic," *Wall Street Journal*, 31 December, http://online.wsj.com/article/SB10001424052748704152804574627523625941690.html accessed on 2 January 2010.

72. Avellanet, John (2009), *Seminar: How to Improve Data Quality & Record Integrity in Your NDA, 510(k) or BLA*. 15 July.

73. FDA (2008) *Guidance for Industry: CGMP for Phase 1 Investigational Drugs*, July.

74. Herbold, Robert J. (2004). <u>The Fiefdom Syndrome: The Turf Battles that Undermine Careers and Companies – and How to Overcome Them</u>. New York: Currency and Doubleday, pages 4-5.

75. Avellanet, John (2009) *Avoid 483 Observations with a Document Control System to Actually Control Your Documents*, Teleconference for FOI Services, March.

76. Ibid.

77. Welch, Jan (2009) *Recent Developments in the International Compliance Landscape: From a US FDA Perspective*. 11 February.

78. Autor, Deborah(2008) *CDER Compliance: 2007-2008 and Beyond*. Speech

at the Joint FDA/FDLI Enforcement and Litigation Conference, 19 February.

79. Berthiaume, Marc (2008) "The Importance of Backing Up Computer Files: Some Interesting Facts," *The Independent*, September/October.

80. Scheier, Robert (2007) "Disk Drive Failures 15 Times What Vendors Say, Study Says," *ComputerWorld*, 2 March.

81. Fisk, Margaret Cronin, Elizabeth Lopatto, Jef Feely (2009) "Lilly Sold Drug for Dementia Knowing It Didn't Help, Files Show," *Bloomberg*, 12 June.

82. Feeley, Jef and Margaret Cronin Fisk (2009), "Glaxo Executive's Memo Suggested Burying Drug Studies," *Bloomberg*, 15 September.

83. Trautman, Kimberly (2007), *Regulatory Perspective on Quality Management Systems in the Medical Device Industry – Lessons Learned.* Speech to the Joint PDA/FDA Conference on Modern Quality Systems, 1 November.

CHAPTER 4

84. McIlroy, Anne (2009) "Canadian Hospital Pioneers Mental-Health Treatment," *The Globe and Mail*, 7 July.

85. McIlroy, Anne (2009) "Canadian Hospital Pioneers Mental-Health Treatment," *The Globe and Mail*, 7 July.

86. Zoroya, Gregg (2009) "Findings May Speed Troops' Recovery," *USA Today*, 20 August, p. 5A.

87. Defree, Suzanne (2009) "Implantable Sensor Device Claims to Offer Continuous Cancer Monitoring," *EDN*, 14 May, http://www.edn.com/index.asp?layout=articlePrint&articleID=CA6658480, accessed on 15 May 2009.

88. Burrill, Steve (2009) "Predicting Alzheimer's," *The Journal of Life Sciences*, 15 May, http://www.burrillreport.com/printer_article-1393.html accessed on 18 May 2009.

89. *FierceBiotechIT* (2009) "App Predicts Drug Interactions," 19 September, http://www.fiercebiotechit.com/story/app-predicts-drug-interactions/2009-09-19 accessed on 21 September 2009.

90. Plotkin, Robert (2009) "The Automation of Invention," *The Futurist*, July-August, page 23.

91. *FierceHealthIT* (2009) "IBM, UNC Partner on Data Warehouse for Clinical Research," 1 June, http://www.fiercehealthit.com/story/ibm-u-north-carolina-partner-data-warehouse-clinical-research/2009-06-01 accessed on 8 June 2009.

92. Abramo, Peter and Edmondson, Michael (2008). BioStory: Assessing a Biomedical Product as a Business Opportunity. MEAPA, LLC, pages 126-131.

93. Lee, Thomas (2009) "A Promising Niche for Nanotech," *Star Tribune*, 21 June http://www.startribune.com/business/48643722.html accessed on 22 June 2009.

94. Steenhuysen, Julie (2009) "Nanotech Gene Therapy Kills Ovarian Cancer in Mice," *Reuters*, 30 July, http://news.yahoo.com/s/nm/20090730/sc_nm/us_cancer_nanotechnology.htm accessed on 3 August 2009.

95. Schimpff, Stephen (2007). The Future of Medicine: Megatrends in Healthcare That Will Improve Your Quality of Life. Nashville, Tennessee: Thomas Nelson, pages 112-113.

96. Hobson, David (2009) "Nanotech Safety, Part II: Gather Your Own Nanomaterials Safety Data to Drive Funding, Regulation," *Medical Device Daily Perspectives*, 24 June, vol. 3, no. 25.

97. *FierceBiotech* (2009) "BioHeart Stem Cell Treatment Achieves Positive Response," 18 September, http://www.fiercebiotech.com/story/bioheart-stem-cell-treatment-achieves-positive-response/2009-09-18 accessed on 18 September 2009.

98. Fraunhofer IGB (2009) "Producing Artificial Skin, Factory-Style," *The Futurist*, May-June, page 2.

99. Thompson, Erin (2009) "More are Searching the Web for Medical Advice," *USA Today*, 17 June, page 6D.

100. Ibid.

101. Harris, Gardiner (2009) "Drug Agency May Reveal More Data on Actions," *The New York Times*, 2 June, http://www.nytimes.com/2009/06/02/health/policy/02fda.html accessed on 3 June 2009.

102. Meier, Barry (2009) "House Bill Would Create Artificial Joints Registry," *The New York Times*, 11 June, http://www.nytimes.com/2009/06/11/business/11device.html accessed on 11 June 2009.

103. Chapman, Glenn (2009) "Pathway Genomics Launches Public DNA Testing," *Yahoo! News*, 15 July, http://news.yahoo.com/s/afp/20090715/ts_alt_afp/usitinternetgeneticshealthcompanypathway.html accessed on 16 July.

104. CNN Money Report, May 2007.

105. *FiercePharma* (2009) "Judge: CafePharma Posts Stay in Schering Case," 3 June, http://www.fiercepharma.com/story/judge-cafepharma-posts-stay-schering-case/2009-06-03-0.html accessed on 3 June 2009.

106. Avellanet, John (2009) "Investors Sue Over Sloppy QS," *SmarterCompliance* newsletter, vol. 3 issue 8, August, page 4.

107. Avellanet, John (2008) "Bioval Sued by Shareholders," *SmarterCompliance* newsletter, vol. 2 issue 10, October, page 5.

108. Pollack, Andrew (2009) "Former Drug Executive Convicted of Wire Fraud," *The New York Times*, 30 September, http://www.nytimes.com/2009/09/30/busines/30drug.html accessed on 30 September 2009.

109. Blumberg, Eric (2008) *Purdue Pharma Case*. Speech at the Joint FDA/

FDLI Enforcement and Litigation Conference, 19 February.

110. Rivera-Martinez, Edwin (2008) *Inspections/Investigations, the CDER Perspective.* Speech at the Joint FDA/FDLI Enforcement and Litigation Conference, 19 February.

111. Johnson, Linda (2008) "Drug Makers Sued Over Cholesterol Pills," *Forbes*, 24 January, http://www.forbes.com/feeds/ap/2008/02/24/ ap4572560.html accessed on 26 January 2008.

112. Smith, Rebecca (2007) "Money Back Guarantee Plan for Cancer Drug," *The Telegraph*, 23 October, http://www.telegraph.co.uk/news/ uknews/1567022/Money-back-guarantee-plan-for-cancer-drug.html accessed on 5 November 2009.

113. Martin, Nicole (2007) "U-Turn on Cancer Drug Offers Hope to Victims," *The Telegraph*, 4 June, http://www.telegraph.co.uk/news/uknews/1553519/ U-turn-on-cancer-drug-offers-hope-to-victims.html accessed on 5 November 2009.

114. Orelli, Brian (2009) "Health-Care Reform: If You Can't Beat 'Em, Join 'Em?" *The Motley Fool*, http://www.fool.com/investing/gen- eral/2009/08/27/health-care-reform-if-you-cant-beat-em-join-em.aspx accessed on 31 August 2009.

115. Perrone, Matthew (2009) "Experts: Key Drug Facts Often Left Off FDA Labels," *Associated Press*, http://news.yahoo.com/s/ap/20091021/ap_on_ he_me/us_fda_drug_labels_1.html accessed on 22 October 2009.

116. Cutler, Charles and Tracey Baker (2000) <u>Navigating Your Health Benefits for Dummies</u>. Hoboken, New Jersey: Wiley Publishing.

117. Pettypiece, Shannon (2009) "Glaxo's Migraine Pill Spurned by UnitedHealth for Generic Combo," *Bloomberg*, 19 June http://www. bloomberg.com/apps/news?pid=20670001&sid=ajEO59qlT0jk accessed on 22 June 2009.

118. Avellanet, John (2009) "Virtual Consultants – Are They for You?" *SmarterCompliance* newsletter, July Vol. 3 Issue 7.

119. Burrill, Steven (2009) "Phoning It In," *The Journal of Life Sciences*, 14 May http://www.burrillreport.com/article-1388.html accessed on 18 May 2009.

120. Fuhrmans, Vanessa (2009) "UnitedHealth, Cisco Plan Medical Network," *The Wall Street Journal*, 16 July.

121. Mathews, Anna Wilde (2009) "The Doctor Will Text You Now," *The Wall Street Journal*, 30 June.

122. FDA (2007) *Guidance for the Industry: Radio-Frequency Wireless Technology in Medical Devices*, January draft, http://www.fda.gov/ MedicalDevices/DeviceRegulationandGuidance/GuidanceDocuments/ ucm077210.htm, accessed on 29 December 2009.

123. *FierceBiotech* (2009) "FDA Unveils Safe Use Initiative that Targets Preventable Harm from Medication Use," 5 November, http://www.

fiercebiotech.com/press-releases/fda-unveils-safe-use-initiative-targets-preventable-harm-medication-use-0 accessed on 5 November.

124. Richwine, Lisa (2009) "US FDA Aims to Fight Avoidable Harm from Medicine," Reuters, 4 November, http://www.reuters.com/articleID=USN044802620091104, accessed on 5 November 2009.

CHAPTER 5

125. Story first related in *Harvard Business School's Dorothy Leonard on Knowledge Capture, Igniting Group Creativity and Empathic Design* (2006), Management Roundtable, Inc. and Knowledge Roundtable Group.

126. One of the documents, *The Information Pump*, treats the Information Pump as a parlor game you can play with your friends or spouse around the kitchen table; it's perfect for quickly seeing how powerful a tool the Information Pump is for gathering voice of the customer data. The whole game can be completed in 20-30 minutes.

127. Readers may download a product concept summary template on the book's website at http://www.Get2MarketNow.com.

128. Readers can obtain a copy of this guidance document from the book's website in addition to the FDA's website.

129. FDA (2009) *Patient-Reported Outcome Measures: Use in Medical Product Development to Support Labeling Claims*, December, http://www.fda.gov/downloads/Drugs/GuidanceComplianceRegulatoryInformation/Guidances/UCM193282.pdf, accessed on 29 December 2009.

130. *Wall Street Journal Health Blog* (2009) "The Changing Landscape of Pharmaceutical Marketing," 20 July, http://blogs.wsj.com/health/2009/07/20/the-changing-landscape-of-pharmaceutical-marketing.htm accessed on 21 July 2009.

131. Huston, Larry and Nabil Sakkab (2006) "Connect and Develop: Inside Procter & Gamble's New Model for Innovation," March, *Harvard Business Review*.

132. Ibid.

133. Smith, Neil and Terri Roberson (2008) "Transforming Drug Development: A Fully Outsourced Model," *Pharma Focus Asia*, Issue 9, http://www.pharmafocusasia.com/research_development/transforming_drug_development_outsourced_model.htm accessed on 5 January 2010.

134. Longman, Roger (2007) "Lilly's Chorus Experiment," *IN VIVO*, Vol. 25, No. 2, February, pp. 35-39.

135. Crabtree, Penni (2006) "Good Old Days Gone for Biotech," *San Diego Union-Tribune*, 26 November, http://www.signonsandiego.com/news/business/biotech/20061126-9999-1n26biotech.html accessed on 16 January 2007.

136. Wechsler, Jill (2006) "Biotech Firms Collaborate on Third-World Drug Development," *BioPharm International*, September, p. 22-24.

137. Hessel, Andrew (2009) "Reinventing the Pharmaceutical Industry, without the Industry," *The Futurist*, January-February 2010, pp. 19-20.

138. At the time of writing, the link to the FDA's sub-site was http://www.fda. gov/AboutFDA/CentersOffices/CDER/ucm167032.htm; visit the book's website for current links.

139. At the time of writing, the link to the NCI's developmental therapeutics program was http://dtp.nci.nih.gov/index.html; visit the book's website for current links.

140. The FDA's Sentinel Initiative is a national electronic system that will track reports of adverse events linked to drugs, biologics, and medical devices, and look for patterns and emerging risk factors; learn more about the Sentinel Initiative at http://www.fda.gov/Safety/ FDAsSentinelInitiative/default.htm.

141. Friedman, Yali, editor (2008) <u>Best Practices in Biotechnology Business Development</u>. Washington, D.C.: Logos Press.

CHAPTER 6

142. Readers can obtain a copy of this guidance document from the book's website at http://www.Get2MarketNow.com as well as from FDA's website.

143. Avellanet, John (2008) *Speeding Time to Market with the FDA's Quality by Design*. Presentation at the BIO-IT Coalition New Year Luncheon, 23 January, Washington, D.C. Readers of the book can download a copy of the slide presentation on the book's website (http://www. Get2MarketNow.com).

144. FDA (2004), *Pharmaceutical cGMPs for the 21st Century – A Risk-Based Approach*, September, http://www.fda.gov/Drugs/ DevelopmentApprovalProcess/Manufacturing/QuestionsandAnswers onCurrentGoodManufacturingPracticescGMPforDrugs/ucm137175. htm, accessed 4 August 2009.

145. FDA (2006), *Guidance for the Industry: Q8 Pharmaceutical Development*, May, http://www.fda.gov/RegulatoryInformation/Guidances/ucm128028. htm, accessed 20 November 2009; readers of the book can download a copy of this guidance from the FDA website or the book's website http:// www.Get2MarketNow.com.

146. Cherney, Barry (2007) *Quality Product Attributes and Linkages*. Workshop presentation at Quality by Design for Biopharmaceuticals: Concepts and Implementation, 22 May, Bethesda, Maryland.

147. Ibid.

148. Ibid.

149. Woodcock, Janet (2007) *The Future of Quality by Design*. Keynote presentation at Quality by Design for Biopharmaceuticals: Concepts and Implementation, 22 May, Bethesda, Maryland.
150. Private conversation with author, June 2007.
151. Wilson, Steve (2006) *FDA Regulatory Perspective: Data Integrity*. Presentation at the National Institutes of Health 4th Steering Committee Meeting of the NIH Roadmap for the Feasibility of Integrating & Expanding Clinical Research Networks, 12 May, Bethesda, Maryland.
152. Avellanet, John (2007) "Data Integrity and Validation: An Interview with Cerulean CEO John Avellanet." *Pharmaceutical Manufacturing*, 16 August; readers can download a copy of the interview from the book's website at http://www.Get2MarketNow.com.
153. FDA (2002) *General Principles of Software Validation; Final Guidance for Industry and FDA Staff*, 11 January, and (1993) *Validation of Cleaning Process*, http://www.fda.gov/ICECI/Inspections/InspectionGuides/ucm074922.htm accessed 23 November 2009, and 21 CFR 820.3 (z).
154. FDA (2009) *Guidance for Industry: End of Phase 2A Meetings*, September.
155. Ibid and (2009) *Draft Guidance for Industry: Postmarketing Studies and Clinical Trials – Implementation of Section 505(o) of the Federal Food, Drug, and Cosmetic Act*, July 2009.
156. Winkle, Helen (2007) *Implementing Quality by Design*. Presented at PDA/FDA Joint Regulatory Conference, 24 September, Bethesda, Maryland.
157. Yu, Lawrence (2006) *Implementation of Quality-by-Design: Question-based Review*. Presented at the 42nd Annual Drug Information Association Meeting, Philadelphia, Pennsylvania.
158. Trautman, Kimberly (1997) <u>The FDA and Worldwide Quality Systems Requirements Guidebook for Medical Devices</u>. ASQ Quality Press, Milwaukee, Wisconsin, pp. 29-30.
159. FDA (2009) *Guidance for Industry: Q10 Pharmaceutical Quality System*, April.
160. FDA (2004) *Guidance for Industry: PAT – A Framework for Innovative Pharmaceutical Development, Manufacturing, and Quality Assurance*, September.
161. FDA (2008), *Q8(R1) Pharmaceutical Development Revision 1*, 14 January, http://www.fda.gov/RegulatoryInformation/Guidances/ucm128003.htm, accessed on 23 November 2009, and ICH (2008) *Pharmaceutical Development Q8(R1)*, 13 November.
162. Cherney, Barry (2007) *Quality Product Attributes and Linkages*. Workshop presentation at Quality by Design for Biopharmaceuticals: Concepts and Implementation, 22 May, Bethesda, Maryland.
163. Nosal, Roger (2007) *Lessons Learned from QbD Experiences on Small Molecules: Pitfalls & Benefits*. Presentation at Quality by Design for

Biopharmaceuticals: Concepts and Implementation, 21 May, Bethesda, Maryland.

CHAPTER 7

164. *Note for the reader*: throughout this chapter I use the terms "quality system" and "quality management system" interchangeably.
165. Paton, Scott (2000) "Consumer-driven Six Sigma saves Ford $300 million," Quality Digest, 1 September, http://www.qualitydigest.com/sept01/html/ford.html accessed on 23 November.
166. FDA (1999) *Guide to Inspections of Quality Systems*, August, http://www.fda.gov/downloads/ICECI/Inspections/UCM142981.pdf accessed on 23 November 2009.
167. Smith, George (2005) *FDA's Current Interpretation and Guidance for Computerized Systems*. Presented at the IVT Computer Systems & Software Validation Conference, 25 April, Philadelphia, Pennsylvania.
168. FDA (2009) *Presenting Risk Information in Prescription Drug and Medical Device Promotion*, May, p. 7 (draft version).
169. Wikipedia (2009) "Flesch-Kincaid Readability Test" http://en.wikipedia.org/wiki/Flesch-Kincaid_Readability_Test accessed on 23 November 2009.
170. Readability scores were determined using Microsoft Word 2007. Note how high these scores are. Achieving an 8th-10th grade reading level is a difficult task in and of itself, which is why executives must make sure to clarify that SOPs, labels, and other text only need to *target* this grade level range.
171. Welch, Jan (2009) *Recent Developments in the International Compliance Landscape: From a US FDA Perspective*. 11 February.
172. HHS (2003) *Compliance Program Guidance for Pharmaceutical Manufacturers*, Federal Register vol. 68, no. 86, 5 May, p. 23731. Readers may download a copy of this guidance from the book's website (http://www.Get2MarketNow.com).
173. Ibid, p. 23740.
174. Intelegen Inc. (2005) "Memory and Related Learning Principles" http://www.web-us.com/memory/memory_and_related_learning_prin.htm accessed on 10 July 2009.
175. Readers of the book may download a copy of my five-slide QSR presentation on the book's website at http://www.Get2MarketNow.com.
176. FDA (1997) *Hazard Analysis and Critical Control Point Principles and Application Guidelines*, 14 August, http://www.fda.gov/Food/FoodSafety/HazardAnalysisCriticalControlPointsHACCP/HACCPPrinciplesApplicationGuidelines/default.htm accessed on 24 November 2009.

177. FDA (2001) *Fish and Fisheries Products Hazards and Controls Guidance*, June, http://www.fda.gov/Food/ GuidanceComplianceRegulatoryInformation/GuidanceDocuments/ Seafood/FishandFisheriesProductsHazardsandControlsGuide/default. htm accessed on 24 November 2009.

178. FDA (2006) *Guidance for Industry: Guidance for the Use of Bayesian Statistics in Medical Device Clinical Trials*, May (draft).

179. Trautman, Kimberly (2009) quoted in "FDA Officials on Supplier Control," *SmarterCompliance* newsletter, October, vol. 3, iss. 10, p. 9.

180. Author conversations with Dr. Rothman and Mrs. Trautman at the FDAnews FDA Supplier Quality Management Congress, 20 August 2009, Arlington, Virginia.

181. Homan, Madeleine (2005) "Have You Mapped Your Key Relationships?" *Harvard Management Update*, 1 August.

182. Ibid.

183. HHS (2003) *Compliance Program Guidance for Pharmaceutical Manufacturers*, Federal Register vol. 68, no. 86, 5 May, p. 23739.

184. ICH (2008) *Pharmaceutical Quality System*, 4 June. Readers may download a copy of this guidance from the book's website http://www. Get2MarketNow.com.

185. Kempic, Annamarie (2008) Living with Consent Decrees Panel Discussion at the Food and Drug Law Institute's 6th Annual Conference on Enforcement & Litigation, Washington, D.C., 19 February.

186. Midbern Pharmaceuticals is an altered name to protect the individuals and company involved, and is representative of the experiences of multiple clients who have adopted the tactics in this chapter.

187. On average, companies have 7.8 suppliers per item purchased. Mark Pagell and Chwen Shu (2001) "Buyer Behaviors and Supply Chain Performance: An International Exploration." Manhattan, Kansas: Kansas State University Department of Management, http://om.aomonline.org/ dyn/award/2001pw.pdf accessed on 25 November 2009.

CHAPTER 8

188. Management Roundtable (2006) "Technology and Strategy Roadmapping Implementation Kit," Waltham, Massachusetts, p. 4.

189. Ibid.

190. Ibid., p. 5

191. FDA (2006) *Guidance for Industry, Investigators, and Reviewers: Exploratory IND Studies*, January, pp. 8-12, http://www.fda.gov/down-loads/Drugs/GuidanceComplianceRegulatoryInformation/Guidances/ ucm078933.pdf accessed on 27 November 2009; readers may also download a copy of this guidance from the book's website.

192. At the time of writing, Amgen is one of the few firms that aggressively uses Phase 0 trials, using them to ensure that no drugs are advanced into clinical trials unless the trial advances the science and knowledge of the drug (*i.e.*, they want to be able to ensure the drug works the way they think it works).

193. FDAnews (2009) "Adaptive Trial Designs Save Merck Millions," *FDAnews Drug Daily Bulletin*, 10 September, Vol. 6, No. 176.

194. FDA (2006) *Independent Evaluation of FDA's First Cycle Review Performance – Retrospective Analysis Final Report*, prepared by Booz Allen Hamilton Inc., January, http://www.fda.gov/ForIndustry/UserFees/PrescriptionDrugUserFee/ucm119469.htm accessed on 27 November 2009.

195. FDA (2009), *Guidance for Industry: End-of-Phase 2A Meetings*, September. Readers may download a copy of the guidance from the book's website (http://www.Get2MarketNow.com) or from the FDA website http://www.fda.gov/downloads/Drugs/GuidanceComplianceRegulatoryInformation/Guidances/ucm079690.pdf accessed on 26 November 2009.

196. The REMS guidance document is in draft format and the FDA's strategic communication plan is labeled Fall 2009, presumably with periodic updates planned. Readers can access copies of the documents through the FDA website or the book's website at http://www.Get2MarketNow.com.

197. FDA (2009) *FDA's Strategic Plan for Risk Communication*, September, p. 10.

198. Food and Drug Administration Amendments Act of 2007, Section 902(4) A.

199. District of Columbia Code, 3-1207.41 *et seq.* (2009)

200. Oroho, John Patrick, Christine Bradshaw, and Christopher Corallo (2009) "Sales Rep Nightmares: Emerging Issues in Marketing Compliance," *Food & Drug Law Institute Update*, May/June, pp. 43-44.

201. Avellanet, John (2008) "Export Compliance for Life Sciences," *Journal of Commercial Biotechnology*, April, Vol. 14, No. 2, pp. 103-105.

202. *Focus* is published by the Regulatory Affairs Professionals Society, Rockville, Maryland, and can be accessed through membership in the society (see http://www.raps.org).

203. *The Silver Sheet* is published by Elsevier Inc., Bridgewater, New Jersey, and can be accessed online at http://thesilversheet.elsevierbi.com

204. *The Burrill Report* is published by Burrill & Company, San Francisco, California, and can be accessed online at http://www.burrillreport.com.

205. *FierceBiotech* is published by FierceMarkets, Washington, D.C., and can be accessed online at http://www.fiercebiotech.com.

206. *The Kiplinger Letter* is published by Kiplinger, Washington, D.C., and can be accessed online at http://www.kiplinger.com.

207. To learn more about this innovative program, see the website of Australia's Department of Human Services, Department of Families, Housing, Community Services and Indigenous Affairs http://www.facs. gov.au/sa/families/progserv/familysupport/Pages/default.aspx or http:// www.humanservices.gov.au accessed on 14 September 2009.

CHAPTER 9

208. Study conducted by author of all warning letters published by the FDA from June 2008 through September 2009.

209. Avellanet, John (2009) "How to Meet Compliance and Records Requirements of the US Food and Drug Administration," *RAJ Pharma*, June, pp. 359-364.

210. Avellanet, John (2008) "Getting the Results You Expect from Consultants," *BioPharm International*, April, Vol. 21, No. 4., pp. 32-36.

211. Consider a litmus test for any outside expert that includes an understanding of the real-world implications of "discovery" and familiarity with the nuances of regulatory health requirements (*e.g.*, agency regulations, statutes, guidance documents, and guidelines from international harmonization efforts must all be factored into any plan and set of controls).

212. Singer, Nancy (2009) cited in the article, "Former FDA Prosecutor on Document Mistakes", John Avellanet, *SmarterCompliance* newsletter, September, vol. 3, iss. 9, p. 6.

213. Rothman, Barry (2009) as quoted in "FDA Officials on Supplier Control," John Avellanet, *SmarterCompliance* newsletter, October, vol. 3, iss. 9, p. 7.

214. This example and suggested corrective action to avoid in the future is drawn from an FDA warning letter to Gaven Medical dated 26 June 2009, http://www.fda.gov/ICECI/EnforcementActions/WarningLetters/ ucm180918.htm accessed on 23 November 2009.

215. HHS (2003) *Compliance Program Guidance for Pharmaceutical Manufacturers*, Federal Register vol. 68, no. 86, 5 May. Readers may download a copy of this guidance from the book's website (http://www. Get2MarketNow.com).

216. The Office of Inspector General has devoted an entire section of its website to corporate integrity agreements; this can be accessed through www.oig.hhs.gov (see the book's website for the most current link).

217. Toffler, Alvin and Heidi (2006) <u>Revolutionary Wealth</u>. Currency Doubleday: New York, New York, pp. 325-326.

218. Machiavelli, Niccolo (1985) <u>The Prince</u>, translated by Harvey Mansfield, Jr., University of Chicago Press: Chicago, Illinois.

219. Ibid, p. 30.

220. Foucault, Michel (1975) <u>Discipline and Punish: The Birth of the Prison</u>.

Gallimard: France.

221. Wikipedia, http://en.wikipedia.org/wiki/Panopticon accessed 29 November 2009.

CHAPTER 10

222. Malone, Michael (2009) <u>The Future Arrived Yesterday: The Rise of the Protean Corporation and What it Means for You</u>. Crown Business: New York, New York, p. 262.

Bibliography

Abrahams, Ed (2009) "How Personalized is Transforming Healthcare."
Interview to *The Burrill Report.* 15 June.

Abramo, Peter and Edmondson, Michael (2008). <u>BioStory: Assessing
a Biomedical Product as a Business Opportunity</u>. Philadelphia,
Pennsylvania: MEAPA, LLC.

Anders, Donald (2004) "Attention ABLS…Are You Undervaluing Your
Borrower's Greatest Assests?" *ABF Journal*, July/August, vol. 2, no. 7

Andrews, Robert (2007) "Strategies for Developing and Commercializing
Next Generation Medical Devices." Foster-Miller Report, July.

Ariely, Dan (2008) <u>Predictably Irrational</u>. New York, New York:
HarperCollins Publishers.

A.T. Kearney (2009) "Report: Pharmaceuticals Out of Balance." December.

Autor, Deborah (2007) *How to Avoid Warning Letters and Other Troubles
with the FDA.* Speech at the Joint FDA/FDLI Enforcement & Litigation
Conference, 6 February.

Autor, Deborah(2008) *CDER Compliance: 2007-2008 and Beyond.* Speech
at the Joint FDA/FDLI Enforcement and Litigation Conference, 19
February.

Avellanet, John (2007) "Data Integrity and Validation: An Interview with
Cerulean CEO John Avellanet." *Pharmaceutical Manufacturing*, 16
August.

Avellanet, John (2008) *Speeding Time to Market with the FDA's Quality by
Design.* Presentation at the BIO-IT Coalition New Year Luncheon, 23
January, Washington, D.C.

Avellanet, John (2008) "Export Compliance for Life Sciences," *Journal of
Commercial Biotechnology*, April, Vol. 14, No. 2, pp. 103-105.

Avellanet, John (2008) "Getting the Results You Expect from Consultants,"
BioPharm International, April, Vol. 21, No. 4., pp. 32-36.

Avellanet, John (2008), *Securing Intellectual Property from the Inside Out.*, in:
Friedman, Yali (ed.) <u>Best Practices in Biotechnology Business Practices</u>.
Washington, D.C.: Logos Press.

Avellanet, John (2008) "Bioval Sued by Shareholders," *SmarterCompliance* newsletter, vol. 2 issue 10, October, page 5.

Avellanet, John (2008) "Want a Good Partnership? Know How to Ruin One First," *BioProcess International*, November (Supplement), pp. 44-47.

Avellanet, John (2009), "Trend Watch: CRO Industry to Double." *SmarterCompliance*, volume 3, issue 4, April, p. 4.

Avellanet, John (2009) *Avoid 483 Observations with a Document Control System to Actually Control Your Documents*, Teleconference for FOI Services, March.

Avellanet, John (2009) "How to Meet Compliance and Records Requirements of the US Food and Drug Administration," *RAJ Pharma*, June, pp. 359-364

Avellanet, John (2009) "Virtual Consultants – Are They for You?" *SmarterCompliance* newsletter, July Vol. 3 Issue 7.

Avellanet, John (2009), *Seminar: How to Improve Data Quality & Record Integrity in Your NDA, 510(k) or BLA*. 15 July.

Avellanet, John (2009) "Investors Sue Over Sloppy QS," *SmarterCompliance* newsletter, vol. 3 issue 8, August, page 4.

BBC News (2009) "Nanoparticle Lung Threat Blocked," 11 June, http://news. bbc.co.uk/go/pr/fr/-/2/hi/health/8091141.stm accessed on 12 June 2009.

Beich, Elaine (2005) Training for Dummies. Indianapolis, Indiana: Wiley Publishing.

Berthiaume, Marc (2008) "The Importance of Backing Up Computer Files: Some Interesting Facts," *The Independent*, September/October.

Bielski, Michael and Christine Ford (2007) "Combination Products and Intellectual Property Strategy: What Drug Companies and Device Makers Should Know", *Regulatory Affairs Focus*, July, pp. 40-42.

Blumberg, Eric (2008) *Purdue Pharma Case*. Speech at the Joint FDA/FDLI Enforcement and Litigation Conference, 19 February.

Bowers, Brent (2009) "Investors Pay Business Plans Little Heed, Study Finds." *New York Times*, 14 May.

Boyne, R. (2000) "Post-Panopticism," *Economy and Society*, May, vol. 29, iss. 2, pp. 285-307.

Brafman, Ori and Beckstrom, Rod (2006) The Starfish and The Spider: The Unstoppable Power of Leaderless Organizations. New York, New York: Penguin Group.

Brue, Greg and Robert Launsby (2003) Design for Six Sigma. New York, New York: McGraw-Hill Companies.

Buckingham, Marcus and Curt Coffman (1999) First, Break All the Rules. New York, New York: Simon & Schuster.

Burns, Lawton Robert, editor (2005) The Business of Healthcare Innovation. United Kingdom: Cambridge University Press.

Burrill, Steve (2009) "Predicting Alzheimer's," *The Journal of Life Sciences*, 15 May, http://www.burrillreport.com/printer_article-1393.html accessed on 18 May 2009.

Burrill, Steven (2009) "Phoning It In," *The Journal of Life Sciences*, 14 May http://www.burrillreport.com/article-1388.html accessed on 18 May 2009.

Chapman, Glenn (2009) "Pathway Genomics Launches Public DNA Testing," *Yahoo! News*, 15 July, http://news.yahoo.com/s/afp/20090715/ts_alt_afp/usitinternetgeneticshealthcompanypathway.html accessed on 16 July.

Cherney, Barry (2007) *Quality Product Attributes and Linkages*. Speech at the PDA Workshop Quality by Design for Biopharmaceuticals: Concepts and Implementation, 22 May.

Clark, Ross (2009) The Road to Big Brother: One Man's Struggle against the Surveillance Society. New York, New York: Encounter Books.

CNN Money Report, May 2007.

Cooper, Robert (2001) Winning at New Products: Accelerating the Process from Idea to Launch. New York, New York: Perseus Publishing.

Christensen, Clayton (2009) The Innovator's Prescription. New York, New York: McGraw-Hill.

Crabtree, Penni (2006) "Good Old Days Gone for Biotech," *San Diego Union-Tribune*, 26 November, http://www.signonsandiego.com/news/business/biotech/20061126-9999-1n26biotech.html accessed on 16 January 2007.

Cutler, Charles and Tracey Baker (2000) Navigating Your Health Benefits for Dummies. Hoboken, New Jersey: Wiley Publishing.

Defree, Suzanne (2009) "Implantable Sensor Device Claims to Offer Continuous Cancer Monitoring," *EDN*, 14 May, http://www.edn.com/index.asp?layout=articlePrint&articleID=CA6658480, accessed on 15 May 2009.

DiMasi, Joseph, Ronald Hansen, Henry Grabowski (2003) "The Price of Innovation: New Estimates of Drug Development Costs." *Journal of Health Economics*, vol. 22, p. 151-185.

Emanual, Ezekial (2002) "Session 2: Regulation 6: Institutional Review Boards (IRBs)," President's Council on Bioethics, 12 September 2002, http://bioethics.gov/transcripts/sep02/session2.html and Nancylynn-GA (2004) "Google Answers," 17 July, http://answers.google.com/answers/threadview/id/374774.html accessed on 17 November 2009.

Eppinger, Steven and Anil Chitkara (2006) "The New Practice of Global Product Development." *MIT Sloan Management Review*, Summer, Vol. 47, No. 4, pp. 22-30.

FDA (1995), *Medical Device Premarket Approval Inspection Process*, 7383.001, p. 3.

FDA (1997) *Hazard Analysis and Critical Control Point Principles and Application Guidelines*, August.

FDA (1999) *Guide to Inspections of Quality Systems*, August.

FDA (2001) *Fish and Fisheries Products Hazards and Controls Guidance*, June.

FDA (2002) *General Principles of Software Validation; Final Guidance for Industry and FDA Staff*, January.

FDA (2002), *Concept Paper, Pharmaceutical cGMPs for the 21st Century: A Risk-Based Approach*, August.

FDA (2003), *Pharmaceutical cGMPs for the 21st Century – A Risk-Based Approach: Second Progress Report and Implementation Plan*, August.

FDA (2004), *Innovation or Stagnation: Challenge and Opportunity on the Critical Path to New Medical Products*, March.

FDA (2004), *Guidance for Industry: Pharmaceutical cGMPs for the 21st Century – A Risk-Based Approach*, September.

FDA (2004) *Guidance for Industry: PAT – A Framework for Innovative Pharmaceutical Development, Manufacturing, and Quality Assurance*, September.

FDA (2006) *Guidance for Industry, Investigators, and Reviewers: Exploratory IND Studies*, January.

FDA (2006) *Guidance for Clinical Trial Sponsors: Establishment and Operation of Clinical Trial Data Monitoring Committees*, March.

FDA (2006), *Guidance for the Industry: Q8 Pharmaceutical Development*, May.

FDA (2006) *Guidance for Industry: Guidance for the Use of Bayesian Statistics in Medical Device Clinical Trials*, May.

FDA (2006) *Independent Evaluation of FDA's First Cycle Review Performance – Retrospective Analysis Final Report*, prepared by Booz Allen Hamilton Inc., January.

FDA (2008), *Q8(R1) Pharmaceutical Development Revision 1*, January.

FDA (2008), *Guidance for Industry: CGMP for Phase 1 Investigational Drugs*, July.

FDA (2008) *Guidance for Industry: Integrated Summary of Effectiveness*, August.

FDA (2009) *Guidance for Industry: Q10 Pharmaceutical Quality System*, April.

FDA (2009) *Guidance for Industry: Presenting Risk Information in Prescription Drug and Medical Device Promotion*, May.

FDA (2009), *Guidance for Industry: Postmarketing Studies and Clinical Trials – Implementation of Section 505(o) of the Federal Food, Drug, and Cosmetic Act*, July.

FDA (2009) *Guidance for Industry: End of Phase 2A Meetings*, September.

FDA (2009) *FDA's Strategic Plan for Risk Communication*, September.

FDA (2009) *FDA's Safe Use Initiative: Collaborating to Reduce Preventable Harm from Medications*, November.

FDA (2009) *Guidance for Industry: Patient-Reported Outcome Measures: Use in Medical Product Development to Support Labeling Claims*, December.

FDA-EMEA (2009) "Medicines Regulation: Transatlantic Administration Simplification Action Plan Implementation Report – 2009."

FDAnews (2009) "Adaptive Trial Designs Save Merck Millions," *FDAnews Drug Daily Bulletin*, 10 September, Vol. 6, No. 176.

Feeley, Jef and Margaret Cronin Fisk (2009), "Glaxo Executive's Memo Suggested Burying Drug Studies," *Bloomberg*, 15 September.

FierceBiotech (2009) "FDA Takes Questions at DIA," 24 June http://www.fiercebiotech.com/story/fda-takes-questions-dia/2009-06-24 accessed on 24 June 2009.

FierceBiotech (2009) "Sanofi Unveils R&D Makeover." 30 June, http://www.fiercebiotech.com/story/sanofi-starts-r-d-makeover/2009-06-30, accessed 27 December 2009.

FierceBiotech (2009) "BioHeart Stem Cell Treatment Achieves Positive Response," 18 September, http://www.fiercebiotech.com/story/bioheart-stem-cell-treatment-achieves-positive-response/2009-09-18 accessed on 18 September 2009.

FierceBiotech (2009) "FDA Unveils Safe Use Initiative that Targets Preventable Harm from Medication Use," 5 November, http://www.fiercebiotech.com/press-releases/fda-unveils-safe-use-initiative-targets-preventable-harm-medication-use-0 accessed on 5 November.

FierceBiotechIT (2009) "App Predicts Drug Interactions," 19 September, http://www.fiercebiotechit.com/story/app-predicts-drug-interactions/2009-09-19 accessed on 21 September 2009.

FierceHealthIT (2009) "IBM, UNC Partner on Data Warehouse for Clinical Research," 1 June, http://www.fiercehealthit.com/story/ibm-u-north-carolina-partner-data-warehouse-clinical-research/2009-06-01 accessed on 8 June 2009.

FiercePharma (2009) "Judge: CafePharma Posts Stay in Schering Case," 3 June, http://www.fiercepharma.com/story/judge-cafepharma-posts-stay-schering-case/2009-06-03-0.html accessed on 3 June 2009.

FiercePharma (2009), "J&J Researchers on the Future of Personalized Medicine," 11 June.

FiercePharma (2009), "Sanofi CEO: Think Small in Big Pharma," 19 June.

FiercePharma (2009) "FDA Experts Reject King's Imaging Drug," 29 July, http://www.fiercebiotech.com/story/fda-experts-reject-kings-imaging-drug/2009-07-29 accessed on 29 July.

Fisk, Margaret Cronin, Elizabeth Lopatto, Jef Feely (2009) "Lilly Sold Drug for Dementia Knowing It Didn't Help, Files Show," *Bloomberg*, 12 June.

Foucault, Michel (1975) <u>Discipline and Punish: The Birth of the Prison</u>. France: Gallimard.

Fraunhofer IGB (2009) "Producing Artificial Skin, Factory-Style," *The Futurist*, May-June, page 2.

Friedman, Yali, editor (2008) <u>Best Practices in Biotechnology Business Development</u>. Washington, D.C.: Logos Press.

Frueh, Felix (2005) *Personalized Medicine: What Is It and How Will It Affect*

Health Care? presented at the 11th Annual FDA Science Forum, 26 April, Washington, D.C.

Fuhrmans, Vanessa (2009) "UnitedHealth, Cisco Plan Medical Network," *The Wall Street Journal*, 16 July.

Gaba, Michael (2009) "Comparative Effectiveness: Will it Foster FDA-CMS Collaboration or Drive the Agencies Apart?" *FDLI Update*, March/April, pp. 14-17.

GPhA (2009) *Economic Analysis of Generic Pharmaceuticals 1999-2008*, Arlington, Virginia, May.

Goldman, Stephen Robert (2003) <u>Handbook of Computer and Computerized System Validation for the Pharmaceutical Industry</u>. Bloomington, Illinois: 1st Books Library.

Goldstein, Jacob (2009) "The Next Step in Cancer Drugs: Who Should NOT Get Them" *Wall Street Journal Health Blog*, 14 January, http://blogs.wsj.com/health/2009/01/14/the-next-step-in-cancer-drugs-who-should-not-get-them/, accessed 4 August 2009.

Goldman Sachs Global Economics (2009) "US Recover: Why V is Unlikely," *US Economics Analyst*, Issue No. 09/19, 15 May, pp. 1-8.

Government Accountability Office (2006) *New Drug Development: Science, Business, Regulatory, and Intellectual Property Issues Cited as Hampering Drug Development Efforts*, November.

Grabowski, H., J. Vernon and J. DiMasi, "Returns on research and Development for 1990s New Drug Introductions," *Pharmacoeconomics* 20 (December 2002): suppl. 3, pp. 11-29.

Hamburg, Margaret and Joshua Sharfstein (2009) "The FDA as a Public Health Agency." *New England Journal of Medicine*, 11 June, 360:24, pp. 2493-2495.

Hanson, William (2008) <u>The Edge of Medicine: The Technology That Will Change Our Lives</u>. New York, New York: Palgrave Macmillan.

Harris, Gardiner (2009) "Drug Agency May Reveal More Data on Actions," *The New York Times*, 2 June, http://www.nytimes.com/2009/06/02/health/policy/02fda.html accessed on 3 June 2009.

Heath, Chip and Dan (2007) <u>Made to Stick</u>. New York, New York: Random House.

Herbold, Robert (2005) <u>The Fiefdom Syndrome</u>. New York, New York: Currency Doubleday.

Hessel, Andrew (2009) "Reinventing the Pharmaceutical Industry, without the Industry." *The Futurist*, January-February, pp. 19-20.

HHS (2003) *Compliance Program Guidance for Pharmaceutical Manufacturers*, Federal Register vol. 68, no. 86, 5 May.

HHS (2008) *Personalized Health Care: Pioneers, Partnerships, Progress*, November.

Hobson, David (2009) "Nanotech Safety, Part II: Gather Your Own

Nanomaterials Safety Data to Drive Funding, Regulation," *Medical Device Daily Perspectives*, 24 June, vol. 3, no. 25.

Hollis, April (2009) "Proposed Rule for Combo Products Offers Streamlined GMP Option." *The GMP Letter*, October, Issue No. 357, pp.1,4.

Homan, Madeleine (2005) "Have You Mapped Your Key Relationships?" *Harvard Management Update*, 1 August.

Hubbard, Douglas (2007) How to Measure Anything: Finding the Value of Intangibles in Business. Hoboken, New Jersey: Jon Wiley & Sons.

Huston, Larry and Nabil Sakkab (2006) "Connect and Develop: Inside Procter & Gamble's New Model for Innovation," March, *Harvard Business Review*.

ICH (2008) *Pharmaceutical Quality System*, June.

ICH (2008) *Pharmaceutical Development Q8(R2)*, November.

Institute of Medicine (2009) *Report Brief: Initial National Priorities for Comparative Effectiveness Research*, June.

Intelegen Inc. (2005) "Memory and Related Learning Principles" http://www.web-us.com/memory/memory_and_related_learning_prin.htm accessed on 10 July 2009.

ISO (2000) *ISO 14971: Medical Devices – Application of Risk Management to Medical Devices*. Geneva, Switzerland: International Standards Organization.

ISPE (2008) GAMP 5: A Risk-Based Approach to Compliant GxP Computerized Systems. Tampa, Florida: ISPE.

Johnson, Linda (2008) "Drug Makers Sued Over Cholesterol Pills," *Forbes*, 24 January, http://www.forbes.com/feeds/ap/2008/02/24/ap4572560.html accessed on 26 January 2008.

Journal of Life Sciences (2009), "The Next Big Thing," 21 May.

Keckley, Paul (2009) "Lessons to be Learned from Comparative Effectiveness Systems Around the World." Interview to *The Burrill Report*. 22 May.

Kelland, Kate (2009) "Interview – UK Watchdog Offers Health Rationing Tips to World" Reuters, 9 October.

Kim, W. Chan and Renee Mauborgne (2005) Blue Ocean Strategy. Boston, Massachusetts: Harvard Business School Press.

Kingsley, Margaret (2009) "Companion Diagnostics Working Group Formed," *IVD Technology*, September, p. 13.

Kucklick, Theodore, editor (2006) The Medical Device R&D Handbook. Boca Raton, Florida: CRC Taylor & Francis Group, LLC.

Langemo, Mark (2002) Winning Strategies for Successful Records Management Programs. Denver, Colorado: Information Requirements Clearinghouse.

Lee, Thomas (2009) "A Promising Niche for Nanotech," *Star Tribune*, 21 June http://www.startribune.com/business/48643722.html accessed on 22 June 2009.

Lesko, Lawrence (2008) *Personalized Medicine: Regulatory Perspective*, presented at President's Council of Advisors on Science and Technology, 8 January, Washington, D.C.

Light, Donald (2009) "Global Drug Discovery: Europe is Ahead," *Health Affairs*, 25 August, pp. 969-977.

Lindpaintner, Klaus (2009) *Biomarkers in Personalized Health Care: Opportunities, Challenges, Approaches* presented at PDA Annual Conference, September, Washington, D.C.

Longman, Roger (2007) "Lilly's Chorus Experiment," *IN VIVO*, February, Vol. 25, Iss. 2, pp. 35-39.

Lyon, David, editor (2006) Theorizing Surveillance: The Panopticon and Beyond. Portland, Oregon: Willan Publishing.

McCormick, Kate (2009) "Global Regulatory Framework Overview: US FDA, EMEA, PIC/S, and ICH." *Pharmaceutical Engineering*, May/June, pp. 40-48.

McIlroy, Anne (2009) "Canadian Hospital Pioneers Mental-Health Treatment," *The Globe and Mail*, 7 July.

Machiavelli, Niccolo (1985) The Prince, translated by Harvey Mansfield, Jr., Chicago, Illinois: University of Chicago Press.

Malone, Michael (2009) The Future Arrived Yesterday: The Rise of the Protean Corporation and What It Means for You. New York, New York: Crown Business.

Management Roundtable (2006) "Technology and Strategy Roadmapping Implementation Kit." Waltham, Massachusetts.

Martin, Nicole (2007) "U-Turn on Cancer Drug Offers Hope to Victims," *The Telegraph*, 4 June, http://www.telegraph.co.uk/news/uknews/1553519/U-turn-on-cancer-drug-offers-hope-to-victims.html accessed on 5 November 2009.

Mathews, Anna Wilde (2009) "The Doctor Will Text You Now," *The Wall Street Journal*, 30 June.

Mathieu, Mark (2005) New Drug Development: A Regulatory Overview. Waltham, Massachusetts: Parexel International Corporation.

Meier, Barry (2009) "House Bill Would Create Artificial Joints Registry," *The New York Times*, 11 June, http://www.nytimes.com/2009/06/11/business/11device.html accessed on 11 June 2009.

Meritz, Judith (2008) *The FDA Landscape* presented at AdvaMed Conference, September.

Michaelson, Steven (2007) Sun Tzu for Execution. Avon, Massachusetts: Adams Media.

Mills, George (2007) "Using Exploratory IND Studies to Reduce Drug Development Costs," *RAJ Pharma*, July, pp. 451-454.

Ng, Rick (2009) Drugs: From Discovery to Approval. Hoboken, New Jersey: John Wiley & Sons.

Nosal, Roger (2007) *Lessons Learned from QbD Experiences on Small Molecules: Pitfalls & Benefits.* Presentation at Quality by Design for Biopharmaceuticals: Concepts and Implementation, 21 May, Bethesda, Maryland.

Ogawa, Susumu and Frank Piller (2006) "Reducing the Risks of New Product Development." *MIT Sloan Management Review*, Winter, Vol. 47, No. 2, pp. 65-71.

Orelli, Brian (2009) "Health-Care Reform: If You Can't Beat 'Em, Join 'Em?" *The Motley Fool*, http://www.fool.com/investing/general/2009/08/27/ health-care-reform-if-you-cant-beat-em-join-em.aspx accessed on 31 August 2009.

Oroho, John Patrick, Christine Bradshaw, and Christopher Corallo (2009) "Sales Rep Nightmares: Emerging Issues in Marketing Compliance," *FDLI Update*, May/June, pp. 43-44.

Page, Stephen (2000) Achieving 100% Compliance of Policies and Procedures. Westerville, Ohio: Process Improvement Publishing.

Page, Stephen (2004) 7 Steps to Better Written Policies and Procedures. Westerville, Ohio: Process Improvement Publishing.

Pagell, Mark and Chwen Shu (2001) "Buyer Behaviors and Supply Chain Performance: An International Exploration." Manhattan, Kansas: Kansas State University Department of Management.

Paton, Scott (2000) "Consumer-driven Six Sigma saves Ford $300 million," Quality Digest, 1 September, http://www.qualitydigest.com/sept01/html/ ford.html accessed on 23 November.

Perrone, Matthew (2009) "Experts: Key Drug Facts Often Left Off FDA Labels," *Associated Press*, http://news.yahoo.com/s/ap/20091021/ap_on_ he_me/us_fda_drug_labels_1.html accessed on 22 October 2009.

Pettypiece, Shannon (2009) "Glaxo's Migraine Pill Spurned by UnitedHealth for Generic Combo," *Bloomberg*, 19 June http://www.bloomberg.com/ apps/news?pid=20670001&sid=ajEO59q1T0jk accessed on 22 June 2009.

PhRMA, *Drug Discovery and Development*, Pharmaceutical Research and Manufacturers of America, Washington, D.C., March 2007

Piche, Greg (2008) *Pfizer's "Double Blind" Bextra Bind – The Value of Clinical Data*, 30 December, Healthcare Law Blog, http://www.holland-harthealthcare.com/healthcare/2008/12/pfizers-double-blind-bextra-bind-the-value-of-clinical-data.html, accessed 14 August 2009.

Pines, Wayne, editor (2003) How to Work with the FDA. Washington, D.C.: FDLI.

Pisano, Douglas and David Mantus, editors (2008) FDA Regulatory Affairs. New York, New York: Informa Healthcare USA.

Pisano, Gary (2006) Science Business: The Promise, the Reality, and the Future of Biotech. Boston, Massachusetts: Harvard Business School Press.

Plotkin, Robert (2009) "The Automation of Invention," *The Futurist*, July-August, page 23.

Pollack, Andrew (2009) "Former Drug Executive Convicted of Wire Fraud," *The New York Times*, 30 September, http://www.nytimes.com/2009/09/30/busines/30drug.html accessed on 30 September 2009.

PriceWaterhouseCoopers (2009) *Pharma 2020: Challenging Business Models – Which Path Will You Take?* 24 April.

Reuters (2009) KV Pharma: FDA Accepts Plan to Resolve Manufacturing Issue, 2 September.

Richmond, Frances J and Nancy Singer (2007) *Hiring and Training Needs in the Medical Products Industry: Focus on Regulatory, Quality and Clinical Professions*, Los Angeles, California: School of Pharmacy, University of Southern California.

Richwine, Lisa (2009) "US FDA Aims to Fight Avoidable Harm from Medicine," Reuters, 4 November, http://www.reuters.com/articleID=USN044802620091104, accessed on 5 November 2009.

Richwine, Lisa and Biane Bartz (2009) "FTC: 12-14 Yrs Too Long to Protect Biotech Drugs," *Reuters*, 10 June http://www.reuters.com/articleID=USTRE55953Q20090610 accessed on 11 June 2009.

Rivera-Martinez, Edwin (2008) *Inspections/Investigations, the CDER Perspective*. Speech at the Joint FDA/FDLI Enforcement and Litigation Conference, 19 February.

Rockoff, Jonathan and Julia Mengewein (2009) "J&J in Setback Over Antibiotic," *Wall Street Journal*, 31 December, http://online.wsj.com/article/SB10001424052748704152804574627523625941690.html accessed on 2 January 2010.

Rockoff, Jonathan (2010) "Lilly Taps Contractors to Revive Pipeline," *Wall Street Journal*, 5 January, pp. B1-2.

Rogers, Michael C. (2008) *Inspections/Investigations – the ORA Perspective*. Speech at the Joint FDA/FDLI Enforcement and Litigation Conference, 19 February.

Rydzewski, Robert (2009) Real World Drug Discovery: A Chemist's Guide to Biotech and Pharmaceutical Research. Amsterdam, The Netherlands: Elsevier, Ltd.

Sadrieh, Nakissa (2007) *FDA Regulatory Consideration for Nanotechnology Products* presented at PDA Meeting, January, San Diego, California.

Saffady, William (2004) Records and Information Management. Lenexa, Kansas: ARMA International.

Sayer, Natalie and Bruce Williams (2007) Lean for Dummies. Indianapolis, Indiana: Wiley Publishing.

Scheier, Robert (2007) "Disk Drive Failures 15 Times What Vendors Say, Study Says," *ComputerWorld*, 2 March.

Scheineson, Marc (2009) "Democrats Focus on FDA to Improve Treatment

Quality and Reduce Cost." *FDLI Update*, March/April, pp. 27-31.

Schimpff, Stephen (2007) <u>The Future of Medicine</u>. Nashville, Tennessee: Thomas Nelson, Inc.

Sherma, Debra (2009) "Abbot, Pfizer in Pact for Lung Cancer Screening." Reuters, 27 August.

Shillito, M. Larry (2001) <u>Acquiring, Processing, and Deploying Voice of the Customer</u>. Boca Raton, Florida: CRC Press.

Silverman, Ed (2008) "Fleeing the FDA for Industry and Retirement," 3 June, *Pharmalot Blog*, http://www.pharmalot.com/2008/06/fleeing-the-fda-for-industry-and-retirement/, accessed on 14 August 2009.

Smith, George (2005) *FDA's Current Interpretation and Guidance for Computerized Systems*. Presented at the IVT Computer Systems & Software Validation Conference, 25 April, Philadelphia, Pennsylvania.

Smith, Neil and Terri Roberson (2008) "Transforming Drug Development: A Fully Outsourced Model," *Pharma Focus Asia*, Issue 9, http://www.pharmafocusasia.com/research_development/transforming_drug_development_outsourced_model.htm accessed on 5 January 2010.

Smith, Rebecca (2007) "Money Back Guarantee Plan for Cancer Drug," *The Telegraph*, 23 October, http://www.telegraph.co.uk/news/uknews/1567022/Money-back-guarantee-plan-for-cancer-drug.html accessed on 5 November 2009.

Somsen, Han, editor (2007) <u>The Regulatory Challenge of Biotechnology: Human Genetics, Food and Patents</u>. Cornwall, United Kingdom: MPG Books, Ltd.

Steenhuysen, Julie (2009) "Nanotech Gene Therapy Kills Ovarian Cancer in Mice," *Reuters*, 30 July, http://news.yahoo.com/s/nm/20090730/sc_nm/us_cancer_nanotechnology.htm accessed on 3 August 2009.

Steenhuysen, Julie (2009) "Risks to Personalized Medicine Seen In U.S. Reform," *Reuters India*, 27 October.

Thompson, Erin (2009) "More are Searching the Web for Medical Advice," *USA Today*, 17 June, page 6D.

Toffler, Alvin and Heidi (2006) <u>Revolutionary Wealth</u>. New York, New York: Currency Doubleday.

Trautman, Kimberly (1997) <u>The FDA and Worldwide Quality System Requirements Guidebook for Medical Devices</u>. Milwaukee, Wisconsin: ASQ Quality Press.

Trautman, Kimberly (2007), *Regulatory Perspective on quality management Systems in the Medical Device Industry – Lessons Learned*. Speech to the Joint PDA/FDA Conference on Modern Quality Systems, 1 November.

Wall Street Journal (2009), "New Recruits: Enlisting Genes in the Campaign Against Cancer," 29 May.

Wall Street Journal (2009), "FDA Approves a Novel Novartis Drug," 19 June.

Wall Street Journal Health Blog (2009) "The Changing Landscape

of Pharmaceutical Marketing," 20 July, http://blogs.wsj.com/
health/2009/07/20/the-changing-landscape-of-pharmaceutical-market-
ing.htm accessed on 21 July 2009.

Wall Street Journal Venture Capital Blog (2009) "Sorting Through Challenges,
Opportunities of Stem Cells," 29 December, http://blogs.wsj.com/ven-
turecapital/2009/12/29/sorting-through-challenges-opportunities-of-the-
stem-cell-space/ accessed on 29 December 2009.

Wechsler, Jill (2006) "Biotech Firms Collaborate on Third-World Drug
Development," *BioPharm International*, September, p. 22-24.

Weissman, Robert and Sarah Rimmington (2008) "Letter to Federal Trade
Commission: Emerging Health Care Competition and Consumer Issues
– Comment, Project No. P083901," 22 December.

Welch, Jan (2009) *Recent Developments in the International Compliance
Landscape: From a US FDA Perspective.* 11 February.

Wikipedia (2009) "Flesch-Kincaid Readability Test" http://en.wikipedia.org/
wiki/Flesch-Kincaid_Readability_Test accessed on 23 November.

Wikipedia (2009) "Panopticon" http://en.wikipedia.org/wiki/Panopticon accessed 29 November.

Winkle, Helen (2007) *Implementing Quality by Design.* Presented at PDA/
FDA Joint Regulatory Conference, 24 September, Bethesda, Maryland.

Winkler, Ira (2005) <u>Spies Among Us</u>. Indianapolis, Indiana: Wiley
Publishing.

Winslow, Ron (2009) "Roche Drug Shrinks Tumors in Study," *Wall Street
Journal*, 3 September.

Wilson, Steve (2006) *FDA Regulatory Perspective: Data Integrity.* Presentation
at the National Institutes of Health 4th Steering Committee Meeting
of the NIH Roadmap for the Feasibility of Integrating & Expanding
Clinical Research Networks, 12 May, Bethesda, Maryland.

Wood, David, editor (2003) "Foucault and Panopticism Revisited,"
Surveillance & Society, vol 1., iss. 3, Newcastle upon Tyne, United
Kingdom.

Woodcock, Janet (2007) *The Future of Quality by Design.* Keynote presentation at Quality by Design for Biopharmaceuticals: Concepts and
Implementation, 22 May, Bethesda, Maryland.

Yank, Kai (2008) <u>Voice of the Customer: Capture and Analysis</u>. New York,
New York: McGraw-Hill.

Yu, Lawrence (2006) *Implementation of Quality-by-Design: Question-based
Review.* Presented at the 42nd Annual Drug Information Association
Meeting, Philadelphia, Pennsylvania.

Zinsser, William (1988) <u>Writing to Learn</u>. New York, New York: Harper &
Row, Publishers.

Zoroya, Gregg (2009) "Findings May Speed Troops' Recovery," *USA Today*, 20
August, p. 5A.

Index

Supplementary materials - templates, to-do lists, helpful internet links, mini-seminars - can all be found on the book's exclusive web page at www.Get2MarketNow.com

Please send correspondence or requests for speaking engagements to:

john@Get2MarketNow.com

About the Author

John Avellanet is the founder of Cerulean Associates LLC—a private FDA compliance and quality systems consultancy. In addition to writing this book, he was a contributing author to the book *Best Practices in Biotechnology Business Development* (2008), is a compliance columnist for three international journals, and has written over 100 articles on lean regulatory affairs and FDA quality systems compliance. He serves on the advisory boards of several trade associations, and is a frequently requested speaker for industry events, business schools, and corporate workshops.

Prior to founding Cerulean Associates LLC, Mr. Avellanet was a C-level medical device and biopharmaceutical executive who created, developed, and ran a *Fortune 50* subsidiary's records management and information technology departments to meet FDA, ISO, ICH, and GHTF compliance requirements. In 2006, he was awarded lifetime membership in the Who's Who of top executives in the pharmaceutical and life sciences industry. And he has been interviewed in print and on radio programs such as *Tomorrow's Business* and *My Technology Lawyer*. He currently lives in Williamsburg, Virginia.

Through his firm, Cerulean Associates LLC, Mr. Avellanet offers a range of independent consulting services and compliance products, all of which are based around the ideas outlined in this book. More information on Cerulean and Mr. Avellanet can be found on the website www.Ceruleanllc.com

Mr. Avellanet would love to hear any feedback on the concepts and advice offered in this book. Contact him through the book's website at john@Get2MarketNow.com

Related titles from Logos Press

http://www.logos-press.com

Best Practices in Biotechnology Business Development

Valuation, Licensing, Cash Flow,
Pharmacoeconomics, Market Selection,
Communication, and Intellectual Property

ISBN: 978-09734676-0-4

Building Biotechnology

*Scientists know science; businesspeople know
business. This book explains both.*

Hardcover ISBN: 978-09734676-5-9
Softcover ISBN: 978-09734676-6-6

9 781934 899120